B
WRIGHT   Farr, Finis

              Frank Lloyd Wright

FRANK LLOYD WRIGHT

1. Frank Lloyd Wright

FRANK
LLOYD
WRIGHT

A BIOGRAPHY BY FINIS FARR

New York

CHARLES SCRIBNER'S SONS

ACKNOWLEDGMENTS

THE AUTHOR hereby expresses his gratitude to the hundreds of people in all parts of the country who were so kind as to assist in the preparation of this book. In addition, special thanks should be accorded Gilmer V. Black, Noel F. Busch, William T. Priestley, and Craig Thompson for generous help above and beyond that of casual interest; to Frank Norris, for manuscript and other materials of value; to Barry Byrne, Thomas Quinn Beesley, Cary Caraway, George H. Dapples, William R. Gerler, and Alfonso Iannelli; and to Mrs. Charles C. Healy of the Chicago Historical Society. The author is also indebted to Christabel Wheeler Priestley of Lake Forest for material on early Chicago; and to W. H. Binford of Pace Associates, Chicago, for information on the practice of architecture. Among other busy architects, William F. Deknatel of Chicago and John B. Rodgers of San Francisco took time to help and instruct the author, as did Miës van der Rohe. Harwell Hamilton Harris of Dallas interrupted work at his distinguished practice to give advice and counsel, a kindness which was repeated by Kelly Oliver of the same city. Thanks also are due the publishers and reference room staffs of the Chicago *Tribune*, Dallas *News*, and Los Angeles *Times*, and the editors of the *Saturday Evening Post*, in which part of this material has appeared in another form. While acknowledging his debt to the persons listed, the author should emphasize that the opinions and judgments offered in this book are his responsibility alone.

In conclusion, the author should record that were this book to carry a dedicatory page, it would be shared by Carl D. Brandt and Wayne Andrews, for their unfailing encouragement and support.

CONTENTS

Chapter   *Page*

ONE *Out of Wisconsin*   3

TWO *Wright and Sullivan*   29

THREE *The Conquest of Chicago*   57

FOUR *Tragedy at Taliesin*   113

FIVE *And Then Tokyo*   143

SIX *Time of Trouble*   177

SEVEN *The Old Great Man*   249

LIST OF ILLUSTRATIONS

Plate

1. FRANK LLOYD WRIGHT
2. RESIDENCE OF JAMES CHARNLEY, CHICAGO, ILLINOIS, 1891
3. RESIDENCE OF W. H. WINSLOW, RIVER FOREST, ILLINOIS, 1893
4. RESIDENCE OF AVERY COONLEY, RIVERSIDE, ILLINOIS, 1908
5. LIVING ROOM, RESIDENCE OF AVERY COONLEY, RIVERSIDE, ILLINOIS, 1908
6. RESIDENCE OF DARWIN D. MARTIN, BUFFALO, NEW YORK, 1904
7. LARKIN BUILDING, BUFFALO, NEW YORK, 1904
8. RESIDENCE OF FREDERICK C. ROBIE, CHICAGO, ILLINOIS, 1909
9. DINING ROOM, RESIDENCE OF FREDERICK C. ROBIE, CHICAGO, ILLINOIS, 1909
10. RESIDENCE OF B. HARLEY BRADLEY, KANKAKEE, ILLINOIS, 1900
11. UNITY CHURCH, OAK PARK, ILLINOIS, 1906
12. RESIDENCE OF WARD W. WILLITTS, HIGHLAND PARK, ILLINOIS, 1902
13. RESIDENCE OF SUSAN LAWRENCE DANA, SPRINGFIELD, ILLINOIS, 1903
14. RESIDENCE OF THOMAS P. HARDY, RACINE, WISCONSIN, 1905
15. MIDWAY GARDENS, CHICAGO, ILLINOIS, 1914
16. IMPERIAL HOTEL, TOKYO, JAPAN, 1915-22
17. MAIN LOBBY, IMPERIAL HOTEL, TOKYO, JAPAN, 1915-22

18. "HOLLYHOCK HOUSE," RESIDENCE OF MISS ALINE BARNSDALL, HOLLYWOOD, CALIFORNIA, 1920

19. RESIDENCE OF MRS. GEORGE MADISON MILLARD, PASADENA, CALIFORNIA, 1923

20. STUDIO, TALIESIN EAST, SPRING GREEN, WISCONSIN, 1925-59

21. TALIESIN EAST, SPRING GREEN, WISCONSIN, 1925-59

22. TALIESIN WEST, PHOENIX, ARIZONA, 1938-59

23. LIVING ROOM, TALIESIN WEST, PHOENIX, ARIZONA, 1938-59

24. RESIDENCE OF RICHARD LLOYD JONES, TULSA, OKLAHOMA, 1929

25. RESIDENCE OF RICHARD LLOYD JONES, TULSA, OKLAHOMA, 1929

26. "FALLING WATER," RESIDENCE OF EDGAR J. KAUFMANN, BEAR RUN, PENNSYLVANIA, 1936

27. *Above, right;* LIVING ROOM, "FALLING WATER," RESIDENCE OF EDGAR J. KAUFMANN, BEAR RUN, PENNSYLVANIA, 1936

28. "FALLING WATER," RESIDENCE OF EDGAR J. KAUFMANN, BEAR RUN, PENNSYLVANIA, 1936

29. INTERIOR, V. C. MORRIS STORE, SAN FRANCISCO, CALIFORNIA, 1949

30. V. C. MORRIS STORE, SAN FRANCISCO, CALIFORNIA, 1949

31. RESIDENCE OF LOWELL WALTER, QUASQUETON, IOWA, 1949

32. BOAT HOUSE FOR LOWELL WALTER, QUASQUETON, IOWA, 1949

33. FIRST UNITARIAN MEETING HOUSE, MADISON, WISCONSIN, 1951

34. INTERIOR, FIRST UNITARIAN MEETING HOUSE, MADISON, WISCONSIN, 1951

35. RESIDENCE OF MRS. CLINTON WALKER, CARMEL, CALIFORNIA, 1952

36. DINING ALCOVE, RESIDENCE OF MRS. CLINTON WALKER, CARMEL, CALIFORNIA, 1952

37. H. C. PRICE TOWER, BARTLESVILLE, OKLAHOMA, 1953-56

38. ADMINISTRATION BUILDING, FLORIDA SOUTHERN COLLEGE, LAKELAND, FLORIDA, 1948

39. PFEIFFER CHAPEL, FLORIDA SOUTHERN COLLEGE, LAKELAND, FLORIDA, 1940

40. ROUX LIBRARY, FLORIDA SOUTHERN COLLEGE, LAKELAND, FLORIDA, 1942

41. INTERIOR, ADMINISTRATION BUILDING, S. C. JOHNSON & SON, RACINE, WISCONSIN, 1936-39

42. RESEARCH TOWER, S. C. JOHNSON & SON, RACINE, WISCONSIN, 1951

43. CONGREGATION BETH SHOLOM, ELKINS PARK, PENNSYLVANIA, 1959

44. INTERIOR, CONGREGATION BETH SHOLOM, ELKINS PARK, PENNSYLVANIA, 1959

45. RESIDENCE OF DAVID WRIGHT, PHOENIX, ARIZONA, 1952

46. KALITA HUMPHREYS THEATER, DALLAS, TEXAS, 1960

47. ENTRANCE, GUGGENHEIM MUSEUM, NEW YORK CITY, 1959

48. INTERIOR, GUGGENHEIM MUSEUM, NEW YORK CITY, 1959

49. GUGGENHEIM MUSEUM, NEW YORK CITY, 1959

FRANK LLOYD WRIGHT

Chapter One

OUT OF WISCONSIN

FRANK LLOYD WRIGHT was born in Richland Center, Wisconsin, on June 8, 1869. At this date, Thomas Jefferson and John Adams had been dead for only forty-three years, James Madison for only thirty-three, and the nation itself was younger than Frank Lloyd Wright would be at the end of the life that lay before him. His mother wished him to be an architect, and looked at pictures of English cathedrals while carrying him before birth. Wright announced, early in his career, that he intended to become the greatest architect who ever lived. The naked self-assurance of this statement is enough to establish him as something of an oddity, but those who are irritated by the remark are also haunted by the thought that he may have made it come true. At the very least, Wright has become part of his beloved southern Wisconsin, and he has given his adopted state of Arizona a voice. When he was buried, the *Journal of the American Institute of Architects* said that the achievements of twentieth-century building would have been impossible without him, that he stood safe in history, and was the teacher of all his colleagues. With this Wright himself would have heartily agreed. Yet no art can be only one man deep, and no profession have only one competent living practitioner. Sometimes he seemed to be claiming exactly that; therefore one must bear in mind, when reading his strictures on other members of his craft, that his writing, like Emerson's, is the transcription of one lifelong lecture, and that there often was a twinkle in Wright's eye that did not come through when his remarks appeared in type. It should also be remembered that no more than he escaped

3

greatness did he escape the human fate of sometimes seeming absurd.

Frank Lloyd Wright—his three short names strike like a pattern of blows by a boxer. He had much in common with two other monosyllabically named great men: like Charles James Fox he delighted in the unorthodox and new; like John Paul Jones he believed in quick decision and swift stroke. Moreover, when he wished it so, Wright could be an enchanter of men and women as Fox had been. And when life attacked him Wright fought back with the courage of Captain Jones. Brave, brilliant, and eternally moralizing, Frank Lloyd Wright was the last great American Victorian.

Such a man must be lucky in his parentage, and Wright inherited much of value from his father, including the long-lived strain of a grandfather who attained the age of ninety-nine. Equally important was the feeling for music and literature that William Russell Cary Wright bequeathed to his son Frank. Some students of the son's career are inclined to pass over William Wright, or relegate him to the ranks of failures. This is an injustice to a man of parts who had a knack for imparting drama to his life. William Wright was the son of a Baptist minister, who came from England to a pastorate in Hartford, Connecticut. Educated at Amherst, William could point to connections on his mother's side with the family of James Russell Lowell, the literary heavyweight champion, and with Alice and Phoebe Cary, whose poems were greatly esteemed.[1] Feeling for his place in life, William Wright tentatively practiced law and even considered medicine before he came to the new state of Wisconsin as a wandering music master about the middle

---

[1] Phoebe Cary was author of the hymn, "One Sweetly Solemn Thought."

of the 1850's. Mr. Wright was no mere rolling stone: many a talented man in that era before the rise of rigid specialization would shop around among the learned professions, as did Emerson's brother William, for example, who turned from preaching to the law. As subsequent events were to show, Wright's real bent was for music. Coaxing a frontier living from the farmers up and down the Wisconsin River Valley, Professor Wright was a man of mark with his swallowtail coat, fiddle, and metronome. Though he sometimes took fees in produce rather than cash, he persevered in hammering the elements of musical notation into children's heads, and showed his own considerable abilities as a performer when he got near one of the few pianos in the region, or was seated at a hand-pumped organ, charming rural ears with "Sheep May Safely Graze," by J. S. Bach. At other times the professor would preside at a singing bee, or start hands clapping and feet flying as he scraped away on his fiddle for a country dance.

William Wright was a widower with three children when he met the woman who would be his second wife and Frank's mother. He was seventeen years older than Anna Lloyd-Jones, daughter of a sturdy Welsh clan of preachers, teachers, and farmers recently migrated from the old country to the similarly rolling lills of southern Wisconsin. Anna's father had been a hatter as well as a farmer and lay minister. Family tradition maintained that the hats manufactured by Richard Lloyd-Jones were tall, black, conical, and suitable for witches. The Welsh neighbors, it seemed, accepted these styles in headgear, but refused the Lloyd-Jones preaching. As a matter of principle, Richard Lloyd-Jones departed from them, leading his family to a homestead in the New World. This established in Anna's mind the idea of a patriarch standing firm at all costs to his own convictions. Richard put before his children a figure of benign dignity as he rode over the fields, a shepherd's crook hanging from his arm, the Bible in a saddle bag. And constantly in the seven children's view was a druidic symbol that family tradition identified as the ancient emblem of the clan. Its meaning was believed to be "Truth against the world."

When Anna Lloyd-Jones met the widower William Wright, she was a teacher, riding to work in a smart blue reefer with brass buttons, and sometimes leading her pupils in a climb up Percussion Rock, a challenging escarpment near the school. The rock was similar to the Craig yr Aderyn in the old country, and might be said to represent, in a way, the Welsh inheritance the Lloyd-Joneses brought to their new home. This was a heritage of many elements, including a mysticism like that of Owen Glendower who could call up spirits and cause music to be heard from the distance of a thousand leagues. "Sit, and attend," said Glendower, and the command was echoed over and over by Welshmen who trusted in the power of persuasion carried to the length of argument as devoutly as they believed their favorite texts from Bishop William Morgan's translation of the Holy Scriptures. To the bent for disputation the Welsh character added an unshakable belief in the virtues of book-learning. The intelligent and literate Welsh workingman or farmer, though poor and liable to suffer from a puritanical lack of general joy, would find a solemn satisfaction in the scholastic attainments of his children. Though he bowed to the schoolmaster, or at least insisted that his children do so, the Welshman mistrusted the Anglican clergy as much as he did the English crown, and Quakers, Baptists, Independents, and Unitarians flourished in the land. An ancestor of Richard Lloyd-Jones preached a heretical sermon in 1726, a date proudly pointed to in the family as ninety-three years before William Ellery Channing established a landmark in American Unitarianism by his Baltimore sermon. But this is not to say that every Welsh preacher was suited with a pliant congregation, as Richard found out. The proverb was that when Welshmen were not talking they were singing, but in this case it seems they were usually shouting, and in uncomplimentary terms. Yet within forty years of Richard's arrival in Wisconsin, a family chapel had been built beside the crossroads near the village of Spring Green, not far from Madison, the capital of the state. In this area, a Lloyd-Jones enclave grew up, with broad fields and snug houses looking down the valley from vantage points on Bryn Mawr, Bryn Canol, and Bryn Bach—the big, middle, and little hills. Five sons and five daughters of Richard Lloyd-Jones and his gentle wife Mary proclaimed the excellence of truth against the world. One son, Jenkin, expounded this doctrine directly as a Unitarian preacher; the rest remained on the farms. Anna's sisters Ellen and Jane also were teachers, destined to eminence in the profession, who would wield important influence in the life of Frank Lloyd Wright. But their noteworthy achievements lay in the future when Anna married William Wright shortly after the close of the Civil War. Their doubts as to the suitability of a forty-six-year-old widower as a husband for their sister were tempered by the consideration that Anna was no girl, but a strong-willed woman of twenty-nine. Moreover, William Wright carried the talisman of education, and the authority of the East, from which the tremendous vibrations of Transcendentalism had come like charges of electricity to the remotest provinces, through the teachings of Emerson, Margaret Fuller, Bronson Alcott, and George Ripley of Brook Farm.

High justification for Anna's choice became evident not
long after Frank's birth, when Mr. Wright accepted a call
to the Baptist ministry, and moved with his family to take
charge of a church in Weymouth, Massachusetts.

Ministers' sons! What remarkable contributions they
have made to the rolls of fame, how they have come to
occupy the seats of the mighty—and in some cases to place
their names on the rosters of prisons and institutes for the
cure of addiction to drink. There can be no denial that the
combination of plain living and high thinking in youth is
a seedbed for talent second to none; the secret perhaps lies
in the opportunity afforded the growing intelligence to
graze in the ministerial library. Moreover, to have a certain
unassailable stature in the community, while at the same
time being poor, is frequently a breeder of indomitable ambition for material success. In addition, the parson's children
learn to live in the public eye; and from his first conscious
moments as a child of the manse Frank Lloyd Wright was
an especially fine example of the type.

Wearing long curls in the fashion of the time, little Frank
attended a private school, though his tuition was doubtless
remitted in view of his father's position, for Mr. Wright's
meagre salary provided no luxuries. Sometimes the minister's
family received a direct handout, to the secret fury of
Anna Wright, who murmured, "No, it's not *possible*,"
when kindly though officious parishioners delivered twenty-
three pumpkin pies at the manse. Plain living did not prevent Anna Wright from exercising her taste in decoration,
which ran to etchings on clean white mats, spotless net
curtains, and bowls of ferns and flowers set about the un-
crowded rooms. Frank had his sanctum, where he kept a
treasure of interestingly shaped stones, and drew with
colored pencils to his heart's content. Throughout his life,

the sight of such pencils was to give him great satisfaction, for they were signs of an interior world, his to command at will. Frank's own first step toward national and world renown was a by-product of the Philadelphia Exposition in this year of 1876. His mother attended the great fair on holiday from the duties of a pastor's wife, and there encountered the aids to teaching that were known as "Froebel blocks." An invention of Friedrich Froebel, originator of the kindergarten system, these blocks were intended to make young children aware of color and form. They were put up in sets called "gifts" to conceal their educational intent from young users—cubes, spheres, and cylinders of clean-cut maple, fitting together in constructions of a highly satisfying kind. The moment she saw these blocks, Mrs. Wright decided Frank should have them, even though he was beyond kindergarten age. Whether or not Anna Wright's prenatal plans had any effect on her son's calling, it has been agreed by all authorities, including Wright himself, that the Froebel gifts were a major influence in his career. Rejoicing in the primary colors and unhesitating shapes, Frank became aware of essential and fundamental design as he arranged the blocks in patterns, first according to the games prescribed in the book of directions, then in structures of his own invention. Wright later said, "Those blocks stayed in my fingers all my life."

Although young Frank was now enjoying the supreme good fortune of discovering his true calling early in life, his father was beginning to doubt that he had found his own vocation in the ministry. Mr. Wright's only comfort was in music, and Frank spent many hours listening as his father played Bach and Beethoven on the church organ. Mr. Wright liked to be caught at the keyboard so wrapped in the music that he would not be aware another person had entered the room. This intense concentration was real: one afternoon in the church auditorium, he forgot that Frank was pumping the organ, and kept playing until the boy collapsed. The incident caused Mrs. Wright to become uncommonly tight-lipped, though her manner toward William Wright was never excessively cordial after the birth of her son. Frank was not consciously aware that most of his mother's emotional funds were now invested in him rather than in his father. But he did realize that his father, though moody and severe, had certain admirable powers that were invoked in drawing the grandeur of great music from church organ and home piano. "Boy, never forget this," Mr. Wright would say, turning from the keyboard, "the music of Beethoven is an architecture—a majestic architecture in sound."

As time passed at Weymouth, Mr. Wright found no majesty and scarcely any dignity in his tall white church. At last he gave up the pastorate and returned to Madison, where he set up a conservatory of music—a venture that was to yield him little income and much nervous strain. In his spare time at night, William Wright read Sanskrit, scraped away on his fiddle, or paced his study reciting "The Raven" in such dramatic tones that his son, listening outside the door, was filled with a sense of tragedy and foreboding.

In Madison, Frank parted with his Lord Fauntleroy curls and went to public school with his two sisters Jane and Maginel. Here he met with strict instruction, that soon had him reading everything from *Hans Brinker, or, The Silver Skates*, which he bought at the bookstore, to the works of Carlyle and Victor Hugo, which he found in his father's library. The chapter on architecture in *Notre Dame* caught Frank's eye, and he was thrilled, as though by the opening of a massive door, when he read that the Renaissance was only a sunset that men had mistaken for the dawn. There was thus planted in Frank's mind an ineradicable conviction that architecture based on historic styles must be esthetically false and morally wrong.

An idea of that complexity was beyond the average youth, in Madison or elsewhere, and Frank could discuss the problem only with a special friend, Robie Lamp, a lame boy who compensated for his handicap by developing his mind. Frank and Robie also carried on the normal activities of painting a bobsled, manufacturing a crossbow, designing an iceboat, and setting up a publishing house with a printing press and seven fonts of type.

In the evening, Frank's sisters would sometimes invite a group of young people to play charades, or sing the scores of the Savoy operas by the new and wonderfully talented team of W. S. Gilbert and Arthur Sullivan. Parlor stunts and recitations contributed to the fun, but Frank was shy in the presence of girls, and though he was to become the most articulate of men found it an ordeal to speak a piece, either at home or in school.

By this time, the Lloyd-Jones family chapel was being built near Spring Green, center of the enclave of flourishing farms that Frank's uncles had established. Every summer the boy worked on his Uncle James's place, where he acquired a muscular physique, and learned the Lloyd-Jones rule: "Add tired to tired." Like the Greeks, Frank was to glory all his life in the sense of sight, and now its possibilities struck him in full for the first time. Even the farm machinery had its beauty: the combine was painted piercing red, and its bright blue, green, and yellow reels ran through yellow grain as the sickle moved rhythmically to and fro. The birds and beasts of the farm also had their great visual values—Frank rejoiced in the sight of the red rooster, strutting at the head of his harem; he appreciated the black, prolific sow, and the brown monarch of a bull. Men and animals fed from simple plenty on the Lloyd-Jones farms; there was green cheese, cream cheese, sorghum, and honey; chicken, ham, turkey, and pork; peas, beans, and ears of roasting corn; apple pies and pickles, cookies and cake, ripe tomatoes and cucumbers eaten in the hand fresh from the garden; milk, buttermilk, clabbered milk, and coffee made on the open fire; and homemade preserves of every kind. Yet as a farm boy Frank dreamed of the day when he himself would control such bounteous acres—he vowed that he would then have "all the cream he wanted." For sound dietetic reasons, his consumption of this item was limited. But the wholesome work and abundant natural food from which Frank benefitted during this period was a contributory factor, together with the longevity of various ancestors on both sides, to the unfaltering physical and mental performance that Wright was to keep up throughout a life that lasted almost into a tenth decade.

Like Nathaniel Hawthorne at Brook Farm, Frank was appalled when he first realized the amount of hard physical work in the world. He did not always take a willing share, and on one occasion ran away from the farm routine. He was found at the ferry over the Wisconsin River and brought back. There was no punishment. Uncle James merely continued to insist, in a kindly but implacable way, that Frank do all the chores assigned to him, until one day the boy felt a sudden access of competence, and began to take pride in endurance and strength. He needed both qualities, for in his sixteenth year an unhappy circumstance made him man of the house in Madison.

William Wright had not been indulging in mere theatrics when he intoned: "Darkness there and nothing more . . .

Merely this, and nothing more . . ." Distraught with melancholia, tired, disappointed, and bored, he reached the conclusion that his home life was unbearable. Anna Wright was equally miserable, and made a decision unusual for a woman of her background at that time: she would agree to a separation.

"Well, Mr. Wright, leave us," said Anna, when she had made up her mind. "I will manage with the children. Go your way." Whereupon William Wright took his violin under his arm, put on his hat, and walked out. His wife and children never saw him again.

Needless to say, the departure of his father was a profound shock to Frank Wright. In addition, he felt a kind of unvoiced public disapproval of his mother, as though a deserted woman was somehow not much better than a divorced woman; but resentment and pride combined to keep his head high. Nevertheless, his father set an example that went deep; a man had a duty, it seemed, to something within himself beyond wife and family; a man might have genius that demanded loyalty above anything the conventional world could know. Of course William Wright had produced nothing of lasting value except some ideas he planted in his son's mind; but whether the idea that genius transcends all ethical rules was a good one is debatable, and will remain so till the end of time. Every selfish and demanding Wagner, perhaps, can be balanced by a great-hearted Beethoven; and the gifted, willful, and dangerous Shelley might be set off by a respectable Tennyson, a chivalrous Browning, or a saintly Blake. But at the time of his father's desertion, Frank Wright felt that he confronted no complicated problem of ethics. The question was quite simple: how was he to help support the family, acquire the education of an architect, and start in practice? It appeared that all this must be done in Madison, a place of limited opportunity in those days even though it was capital of Wisconsin and seat of the state university. It was true that the unbounded opportunities of Chicago, fastest-growing city in the world, lay only 139 miles to the south. But from Chicago Frank's Uncle Jenkin, now one of the most powerful Unitarian preachers in the Middle West, sent word that Frank should stay in Madison, as the city's temptations were too much for young men. Jenkin Lloyd-Jones was a bearded person with a piercing eye, greatly deferred to by his sister on account of his prodigious learning, and the warning could have had no more effect if it had come direct from President Grover Cleveland.

An opening of sorts developed in Madison where Frank got a job as general helper in the office of Allen D. Conover, contractor, man of good will, and Dean of Engineering at the university. Conover arranged Frank's schedule so that he could attend classes and earn a small salary as well. In later life Wright had a poor opinion of higher formal education, and one not entirely unjustified, to be sure; but he also liked to say that his own college courses had taken up nearly four years. In this his memory deceived him, for the records show that he finished only two-thirds of sophomore year. Perhaps the most valuable course was his two terms of descriptive geometry, dealing as it does with forms in three-dimensional space. No architecture as such was ever formally taught to Frank Lloyd Wright; his experience in the Conover office was that of a practical draftsman and engineer.

Although Madison was in many ways no more than a provincial village in 1885, the year Frank entered the university, it was by no means out of touch with a country that was literally on the boil with artistic, intellectual, and polit-

ical ideas. Impressive testimony to the power of ideas had
been furnished by the Civil War that had sundered the
nation; and though the South had recently been strangling
in the throes of Reconstruction, some of the old agrarian
doctrine was still coming through clear and strong to southern Wisconsin. But this was a northern state, and the dom-
inant intellectual strain that set the mental climate in which
Frank Wright developed his ideas was out of the New
England from which abolitionism and Transcendentalism
came. Drawn in general from the intellectual ambience
of Madison, and in particular from his schoolteacher mother,
the complete set of Transcendentalist doctrines was planted
in the mind of Frank Lloyd Wright. Granted that the movement as a formal thing had ended forty years before, its
high-minded basic notions of idealistic individualism and
self-reliance, and its theory that human perfectibility could
be coupled with social reform—these were in the American
air. It was true that Emersonian self-reliance might have its
aspect of intellectual arrogance; and a faint but unmis-
takable tone of priggishness could be detected at times. For
example, Emerson was not at his most attractive when he
said at the outbreak of combat in the Civil War that for
once gunpowder smelt good. For all of that, it was primarily
Emerson who spoke through all the subsequent philoso-
phizings of Frank Lloyd Wright.

Ralph Waldo Emerson had a number of helpers, however, at laying down the basic stock of ideas in young
Frank Wright's mind. There was John Ruskin, whose *Seven
Lamps of Architecture*, the gift of Aunts Jane and Nell, was
the first book of esthetic criticism Frank read. Ruskin held
that art and architecture are national expressions and ruled
by laws of integrity and morality. If this is a fallacy, it is one
of the most powerful ever generated, and today largely

unquestioned. Frank Wright welcomed the idea that a
building could be honest or dishonest. Most of those he saw
and heard of, he decided, fell into the latter category. He
was also exposed to the belief that if the truths of esthetic
ethics were handed down from on high by Ruskin, Matthew Arnold was their chief earthly prophet and interpreter. Like all schoolteachers of the time, Mrs. Wright and
her sisters venerated Arnold, himself an educational official
as well as professor of poetry at Oxford. Wright's thinking
as he recorded it from early youth was clearly organized
around Arnold's doctrine of a high general good called
culture, that shed over mankind the light of ethical and
artistic excellence. The enemies of culture were the Bar-
barians or aristocrats, allied with the Philistines or bour-
geoisie. For a poor, ambitious and yearning young man
who felt within himself a bursting talent, this was com-
forting doctrine indeed. It made one automatically wiser
and better than almost anybody one might meet.

Partly from this conviction, and partly because of the
architectural poverty of Madison at the time, Frank Wright
as a college student had the notion that all America was as
much deprived of esthetic values as the place in which he
found himself. Especially lacking, as young Frank Wright
saw it, was an essentially American expression of the spirit
of the times. In this he was mistaken. Largely or entirely
unknown to Wright as a young student, three fine artists
had come to maturity, and each according to his bent treated
the American scene in a native manner. Winslow Homer,
Albert Pinkham Ryder, and Thomas Eakins were the three
painters whose work Wright might profitably have studied.
Indeed, James Abbot McNeil Whistler had shown "The
White Girl" at the Salon des Refusés in Paris three years
before Wright was born. However, one might concede

Whistler to European and Japanese art, reserving only the right to point out something uncompromisingly American in his approach to work and life. But the other three were in the pure American grain. The year before Wright's birth, Homer painted "The Bridle Path, White Mountains," with its keen feeling for that part of the native landscape; and by the time Wright entered college, the great water-colorist and draftsman had added to his oil paintings a record of American life, mostly on the Eastern seaboard, that was to stand as the finest sort of dramatic realism. And his "Landscape With Figures," showing children crossing a wooden bridge to school, combined a recognition of the nature of materials with the artist's feeling for geometric forms in space. Against this triumphant realism stood the work of Albert Ryder, painter of fabulous landscapes under moonlit clouds. Though he had toured England, France, Holland, Italy, and Spain, it was the American scene that Ryder veiled with mists of romanticism from a deeply-felt inner life. He studied the forms of nature on his long, lonely walks, and his primary material was light and shadow. Years after Ryder's death in 1917 Frank Lloyd Wright made a penetrating remark about the powerful effects of light and shade "used as a painter uses them." Always he was closer to Ryder than he might have thought, but Thomas Eakins, the third of the great triumvirate, was completely Wright's man. Much as Wright might deride realistic painting—and he went on record in maturity to the effect that non-representational pictures were the better kind—still there was a deep kinship with Eakins. Wright maintained, for example, that a brick should be a brick, that its excellence lay in its quality of being a "brick brick." Eakins could find no fault with this.

When it came to architecture Wright, as a young student,

was living in a country that flashed and crackled with imaginative and splendid works of building, whether he knew it or not. He had been born just at the time when the romantic revivals were coming to a close.

The Greek and Gothic revivals had been flourishing for over forty years. Indeed, there were architects who worked in either style, like Alexander Jackson Davis, who erected a Gothic mansion straight out of the Waverley novels for the mercantile William Pauldings at Tarrytown, New York, and seven years later, in 1845, built a Grecian palace in the city for John Cox Stevens, founder of the New York Yacht Club. Long previous to this, in 1799, the classicist Benjamin H. Latrobe, chief architect of the U. S. Capitol, had erected one of the earliest American Gothic mansions for the Philadelphia merchant William Crammond. But the romanticists were not confined to what they called Gothic; in a riot of imagination, they ran freely over Turkish, Moorish, Venetian, Swiss, Egyptian, and Italian styles. In the latter manner, they designed some of the finest American houses of the mid-nineteenth century, such as John Notman's residence for Bishop Doane at Burlington, New Jersey, and Sikes's beautifully proportioned Stebbins house at Springfield, Massachusetts. In public structures something that might be called American Empire Monumental was evoked in the massive State, War, and Navy Building in Washington, and the Philadelphia City Hall. Picturesque to a startling degree was the Smithsonian Institution by James Renwick, Jr., a work sometimes unjustly dimissed as absurd; but Renwick's Grace Church, and Richard Upjohn's Trinity Church, both in New York City, were properly hailed as masterpieces from the beginning.

It was by no means miraculous that the America in which Wright went to his first studies should have a tradition of

fine building for public and private use. Even the Puritans
had craved at least the beauty of seemliness and order, causing Edward Johnson to say in 1654: "Further the Lord hath
been pleased to turn all the wigwams, huts and hovels the
English dwelt in at their first coming into orderly, fair and
well-built houses, well furnished many of them."

Two hundred and thirty years later the professional architect had risen in the land. Henry Hobson Richardson had
completed the Trinity Church of Boston, and was in the full
flight of his series of libraries, city halls, courthouses, and
commercial structures in which he demonstrated his mastery
of Romanesque forms. Equally interesting was a comparatively modest Richardsonian commission, the Stoughton
house in Cambridge, with its wide windows and romantic
shingled tower. Richard Morris Hunt had embarked on his
career of building majestic mansions for the captains of industry who had risen in the wake of the Civil War. Even
more significant than the launching of Hunt was the founding, three years before the start of the Stoughton house, of
the architectural firm of McKim, Mead, and White. Setting
up their office in 1879, Charles Follen McKim and Stanford
White, who had both studied with Richardson, and William
Rutherford Mead were to leave their impress on the cities
of the nation through a revived classicism that can be described as the American Renaissance. Some of their club-
houses and city mansions remain to this day, together with
New York's Pennsylvania Station, to show what wealthy
patronage and superb professional competence can do when
teamed in search of a metropolitan style. Not so well known,
and presumably almost completely unknown to Frank
Wright in Wisconsin, were the fine seaside houses done by
this firm in the early eighties, along with the work of such
men as William Ralph Emerson and Arthur Rich. These

wonderfully charming shingle mansions, that seemed to grow naturally on the dunes above the beaches, were backgrounds for the sort of life that Homer's pictures recorded, and that Henry James mentioned in the short novel *An International Episode*. It will be recalled that in this story Lord Lambeth, the visiting Englishman, and his friend Mr. Beaumont went to Newport to stay at the Westgate house, finding it "a very picturesque structure, resembling a magnified chalet," with "a veranda of extraordinary width all around it, and many doors and windows open to the veranda." These openings had in common "such an accessible, hospitable air, such a breezy flutter within of light curtains, such expansive thresholds and reassuring interiors," that the visitors "hardly knew which was the regular entrance, and after hesitating a moment, presented themselves at one of the windows." Soon they were established on the shady side of the piazza, which they found spacious and pleasingly proportioned, noting that "with its awnings, its fanciful chairs, its cushions and rugs, its view of the ocean, close at hand, tumbling along the base of the low cliffs whose level tops intervened in lawn-like smoothness, it formed a charming complement to the drawing-room." This house impressed Lord Lambeth as "a very jolly place," and the modern reader is justified in assuming that it mingled inner and outer space as though its designers were prescient of laws later to be laid down in Vienna, Paris, and Wisconsin.

America's first architectural school was that of the Massachusetts Institute of Technology, founded in 1865, and from this school, with additional study at the Beaux Arts in Paris, had come the one architect of his time, other than Richardson, that young Frank Wright could respect. Wright particularly revered Louis Henri Sullivan, who was working with the engineer-architect Dankmar Adler in Chicago by

1879, and of Sullivan's originality and artistic integrity
there could be no doubt. A few years before, the gifted
Sullivan had walked out of the Philadelphia office of Furness
and Hewitt because of his resentment over what he considered discourteous treament by George Hewitt, the junior
partner. By the time Wright entered college, Sullivan was
in the front rank of Chicago architects not only as a practitioner, but as a theorist who had a remarkable amount to
say about the nature of design, even for his highly articulate
profession. Carrying a textbook of botany in his pocket, Sullivan held forth about the natural forms that he believed
should lie at the heart of all honest architecture. His ornamentation was already gaining notice; perhaps it owed something to the influences now starting the European Art
Nouveau, and something to the initial letters of the Book of
Kells; but most of all it was an expression of Sullivan's
overflowing talent, which might lead to the conclusion
that Sullivan did the thing first as his daemon compelled
him, then sought to create, in conversation and writing, a
philosophy to explain why it was so. In this, and in much
else, Frank Lloyd Wright was to be Sullivan's follower.

The Transcendentalist magazine, *The Dial*, had featured
architectural criticism as early as 1840; the American Institute of Architects was founded in 1857, and eleven years
later the first professional journal was published. It will be
noted that American architects organized in a trade group
before there was formal schooling available to their craft.
The engineers whose art and science was the literal support
of architecture also organized themselves at an early date,
setting up the American Society in 1852. Two years later
Elisha Graves Otis gave the first demonstration of a trust-
worthy passenger and freight elevator, calling out, "All safe,
gentlemen!" when his platform rose to the second floor. To-

gether with the achievement of James Bogardus of New York, who erected an iron-membered business building in 1848, this was one of the greatest gifts engineering ever made to architecture. Other magnificent feats of American Victorian engineering were the railroad viaducts, such as that put up at Carrolton, Maryland, by the Baltimore and Ohio Railroad in 1829. The mile-long railroad bridge at Louisville came in 1868, but the highest glories of American Victorian engineering were probably the bridges for general traffic that slowly conquered the great rivers of the land: that of James Buchanan Eads, spanning the Mississippi at St. Louis, with a structure of steel arches that was started in 1868, completed in 1874; the Suspension Bridge over the Ohio at Cincinnati, that took from 1856 to 1866 to build; and noblest of all, the Brooklyn Bridge, which might be said to have cost the lives of its builders, John Augustus Roebling and his son Washington Augustus, in the ordeal that lasted from the year Frank Lloyd Wright was born to 1883. Thomas Eakins of the penetrating eye and unwavering sense of actuality expressed the debt of art to engineering when he visited the Paris Exposition of 1867 and withheld praise from everything he saw except an American locomotive. A few years later, he showed what he was getting at in his picture called "The Oarsmen." Here was a pair of racing men in a two-oared shell—itself no mean piece of engineering—swinging past a massive pier of the Schuylkill River Bridge. Masonry, machinery, and human purpose were combined to symbolize Eakins'—and Wright's—contemporary America.

Further and perhaps more nearly complete understanding of Wright may come from a survey of what this America amounted to in the aggregate at the time his father's departure made him a young adult at an early age. In 1840, a population of about 17,000,000 had been centered near Charleston, West Virginia, so that more than half the people of America were seen to be living west of the Appalachian barrier, out of direct touch with Europe. Forty years later, the population had grown to more than 50,000,000, with its center a few miles west of Cincinnati. Although the first transcontinental railroads had joined in Utah about the time Wright was born, the West was still regarded as an undeveloped region of boundless opportunity in his late adolescence; to the popular mind it stood for adventure and high returns as against a presumably conservative and low-earning East. So too the rewarding ideas of Transcendentalism had been rooted out of New England soil into the West of which Wisconsin might be called a part. Though Emerson and Channing and their friends had serious faults, they spoke for the grandeur of the human mind and will; against this there seemed to rise from the city countinghouses a dry unhuman voice like that of Daniel Drew, who liked to say, "The dog that snaps the quickest gets the bone." Yet even Drew had respectable allies: Charles Darwin's *Origin of Species*, published in 1859, had set loose in the English-speaking world the idea that nature's first law said only the fittest would survive, and though this was a considerable distortion of the great observer's rule of natural selection by inherited favorable variations, it admirably suited the temper of the time. In social philosophy, this "Darwinian" idea agreed with the popular notion of what Herbert Spencer was teaching in his *Principles of Sociology*, the entire conception being wrapped up in the homely maxim that every tub should stand on its own bottom. Thus, while Wright's head was filled as a youth with notions of the higher unity and the perfectibility of man, he also acquired a lifelong suspicion of nonproducers, bureaucrats, professors, and committees. But here too he was backed by Emerson, who had tartly expressed his disapproval of providing "alms for sots," and of schemes for "the education of fools at college."

Frank Lloyd Wright was neither a fool nor a failure at college. He even achieved social success, though most of his slender pay went to his mother, who was struggling to keep the family going on what she could earn as a teacher, plus frequent consignments of produce from the Lloyd-Jones farms. But Mrs. Wright wanted her son to enjoy some college life, and took her gold Swiss watch to Old Man Perry, the pawnbroker, when Frank was tapped for the Phi Delta Theta fraternity. Anna Wright also managed to get a mink collar to sew on his overcoat when he went to his first college prom.

On this occasion Frank's date was arranged by a classmate, the sophisticated Charlie Ware, who persuaded a pretty cousin, May White, to attend the dance as the partner of his diffident friend. The man of the world said everything would go off with ease, but Frank was nervous, as he was still shy around young women.

Suffering agonies much like those of another Middle Westerner, Booth Tarkington's William Sylvanus Baxter, Frank presented himself at May's dormitory in a hired carriage, wearing evening dress with patent leather pumps, and carrying white gloves in his hand. At the hall, Frank managed to lose his lady in the crowd, and several dances went by before she located him. The kindly Charlie Ware smoothed things over by seeing that May's dance program was filled—a detail Frank had overlooked—but she seemed rather distant all evening long.

After the ball, when Frank deposited May at her door, he had an idea he was supposed to kiss her good night, but instead, he muttered something about having had a good time, and rushed back to his carriage as though escaping from a great natural disaster. All his life Frank used to wonder if May had managed to open the door and get inside the dormitory. He said he always assumed that she had.

That was in Wright's freshman year, and when this annual dance came again, he gamely gave it another try, with a nice town girl named Blanche Ryder. He had a more assured air and enjoyed himself, being honest enough to admit afterward that most of the smooth going was due to the lady's tact. But in spite of the joy of being alive and young, Frank was restive in Madison. He suffered with a ceaseless fear that both town and university lacked almost everything he needed. And he was certain that with all its pitfalls, Chicago held the answer.

"There are great buildings in Chicago, mother," he argued. "There must be great architects too. I am going to be an architect. I am nowhere near it here." One remark would lead to another, and he would lose his temper, and say that his mother was willing for them all to starve because the Lloyd-Joneses were "cracked about education." Sorry for the hurt he inflicted, he would then quiet down for a while. But one day, after much thought alone in his room, on whose walls his mother's cathedral prints were still displayed, Frank walked downstairs and into the study where William Wright's books stood on the shelves. He took down the calf-bound Plutarch and a good set of Gibbon. He bundled up the books and the mink collar from his overcoat, and went to Old Man Perry, who advanced him seven dollars for the lot. Without going home to say good-by, he went to the station and boarded the next train for Chicago.

The train rolled on, the hills began to flatten into prairie, and darkness fell. After a while he saw a glow along the skyline to the south. Frank Lloyd Wright knew this was the city, but he had no way of knowing that in the next few years he would find within himself a strength and energy to match Chicago's own.

Chapter Two

WRIGHT AND SULLIVAN

When Frank Lloyd Wright came to Chicago in the spring of 1887, he carried his entire property in a carpetbag, and had cash resources of seven dollars, minus the fare from Madison. His courage almost failed him at the sight of the roaring, bustling, gaslit streets which struck him as indescribably ugly and unfriendly. He put up at a cheap hotel, cut his diet to doughnuts and coffee, and set out to find a job in one of the many architectural offices in the swiftly building city.

Chicago had almost entirely burned down less than twenty years before, and within the memory of man had been little more than a mudflat. Indeed, mud was still a major municipal problem at the time Frank Lloyd Wright arrived. The city fathers had tried the experiment of paving Wabash Avenue with stove lids not long before, and the tale was told that rescuers pulled a man from mud up to his neck in Lake Street, whereupon it was discovered he had been standing on a mule. Only thirty years ago the city had been a frontier outpost where deer drank from the river and wolves howled at night. Now it was the most explosively growing place on earth. Timber from the far west, ores from the Mesabi range, the trade of the surrounding Middle Western hinterland—all flowed through Chicago because of its supremely advantageous location at the foot of Lake Michigan, and caused wealth to pile up as rapidly as buildings. There was created a new class of millionaires, and these men needed architects to put up palaces on Prairie Avenue, and massive commercial structures in the Loop. Some of these lords of Chicago had arrived in town as ped-

dlers with packs on their shoulders, and all of them were
fond of remarking that they had not come there for their
health. The moneymen built their great houses for the sound
reasons of glorification and display, but usually insisted they
were only plain citizens who wanted nothing more than
adequate shelter for their wives and children. This was the
tone of Gustavus F. Swift, for example, when he remarked,
in the measured manner suitable to a leading meat packer,
"To those men who have families and who find in their
homes the greatest of their pleasures, Chicago offers all that
New York offers, and in my opinion, more. A man can
get wholesome food in Chicago more cheaply than he can
in the East, and he can live as well on a smaller amount of
money. I do not go in for luxuries myself. Chicago is good
enough for me. I can spend my money fast enough here."[1]
Perhaps Mr. Swift did not escape a suggestion of complac-
ency in that statement. But one cannot help admiring the
spirit displayed at the time of the great fire by a group of
his contemporaries that included Generals Corse and Ledlie,
George and James Young, J. K. Fisher, and John Janes.
These men were completely burned out during the night,
and having had no sleep, assembled at the Chicago Club for
what they called "a champagne supper for breakfast." While
they were drinking wine, fire spread to the clubhouse. Rally-
ing their forces, the clubmen filled their pockets with cigars,
took a demijohn of whiskey from the cellar, and carried a
red satin sofa out to the lakefront, where they finished their
breakfast in peace. That was Chicago. No one could sum
up the city in a few words, but Theodore Dreiser had a try
at it, in his best concrete-mixer prose: "By its shimmering
lake it lay, a king in shreds and patches, a maundering yokel

---

[1] Quoted by Wayne Andrews in *Architecture, Ambition and Americans.*

with an epic in its mouth, a tramp, a hobo among cities, with the grip of Caesar in its mind, the dramatic force of Euripides in its soul. A very bard of a city, this, singing of high deeds and high hopes, its heavy brogans buried deep in the mire of circumstance."

What confronted Frank Lloyd Wright as he set out on his fourth morning in town was not the mire of circumstance, nor even the heady air of disaster, but the cold emptiness of fear. With no breakfast in his stomach, and only a few coppers in his pocket, Wright summoned reserves of resolution to face what might well be another day of discouragement, administered by insolent office boys and patronizing junior draftsmen. Today he would have to land a job, or start beating his way back to Madison. As Wright remembered it afterward, he had promised himself he would not apply for help to his Uncle Jenkin, for he wanted to hear a sermon by that notable clergyman only from the pulpit. Now he needed the help of his uncle—or the essential stroke of luck that gives a creative man his first chance to show what he can do.

As it happened, this good fortune came when Wright walked into the office of Joseph Lyman Silsbee and was interviewed by a draftsman named Cecil Corwin. This young man appears to have been one of those persons, like Keats's friend Severn, who show up over the years without a flaw. As courteous as Wright's previous interviewers had been surly and rude, Corwin sat down in the outer office, put aside Wright's roll of sample drawings, and looked instead at the young man who proffered them.

"You're a minister's son," said Corwin.

"Yes, how did you know?"

"I'm one myself, so I can always tell. So is Silsbee, and

two other fellows here. If you come in, there would be five of us."

"Well—*could* I by any chance come in?" Wright asked.

"Let's see what you have here," Corwin answered, as he unrolled the drawings. After a moment he said, "You have a good touch. Wait a minute."

Corwin went away and came back with a tall, distinguished-looking man whose eyeglasses hung on a long gold chain. This was Silsbee himself, a transplanted New Englander like so many Chicagoans, and one of the most successful house designers in town. He glanced at Wright, and then made him a professional by saying, "Take him on as a tracer—eight dollars."

Wright was pleased at landing a job, but disappointed at the wages, for he had hoped to start at three times Silsbee's offer. He turned to go, and the sound-hearted Corwin followed him, correctly guessing that the youth was broke. Corwin suggested that he be allowed to act as host for lunch at Kinsley's, a restaurant widely known for its nourishing corned beef hash. After eating his first decent meal since arriving in Chicago, Wright accepted Cecil's invitation to stay with the Corwins until he could find better lodgings than those at the dingy hotel.

That night, Frank found himself in a wholesome and familiar atmosphere as he played and sang after supper at the piano with Cecil's sister, who looked after her bachelor brother and their father, a retired Congregational missionary whose wife had died some years before. Then when Cecil showed him to the clean and tidy guest room, Frank said he wanted to write to his mother, and asked for a pen and paper. With this supplied, he added a characteristic request: "Could you lend me ten dollars? I'll pay you back two dollars a week." Corwin put a ten-dollar bill on the writing table. In a few minutes Wright stood before the mail box on the corner, and dropped in the envelope containing the money. It was a great moment—the sending back of the first money, though borrowed, that his venture to the ctiy had brought in.

This happened on a Saturday, and early the following Monday, young Wright reported for work. He found on the boards a number of houses in the Queen Anne residential style of which Silsbee was a polished master. A nearly completed commission was the Unitarian Church of All Souls, and this building was of especial interest to Wright, since the congregation was presided over by his uncle. After work Corwin and Wright went out to Oakwood Boulevard to see how the job was going. Frank noted that it looked more like a clubhouse than a church, and then was startled when someone seized him by the collar from behind. He wrenched around and saw that his assailant, who had leaped from a place of concealment, and now stood accusing, bearded, burly, and wearing a long-tailed coat, was none other than his uncle, the Rev. Dr. Jenkin Lloyd-Jones.

Uncle Jenkin said his sister had written that she was distracted with anxiety about Frank, and he seemed in a considerable temper himself, but became calmer when told that Frank was employed and had already sent money to Madison. The pastor of All Souls was further mollified when Corwin assured him that Frank had landed his job solely on the merit of sample drawings, and had not mentioned that he was a client's nephew. Dr. Lloyd-Jones then had to admit the boy had done well in finding a respectable place to stay, in a clergyman's home.

"I promise you, Uncle Jenk," said Wright, "I'll soon be able to send for Mother and the girls."

But it was evident as the weeks went by that Wright could

scarcely support himself on his wages from the Silsbee office. He got a four dollar raise, but that was eaten up by the rent of the furnished room on Vincennes Avenue to which he had moved, though urged to remain without payment at the kindly Corwins'. The money shortage was so painful that Wright soon asked for a raise to fifteen dollars a week. When Silsbee refused, Wright went to another firm, but found it unsatisfactory and came back. Peering over his gold-rimmed glasses, Silsbee merely said, "Ah, Wright. Here you are again, eh? You may have eighteen dollars."

Meanwhile, Dr. Lloyd-Jones kept in touch with his nephew and saw to it that he took part in the social life of All Souls parish. Frank conquered his shyness in the presence of girls at a round of parties, concerts, and amateur plays, like the production of *Les Misérables*, in which he impersonated a French officer with a sword, cavalry boots, and red coat. At the dance after the performance, he bumped into a girl named Catherine Tobin with such force that they both fell down. As he helped her up, Wright saw that she was uncommonly graceful and pretty, with fine coloring, blue eyes, and curly auburn hair that seemed to have sunshine in it. A member of the chorus of village girls, Catherine was wearing a bright bodice and cap, and a peasant skirt that swirled when she danced away.

Formally presented as soon as he could find a chaperone to perform that service, Wright immediately became interested in Catherine—and on her part, she was fascinated with this bright and handsome admirer, and life became delightful for them both. Frank escorted Catherine on walks and picnics, took her to parties and concerts, lectured her on literature, life, and art. Catherine's response soon showed that Wright was her favorite among all who competed for her smiles, and her parents began to worry for fear he was not a sufficiently substantial young man. On his part, Frank showed he could take responsibility by bringing his mother and sisters to town, and arranging for board at the home of Miss Augusta Chapin, a lady who held the position, unusual for one of her sex, of Universalist pastor in Oak Park.

This western suburb, which was to become famous because of Frank Lloyd Wright, was a conservative, churchgoing community whose leading residents all enjoyed what were known as easy circumstances in the polite idiom of the time. The straight, shady streets were lined with big frame houses, many of them in the turreted shingle style in which Silsbee was so accomplished. As Wright inspected these houses, he found that the sight of their spreading, fretworked porches made him furious, and the "murderous corner-towers" that frequently provided a bay window on the ground floor made him ill. In truth, the best of these houses were as comfortable as they were picturesque, with a spacious plan that provided pleasing nooks and crannies opening from a central hall. Wright also failed to observe that these houses had one characteristic for which he might in all consistency have expressed approval: this was their almost complete lack of historic style. Perhaps overlooking this aspect of Oak Park, Wright felt that an entire new system of architectural ideas was taking shape in his mind.

Wright admitted influences, to be sure. At this period, he was reading the works of Eugène-Emmanuel Viollet-le-Duc, the French architect, critic, and restorer of Notre Dame and the Ste. Chapelle in Paris and the cathedrals of Amiens and Laon. Viollet-le-Duc taught "rational architecture," and stated that a building should express its purpose. In addition, Wright found in the library at All Souls parish house a book called *The Grammar of Ornament*, by Owen

Jones, an English architect with a Welsh name. Five of Jones's general propositions struck Wright as absolutely sound:

1. The Decorative Arts rise from, and should be properly attendant upon Architecture.

2. Architecture is the material expression of the wants, the faculties, and the sentiments, of the age in which it is created. Style in Architecture is the peculiar form that expression takes under the influence of climate and materials, at command.

3. As Architecture, so all works of Decorative Arts, should possess fitness, proportion, harmony, the result of all which is repose.

4. True beauty results from that repose which the mind feels when the eye, the intellect, and the affections, are satisfied from the absence of any want.

5. Construction should never be decorated. Decoration should never be purposely constructed. That which is beautiful is true; that which is true must be beautiful.

Whether or not the successful architects of the time were following these principles, the most lucrative commissions to be obtained in domestic work were the stone castles of the new millionaires. In Chicago, an outstanding example of such an assignment was the house at Eighteenth Street and Prairie Avenue, recently completed for John J. Glessner, a founder of the International Harvester Company, by Henry Hobson Richardson, who was also represented in Chicago by a massive "wholesale store" built for Marshall Field. Richardson's work had strength and character, but sometimes received praise for qualities not perceptible to the average viewer. In the Glessner house, indeed, one might well imagine that Richardson had fortification in mind, and against an army specializing in heavy artillery. Some sensitive persons regarded the mansion as directly threatening in its effect; but nothing took place behind its thick walls more reprehensible than the dowager Mrs. Glessner's Sunday morning reading class, a generally admired cultural activity, attendance at which was a sign of high social standing.

Richardson made an impression on Chicago, with his bright-colored waistcoats, lordly but genial manner, and exceptionally large capacity for champagne. But his health was bad and his habit of high living may have hastened his end, which came three weeks after the completion of the Glessner house. Though Wright could not have given full approval to the historical element in Richardson's work, he was undoubtedly influenced, and in a perfectly proper direction, by Richardson's insistence that the architect's craft and profession was important and worthy of high respect— and high pay.

Though the Glessner house was by far the weightiest composition on the Prairie Avenue scene, there were many other notable domestic structures in the neighborhood. Across the street, for example, was the many-windowed mansion designed by Solon Spencer Beman for W. W. Kimball, head of a piano- and organ-manufacturing firm. Beman, who drew his inspiration from a French château, raised his handsome towers of limestone over a marble porch. Such assured elegance, and that of many other houses of this sort in Chicago, aroused objections in Frank Lloyd Wright —these styles were not the American thing. Beman did better, Wright thought, in Chicago's Grand Central Station, where the architect and his collaborating engineer, W. S.

Jones, placed a light and airy train shed under a great roof of iron and glass. This was direct, good, and new. Wright also may have pondered on the construction of the new Union Station, and noticed its engineering, with members bolted to monolithic piers for support in the soft earth of the site beside the Chicago River. Great railroad stations had sprung up throughout the country—a notable example being erected at Cleveland in 1884, with the most remarkable of them all, the St. Louis Union Station, designed by Theodore C. Link and Edward Cameron, rising from 1891 to 1894. This wonderful structure had a splendid exterior, with a delightfully romantic tower over a cave-like Great Hall with a barrel-vaulted roof that seemed to spring from the floors on either side, so low were the side walls in proportion to the arch, all climaxed in a train shed, engineered by George H. Pegram, that covered several acres. The station expressed all the exuberance and confidence of the time, and seventy years later was still there, holding its own esthetically, if not in volume of traffic, with an airport of concrete and glass.

Important as they were, the railroad stations represented only one aspect of the architectural opportunity in the cities of the country, and especially in Chicago, where Wright could see a new approach to construction in the office buildings, forced higher and higher by the rocketing value of the land, that a new school of designers was putting up, to usher in the age of the skyscraper. There was nothing quaint or picturesque in the Home Insurance Building, recently built from plans by William Le Baron Jenney, a Massachusetts man who had seen action in the Civil War. Jenney devised a skeleton framework for the ten-story building, using wrought iron through the sixth story, and Bessemer steel from there on up. During the same period the energetic and far-seeing Daniel H. Burnham encouraged his partner, John Wellborn Root, to design the Monadnock Block, a retro-gression in that it had no steel construction, but a fine building nevertheless—a mass of masonry that needed no explanation. Root also designed the Reliance Building, a tower of terra cotta and glass, that still adorned the Loop along with the Monadnock in the middle of the twentieth century. Wright cast an appreciative eye on such structures, and on some of the work of William Holabird and Martin Roche. He also was undoubtedly aware of the achievement by the firm of Bauman and Huehl, in their Chamber of Commerce, at La Salle and Washington Streets. Here there was a central court, with balconies running around the periphery at each floor, partly supported by iron beams cantilevered from the central columns.

Such were some of the great buildings that must mean great architects in practice, as Wright told his mother in Madison. These men were as impressive in their persons as in their work: to meet the grueling demands of their profes-sion, they were physically strong, and each in his way a striking personality. Major Jenney was a sturdy man with astonishing energy and a taste for high living like that dis-played by Richardson. John Root, a red-haired Georgian, was at home in the world of fashion, though he liked Bo-hemian parties, and as a good amateur musician was always willing to take a turn at the piano. Daniel H. Burnham was in some ways the most impressive member of his craft at the time Wright came to Chicago. Broad and tall and radiating a blunt force of character, he deferred to his part-ner Root as the creative member of the firm. Burnham's contribution was in engineering, and in his ability to take a firm line with clients, who in themselves were all decisive personalities. Detractors who said this was mere salesmanship on Burnham's part were unfair to one of the most important men of his time. Burnham pointed out the possibilities of the Chicago lakefront, and was its first planner. Had he done no more than this, he would have deserved permanent remembrance. He was also the leading spirit in laying out the World's Columbian Exposition in 1893, and left for all time to his professional colleagues and fellow citizens the bold maxim, "Make no little plans."

But of all the architects who were meeting the challenge of Chicago's unprecedented growth, none appealed to Wright so directly as Louis Henri Sullivan, who was planning a tremendous business block, hotel and opera house for Congress Street and Michigan Avenue. And the second major stroke of luck in Wright's life was his chancing to hear on the architectural grapevine that Sullivan was looking for a draftsman with sufficient taste and skill to help him finish the drawings for the great new structure. When Wright investigated the rumor, he was ushered so promptly into Sullivan's office that he decided to ask for a good salary. Mr. Sullivan, it turned out, was a small, brown man of aristocratic bearing, with a number of sharp pencils on his desk, and an equally pointed glance, that seemed to go clear through his caller. Looking over Wright's drawings, Sullivan's eyes appeared to be photographing each sheet. Then he remarked, "Traced, I suppose?"

"No, sir—free hand."

Wright had taken the precaution of submitting a few samples in Sullivan's own flowing ornamental style, and whether or not he took this as a compliment, Sullivan asked, "What have you been getting in the way of salary?"

"Not enough."

"How much is enough?"

"Twenty-five dollars."

"Come to work Monday morning."

Lyman Silsbee was displeased when Frank reported he was leaving, and said, "This doesn't seem worthy of you, Wright." Frank was momentarily depressed, for he felt he was letting Silsbee down, and he also had a nagging notion he could have obtained forty dollars a week from Sullivan. But these thoughts disappeared as Wright got down to work with Sullivan and his partner, the engineering and business-getting member of the firm, Dankmar Adler. In much the same relation to his twelve-years-younger partner as that of Burnham to Root, Adler seemed to have all the physical and mental strength and endurance that his calling required in a mercilessly competitive city. Adler had served in the Civil War; he was deep-chested and heavy, and stood so solidly on his feet that he reminded Wright of an old Byzantine church. This formidable man could handle clients or contractors with equal firmness. He was also a judge of talent, and concurred when Sullivan raised Wright's salary after a trial period and put him in a private office just outside his own workroom.

In those days, the science of personnel relations had not yet been thought of, and bosses would have considered anyone insane who suggested they curry favor with the help. Louis Sullivan, therefore, was quite in step with his time when he habitually and freely expressed his contempt for draftsmen who failed to understand his ideas or turned in unsatisfactory work. But he was courteous to Wright, and treated him with respect. Indeed, Sullivan valued his new man so highly almost from the very first days of their association, that he employed an understudy "in case anything happened to Wright." This was George Grant Elmslie, a talented youth who some years later would be a partner in the eminent firm of Purcell and Elmslie. Now he was happy to be in the Adler and Sullivan office as Wright's backstop—and was a most pleasant-natured and loyal young man. All this came under the close scrutiny of the rest of the employees, and caused resentment among a clique of draftsmen. The unconcealed bad feeling of this group made Wright resolve that he would be prepared for action.

Accordingly, he went to a professor of mayhem during the noon hours, learning the holds and punches of rough-and-tumble fighting, keeping this training a military secret. Soon he was challenged to boxing matches that were undisguised grudge fights. He more than held his own, not so much from the science of the professor as from the fact that he was in better shape than his assailants, since he neither smoked nor drank, and walked to and from work a total of eighty blocks every day to save carfare. The wearing of boxing gloves kept the office encounters technically on a sporting level, but Wright had added something of Sullivan's imperious attitude to his own naturally self-confident manner, and sooner or later serious trouble was bound to break out.

It came late one afternoon after the bosses had gone, when the leader of the office bullies threw Wright's hat down the stair well and said, "You're just a Sullivan toady anyway. We all know it."

Wright had absorbed one invaluable lesson from the teacher of miliary tactics: if there is going to be trouble, hit first. He threw a hard punch that broke the bully's glasses and knocked him off his stool. Wright showed extra courage in this, for it was an unquestioned belief in saloons and livery stables at the time that hitting a man with glasses was a penitentiary offense. As it was, the fellow jumped up screaming, seized the knife that was used for sharpening pencils, and inflicted several deep cuts before Wright managed to knock him unconscious with a T-square. Blood was running into Wright's shoes, and George Elmslie, who had taken no part in the baiting, hurried him to a doctor. Meanwhile, the others threw a bucket of water on Wright's opponent, who came to, gathered his drawing implements and walked out.

After that, there was no more brawling in the offices of Adler and Sullivan. Both partners heard of the affair, but neither mentioned it. Adler liked a man who stood up for himself, and Sullivan didn't care what happened to a common draftsman, so long as nothing interefered with Wright, "the good pencil in his hand."

For six years that were to have an unhappy ending, Wright worked at the Adler and Sullivan office, not only as a pencil in hand, but as a pencil that could propel itself, so to speak, in a highly commendable way. He became a friend of Sullivan—or perhaps it is more accurate to say that he entered into a relationship of disciple to teacher. "Lieber Meister—" beloved master—was the title he gave Sullivan, and masterful indeed was Sullivan's performance on the great commission for which Wright had originally been hired. The Auditorium, a promotion of a businessman named Ferdinand Peck, who got the idea from a temporary lakefront opera house constructed by Adler and Sullivan, was to contain a magnificent concert hall seating 4,000 people, a hotel of four hundred rooms, and rentable office space as well. The main mass of the building rose twelve floors, with a seventeen-story tower on Congress Street. The backers had a moment of doubt when they saw Sullivan's severe Romanesque façade, and realized the magnitude of what he and his partner had conceived for them. Accordingly they sent for Prof. William R. Ware of the Massachusetts Institute of Technology, Sullivan's old teacher, and asked him to look over their plans and give a critique for a fee of one thousand dollars. After inspecting the drawings, Ware came before the syndicate members with a grave expression on his face that indicated his full sense of the responsibility with which they had entrusted him. Perhaps hoping that the expert would suggest a modification in the plans, or the appointment of other architects, Peck asked Ware if he himself would have produced a similar design.

"I do not believe I should have reached the same result," said Ware, and the backers looked at one another. Then he went on, "But had I reached such a result, I should consider it the inspiration of my life." There was no further talk of changing plans or sending for consulting architects.

All this was noted by Frank Lloyd Wright as he willingly toiled away on the back-breaking work at the drawing boards, and many years later he was to point out what he identified as his own contribution to the grand hall of the Auditorium. Here Adler's justly acclaimed genius as an acoustical engineer insured that the music would swell out full and undistorted to every listener beneath Sullivan's wonderfully decorated golden arches. There was no finer setting for opera in the world, and many a great performance was given there until 1929, when Samuel Insull, the Mr. Merdle of Chicago, managed to get the company of artists moved into a building he had financed on Wacker Drive, overlooking the river. But all that, and the shabby decline of the entire complex, lay in an unconceivable future on the night of December 9, 1889, when the Auditorium was formally opened. Chicago's leading citizens were there in the packed house, of course; but the national importance of the mighty building was symbolized by the presence of the President and Vice-President of the United

States. And Benjamin Harrison and Levi P. Morton knew that international artistic eminence was represented by the world's most famous diva, Adeline Patti, when she stepped forward and sang "Home, Sweet Home."

Other noteworthy features of the Auditorium were its fine public halls and stairways, quite the proper setting for handsome and well-dressed crowds, and its banquet hall that was suspended within the shell of the building by Adler's cunning engineering plan. There was also an excellent bar, one of the longest in Chicago. Here Sullivan stood amid admirers on the opening night. He downed a drink, and tossed the empty glass over his shoulder. Sullivan did not know it, but he had just passed the high point of his life. Never would there be another such triumph: after that, he would be going down hill. But his young friend Wright, impressed as he was with this success of his master, was to go from one pinnacle to another, always climbing out of the deep and dark valleys that stretched between.

The Adler and Sullivan firm now set up quarters at the top of the seventeen-story Congress Street tower of the Auditorium. Sullivan often talked there in the evening with Frank Lloyd Wright, the two of them looking out with appreciation on the lake, heaven-blue in the summer, gray-green under the patterns of broken ice in winter time. Or they would look south and west, and see the vast fires of mills and factories glowing for miles along the prairie after the sun went down. There was high talk in this high chamber: and Sullivan sometimes tried out the speeches he prepared for fellow architects and cultural groups around the city. He liked to shake up an audience, and got complete prior agreement from his acolyte when he experimented with such remarks as, "American architecture is composed, in the hundred, of ninety parts aberration, eight parts indifference, one part novelty, and one part Little Lord Fauntleroy. You can have the prescription filled at any architectural department store or select millinery establishment." As he made his points, Sullivan would walk around the room; a man of medium size, he took the strides of a giant, as though to compensate for his lack of commanding height. On his part, Wright stood so straight and held his head so high when speaking, that throughout his life trained observers would sometimes report him as a tall man. His height was five feet, eight and one-half inches. He imitated his employer by careful attention to his dress, though his noticeably long hair contrasted with Sullivan's neatly trimmed hair and beard. Wright exchanged ideas with Sullivan on other matters than dress, trading him Owen Jones for a volume of Herbert Spencer, and when Sullivan remarked that most architectural students would be better employed studying to become errand boys or butchers, Wright tossed back the idea that nothing worth while would be accomplished in the building line until between them they revived "the Gothic spirit in the middle west."

On and on flowed the torrents of talk, rushing like a river between hard banks of work. The conversation continued over the lunch table at Kinsley's, and even on the seat of the open carriage in which Sullivan liked to ride up Michigan Avenue. "Viollet-le-Duc is the man," Wright would say, without opposition from Sullivan, who had studied at the École des Beaux Arts in Paris, as well as at the Massachusetts Institute of Technology. Wright pointed out that Viollet-le-Duc had even speculated that a building might be constructed on a bolted metal frame—nothing more nor less than the skyscraper as it was now developed. Sullivan agreed; but he had certain reservations about the skyscraper—the end was not yet, he implied, saying, "Wait a while, and I'll show you what I mean." The tall business building, he said, must not be merely a pile of stories— it must have harmony among its elements. He would ponder this problem as Wright continued to expound how Viollet-le-Duc had said that design must result from the logic of plan, construction, and materials. Necessity, not imagination, was the mother of design. Sullivan may have known that something like this had been stated as early as 1753 by a learned Jesuit, the Abbé Marc-Antoine Laugier. Writing on architecture in general, the Abbé had stated that "one should put nothing into a building that was not excused by sound reason." Such statements fascinated Sullivan. He told Wright that one of his instructors in Paris had told him that it was possible to lay down a general proposition so broad as to admit of no exception. Sullivan thought he might have such an impregnable maxim in the statement: "Form follows function." This apothegm might logically cause Sullivan to search in vain for an explanation of his own delightful ornamentation, but Wright helped him there by saying that Sullivan's decoration was in and of the structure, and not *on* it. Be that as it may, Sullivan could draw with a fine flowing line, and sometimes when he watched Wright working, he would cry, "Make it come alive, man!" On his part, Wright talked a great deal even in these early days of natural forms as the prime architectural source, but his personal module was the geometric form. To be sure, this too exists in nature, as analysis of crystalline structures will show. And Wright proved that it was possible to create ornament of a sort, and at times a quite acceptable sort, with a ruler and T-square. Organic architecture was what Sullivan and Wright incessantly talked about; beautiful, long-lived, and important architecture, by any name, was what they produced. It almost seemed that nothing else was possible in the stimulating air of Chicago in those days. Sullivan remembered later how he felt: "The future looked bright —the flag was in the breeze . . ."

With wonderful things happening every day, it was not surprising that Frank Lloyd Wright asked Catherine Tobin to be his wife, and Catherine accepted him. His mother immediately leagued herself with Catherine's parents and Uncle Jenkin to convince Frank that this was foolish. It *was* foolish, and for that reason they all might have saved their breath. When a three-month exile on Mackinac Island failed to make Catherine give Frank up, the older people surrendered as gracefully as possible, amid a volley of platitudes from Dr. Lloyd-Jones. More to the point was the gesture of Adler and Sullivan, who gave Wright a five-year contract and advanced money for him to build a house in Oak Park on a lot where there already stood a small carpenter Gothic cottage that would be suitable for Frank's mother.

Life now opened out in entrancing vistas for Frank Lloyd Wright. He had a beautiful bride, a home of his own, and plenty of work with congenial employers. At the office, Sullivan seemed to have tapped a new level of talent within himself, as his assistant grew and developed. One day he brought Frank the sketch for a commission he had received in St. Louis, an office building for the rich brewer, Ellis Wainwright. Years before in Philadelphia, Sullivan's eye had fallen on a nine-story building that had been constructed in 1849 from designs by William Johnston. This Jayne building, as it was called, had slender granite piers that rose straight up its façade to conclude in arches, above which a row of circular windows ran beneath the cornice. The Wainwright building also

emphasized its height with continuous piers, rising from the
first three floors that constituted its base, ending with a
course of round windows and a cornice drawing a line over
all. Sullivan was saying that the important thing about a
tall building was that it was tall: a designer should exploit
this—start it, keep it going, and finish it off in the three
essential elements of beginning, middle, and end. Wright
was enchanted with the Wainwright sketch, and gave it
sincere praise. He felt generous joy that he should be in the
confidence of a master whose gifts were so great and whose
vision put beauty and fitness into common things. Indeed,
Wright had the great satisfaction of being entrusted with
more and more of the work when Sullivan was away visiting clients or resting in his retreat at Ocean Springs,
Louisiana, beside Biloxi Bay. Wright felt the pleasure of one
in whom trust is reposed by a respected superior, and gloried
in the thought that he was the highest-paid draftsman in
Chicago. In fact, he might with justice think of himself
as head designer for the Adler and Sullivan firm. But amid
this there was a flaw—high as his salary was for a draftsman,
or even for a designer, there was still not enough money to
support Wright and his family in the way he felt he ought
to live. Wright was entirely justified in creating the need
for extra money—he was not spending on foolishness, dis-
sipation, or mere social display. He wanted to fill his house
with beautiful things, to make an atmosphere of beauty for
the children who were beginning to come along, to have
books and music for himself; and he wanted to do this here
and now. To increase his income, therefore, Wright took
on overtime work at Adler and Sullivan; and one of the most
important of these assignments was the planning of a town
house for the wealthy lumberman, James Charnley. This
client wanted something different from what might be

expected of architects like Beman, or from such Easterners as Hunt, who built the Borden mansion on Lake Shore Drive, or McKim, who was busy in his New York office on the plans for Bryan Lathrop's Georgian house on East Bellevue Place, that later became the home of the Fortnightly Club.

The Charnley house was to stand on a new thoroughfare called Astor Street. Running from Division Street to North Avenue, these six blocks were to become one of America's most remarkable exhibits of fine houses, and Wright knew that on the Charnley job he was performing in the center ring of the Chicago architectural show. He produced a balanced composition of Roman brick on a stone base, with sharp outlines that recalled the strict geometry of the Froebel blocks. Possibly there was in his mind an echo of the fortieth chapter of Isaiah, that he had been compelled to learn in childhood, to the effect that the crooked shall be made straight, and the rough places plain. At any rate, nothing exactly like this had been seen before: it was serene, self-contained, and more than a little cold. In comparison with this chilly reticence, houses in traditional style were likely to seem overstated unless they were very good indeed.

However, the traditional approach to architecture was nearing a great victory. The Chicago World's Columbian Exposition, popularly called the World's Fair, was to be held in 1893, and preparations started two years before. Prime mover among local architects was Daniel Burnham, whose conservatism was mitigated only by the influence of his more enlightened partner Root, or so Sullivan and Wright believed. Now, on the eve of the Fair, Root died, which was more than a sad personal blow to Sullivan and his young assistant. For just as they feared, Burnham invited the most

2. Residence of
   James Charnley,
   Chicago, Illinois, 1891

3. Residence of W. H. Winslow, River Forest, Illinois, 1893

4. Residence of Avery Coonley, Riverside, Illinois, 1908

5. Living Room, Residence of Avery Coonley, Riverside, Illinois, 1908

conservative men in the East to take the lead in planning—
and the forces of classicism included such redoubtable
figures as Hunt, McKim, Mead, White, George B. Post, and
the firm of Peabody and Stearns.[2] It was announced that the
general style of the fair would be classical, with buildings
of uniform height around a Great Court. But the planners
did not neglect Adler and Sullivan—that firm was to design
the Hall of Transportation, standing outside the Court, and
the only conformity requested was in the matter of height.
The entire Fair would be given coherence by its setting
among the lagoons laid out by Frederick Law Olmsted,
designer of New York's Central Park.

Sullivan well understood that such accomplished per-
formers as Hunt and McKim, Mead, and White would make
an impressive show, and that millions of Americans would
pass through the turnstiles to see, and be amazed—and
influenced. He was heartsick. "The damage wrought by
the World's Fair," he wrote, "will last from half a century
from its date, if not longer. It has penetrated deep into the
the constitution of the American mind, effecting there
lesions significant of dementia."

Few of the twenty-eight million visitors, of course,
came to the fair because of an interest in architecture or
were conscious of it. That was what infuriated Sullivan.
These defenseless members of the public would be drawing
in classicism through their pores, so to speak. Of course
this was by no means the disaster that Sullivan claimed; the
architectural triumph of McKim and White led to an
American Renaissance that benefitted the country with
many a fine building. In any event, people had a way of

[2] Influenced by the Palladian element they found in the American
Colonial, the Eastern men had turned away from Richardson's Romanesque, and from the free style of their own seaside "cottages."

enjoying the fair without giving a thought to the why and wherefore. Mrs. William Calhoun, a Chicago lady, tried to give some idea of the magical effect of it all when she later recalled that a radiance hung over the entire summer of the fair. There was some good spell in the atmosphere when the visitors floated in gondolas at dusk around the Wooded Island and glided out upon the splendid Court. Evanescent though these sensations might be, there was sound and practical construction behind the classic façades. Knowledgeable about engineering though they were, Wright and Sullivan may not have given sufficient credit to the highly sophisticated systems of hinged-arch framing that carried the great vaults and domes of glass. Be that as it may, they were wrapped up in their own contribution; except for the Fisheries Building in the Richardsonian manner designed by their fellow townsman Henry Ives Cobb, the Transportation Building was the only departure from the classical canon to be seen among the major structures at the fair, and so was of the greatest importance as a sample of Adler and Sullivan work. Its most striking feature was the central door, surmounted by five arches set one within another, and reminiscent of the treatment Sullivan had given the main hall of the Auditorium. Richly decorated in gold leaf, and orange, red, and yellow stucco, the springing arches were yet subdued by the spreading eaves of a flat roof. It was seen that the secondary elements of this great portal, as well as the roof, had in them a geometrical quality, an insistent horizontality that pointed to the hand of Frank Lloyd Wright. At the time these plans were in the Adler and Sullivan office, Wright was at the top of his authority and influence there; and many critics are convinced that the master, Sullivan, went some distance toward actual collaboration with his pupil in this building—and that the essential architectural convictions of each man were brilliantly blended in what was by far the most notable structure at the great Exposition. Disturbed as Sullivan and Wright might be at the general triumph of the historic style, their own dissenting vote had been registered in a performance for which Sullivan could take a well-earned bow—and summon Wright from the wings, as it were, to share in the applause.

This building was the last important work that Wright shared with Louis Sullivan. They separated in the spring of 1893 because Wright began to work on his own time designing houses for clients of his own. When Sullivan found this out, he ordered Wright to stop his extra activities at once, even though the office was not primarily interested in domestic commissions. But the firm had given Wright extra pay for extra work on the Charnley plans, and Wright asked, so long as he fulfilled his office contract, why could he not work overtime for himself? He now had two children, and was determined to live on a proper scale, as we have seen. Some compromise might have been effected by an appeal to Dankmar Adler's steadiness and common sense. But this was not to be, for Sullivan, who in spite of their intimacy was yet to address Wright by his first name, now spoke to him in the icy manner he had hitherto reserved for occupants of the outer office. Wright found this tone insufferable, hurled down his pencil, and walked out. He later decided he had been the one in the wrong; but twenty years were to pass before Wright again spoke to his "beloved master." During this time Wright was to move on to world renown, while Sullivan continued steadily in his giant strides toward frustration and despair.

Chapter Three

THE CONQUEST
OF CHICAGO

It was a two-and-a-half story shingled house, with a high gable, and a bank of five casement windows on the second floor. Characteristic of everything its owner and designer would create were the curved brick garden wall and the gently rising stone steps that led to its front door. Uncharacteristic, however, was the fact that this entrance was plainly defined and easy to locate. Exactly the opposite might be attributed to many of the great suburban villas to be created by Frank Lloyd Wright. But for all of that, his new small house at 428 Forest Avenue, Oak Park, had the air of privacy, and above all of shelter, that he more than any architect was able to impart. When all was said and done, the design of houses would be the chief glory of this artist. It also would lead him, by way of his relations with a client, into a tragedy so vast and inconceivable that his enduring that agony alone would be his insurance of a sort of fame.

Tragedy and pain were far from the minds of Frank and Catherine as they settled in. An independent architect, like any other man, was facing a national depression in 1893; and the Populist farmers of the West, who had an eloquent champion in William Jennings Bryan, cried that the eastern moneymen woud ruin the country and starve the poor. Yet in hustling Chicago, still growing visibly from day to day, there might be a prospect of as much work as ever for persons connected with the construction of houses and business buildings. Wright of all people had high hopes in this direction, for during the first five years of his independent practice, four more children were to join the two already born. The first five Wright offspring—two girls and three boys—were so close together in age and size, and so similar in their wholesome good looks, that a playful neighbor could sometimes confuse their father by suddenly holding one of them up and crying, "Quick now, Frank! What's the name of this one?"

To do the work needed to support this establishment, Wright supplemented the office space he rented in downtown Chicago by building a studio around the corner from his Forest Avenue house. The two structures were connected, and frequently altered and added to, as was to be the case in every house that Wright inhabited. A willow tree came up through the roof of the corridor that connected the living quarters with the drafting room, and the establishment was known far and wide as "the house with the tree growing through it."

There was also a playroom, with a mural from the Arabian Nights over its big fireplace, filled with all sorts of games and toys, made by Wright. Fifty years afterward, the son John Lloyd could easily recall that "you came into the room from a narrow, long, low-arched, dimly lighted passageway, and got a strong first impression of great height and brilliant light." It was an effect that Wright used often enough thereafter, but at the time the vaulted room was personal and private to his family and his close associates. He planned it to contain the children's "milestones to maturity—their treasures, friends, comrades and ambitions."

This dual house, with its extra frontage on Chicago Avenue, carried an extra load of mortgages and bills. But no debts could dull the sheen of silk, the glint of silver, the blaze of fresh-cut flowers, and the deep glow of rare Persian rugs, which surrounded the family. The benefits of Wright's taste were also conferred on the people who came to work with him. He had talent of the highest grade in such helpers as Marion Mahony, the first woman licensed to practice architecture in Illinois; Barry Byrne, who joined Wright's forces as something in the nature of an office boy, and later became a fine church architect; and Walter Burley Griffin, who was to lay out the entire Australian capital city of Canberra and practice on three continents before he died in India in 1937. Marion Mahony married Griffin in the first of several such matches among Wright's associates. A sculptural feature of the workshop wall showed a tree of knowledge, a book of specifications, and a blueprint, flanked by two long-legged creatures known as "the secretary birds" that were actually a pair of storks, symbolic of fertility in general.

From the time they could walk, the Wright children had the privilege of wandering in and out of the drafting room, often with good prospects of being able to persuade their father to leave his work and join them in a story or game. Wright was a fine father, who charmed his children with his gaiety and imagination; he was able to keep up with all six of them because of the never-failing energy that would last throughout his life. Another lifelong characteristic was shown in his organization of a family orchestra, in which the eight Wrights set up a terrific din with piano, drums, horns and strings. The strenuous family life at the Studio, as Wright called his establishment, was rather like that of the Theodore Roosevelts at Oyster Bay.

However, one of the several important elements in which Frank Lloyd Wright and Theodore Roosevelt differed— though each was a splendid American Victorian—was in the matter of accepting fatherhood as a natural thing. Roosevelt liked the title of father and made his position plain even while romping with his children. But there was something in Wright that made him hesitate at the thought of being in a position of authoritative responsibility to the young—of being, that is to say, a mature parent. He was not entirely pleased when those who were introduced to him asked if he had children, and showed amazement when the slender and youthful architect would answer, "Yes—five." This was even more unsettling to Wright after the birth of his son Llewellyn, when the answer became "Six." One can understand his irritation at the tasteless neighborhood remark, "If that fellow Wright doesn't stop having children he'll overcrowd this town," though it was true that large families in those days were most likely to be seen in the poorer districts. But the idea of fatherhood itself disturbed him in some obscure way—he perhaps felt that it was a danger to the inner daemon that his father had cherished, the creative man's sacred independence of child, of wife, of everything but art. So it was that Wright told himself each of these bright and beautiful children had come into the world almost of its own volition, already certain of aim and free in spirit. He liked to think that often enough the two young parents and their six offspring were actually eight children together. Catherine, doubtless with the approval and encouragement of Wright's mother, established a neighborhood kindergarten when the playroom was built, which sometimes added to the uproar around the place, when the children were not fitting together the Froebel blocks, and turned to the beating of drums and the bawling of songs about billy-goats, lambs, and chickens. That he tolerated this would seem to indicate in Wright a certain benignity where children were concerned. Yet he was capable of putting a neighbor boy to work mowing his lawn, then arguing over the fifty-cent payment until the boy gave up in disgust—to remember the incident for sixty years, until he realized that

Wright "simply didn't have the money." Creditors for larger amounts found out the same thing; once the Wrights' grocer called attention to a bill that had risen to eight hundred and fifty dollars. Wright met this by negotiating a loan, though he knew this only postponed a day of reckoning, while adding interest to the load. But the children must be well dressed—it would be a shame not to set off their good looks with good clothes. There must be season tickets at the Chicago Symphony, where Theodore Thomas was conducting great music. There must also be tickets to other concerts and the theater, and the Wrights must entertain; this was one way of attracting clients, as all architects know.

Tradesmen, creditors, and the landlords of the buildings downtown where Wright had his succession of city offices all recognized one thing: this man had earning power. Obviously he meant to make his way through life on that power, paying his way, when necessary, by pledging his future pay. Such men are made to order for those who exact interest charges; indeed, had Wright been starting out as a young family man in the mid-twentieth century, instead of at the close of the nineteenth, his budgeting methods would have met with public encouragement. One can easily imagine his cordial reception at the desks of those metropolitan advertising characters, Mr. Citibanker and Mr. Redikredit, whose dearest wish is to ease the path of those who want to buy what they do not have money to pay for. But things were much different in Wright's young manhood, when there was a distinct odor of social disapproval about being in debt. It was a situation that "nice" people avoided except after dire catastrophe. This was the middle-class attitude; but Wright had the apparently light-hearted approach to finances of a Regency rake, or of the celebrated eighteenth-century spendthrift who complained, when friends begged him to retrench two thousand guineas a year for a pastry cook, "Can't a man have a biscuit?"

That there were biscuits in plenty at the Studio was the outward impression the young architect and father wanted to give, and he presented a spruce and attractive figure to the world. He could be seen in the open area beyond Oak Park and River Forest riding his black horse Kano—named for a famous family of Japanese artists—or marching with soldierly bearing to take the Chicago North Western commuters' train. Modelling his dress on Sullivan's, Wright had a closet full of clothes by Hutchinson, one of Chicago's smartest tailors; the cut was conservative, but he proclaimed his association with the arts by continuing to wear his reddish-brown hair longer than a businessman would wish to, and by a certain freedom in the arrangement of his necktie. During his life, Wright frequently wore neckties knotted in the manner of any well-dressed man; he also showed many odd and original arrangements of this article of dress when the spirit moved him. But never at any time did he approach the enormous knots affected by his contemporary, the Scottish architect Charles Rennie Mackintosh, who in this department admittedly stood supreme.

In the Oak Park days Wright would tone down his Bohemian aspect on Sundays when going to church, pacing gravely beside his wife, and sometimes accompanied by a neighbor couple, Mr. and Mrs. James Robert Mann. Though he never touched liquor and took but little wine, young Mr. Wright was always in good form at parties, where he excelled in organizing charades and games. During this period he fascinated many people, and it is not surprising that a number of those who felt the force that radiated from Frank Lloyd Wright became his clients.

An eminent Chicago physician, Dr. A. W. Harlan, was

one of the first to engage Wright as an independent architect. The resulting house, on Greenwood Avenue, had an admirably open plan and a balcony carrying Sullivanesque detail. That was in 1891. Next year, George Blossom of Kenwood Avenue, also on the residential South Side, came to Wright with the order for a house that could be called a mansion, and was indeed a handsome addition to the neighborhood. As a product of its architect, it was remarkable in being his only completely Colonial job. It bore a certain resemblance, whether or not intentional it is impossible to say, to the residence designed for H. A. C. Taylor at Newport, Rhode Island, by McKim, Mead, and White. At that time, what was called Colonial architecture was a coming thing, and Wright showed in Blossom's house that he could perform in this manner with the best of them. Perhaps his achievement was something on the order of a cubist painter showing that he can turn out an acceptable picture in the academic style. At any rate, the yellow-painted clapboards trimmed in white with a fan-light over the doorway pleased the client, if not the architect. But even here the stamp of Wright's individuality was seen, in a massive chimney of Roman brick. In that same year came another important client, Warren McArthur, whose problem was what to do with a narrow lot next door to the Blossoms' place on Kenwood Avenue. Wright's solution was to set a considerable house the long way on the lot, with its narrow end toward the street. Architecturally, Mr. McArthur got his money's worth: there was a feeling of Richardson, of Sullivan, and even of Silsbee's picturesque in the steep-roofed three-story structure. Polygonal bay windows projecting on either side of the porch at the street end added a note of gaiety, and there was a touch of the primitive national vernacular in the early American overhang of the side walls. Brick and plaster clothed the house, and within Wright designed all the fittings and trim, and some of the furniture, for his well-to-do client. This work is of interest because, like the house itself, it holds several elements: Wright's own touch, a dash of Art Nouveau, and a fairly heavy helping of William Morris' arts and crafts. Morris and his disciples had founded a movement in England twenty years before on the basis that life in general might be considerably improved if objects in ordinary use were designed by artists. No one has yet proved Morris wrong in this, and Wright supplied good evidence that Morris was on the proper track, with the domestic furnishings he supplied for the McArthur house. Interior glass doors, built-in cabinets, and woodwork had the purely Wrightian touch, as opposed to Sullivan's ornamentation. Geometric forms were the modules of this decoration; they foreshadowed the linear effects of the Flemish artist, Piet Mondrian, who was at the time only twenty years old; and they showed that when handled by a large talent the T-square could in itself come alive as Sullivan had so often commanded.

More of a milestone perhaps, was the mansion in Oak Park's neighboring suburb of River Forest that Wright designed for William H. Winslow of the Winslow Ornamental Iron Works, who had met the architect in the Adler and Sullivan office. Winslow was no ordinary businessman, for he collaborated with Wright in designing and printing a sermon on artistic principles, written by the Reverend William C. Gannett, called *The House Beautiful*. This was an excellent essay, with the type-dress very much in the manner of the 1890's, carrying like the McArthur decorations a number of contemporary elements, such as the Art

Nouveau feeling in the initial letters, together with a rather insistent quaintness of layout.

In front, the Winslow house was simply proportioned, with a suggestion of the clean-cut Charnley design, plus a massive hipped roof that formed a long horizontal element when seen from in front, and projected deeply. This house could be said to have an ancient Oriental ancestor—for the proportions of its main façade, probably by the coincidence of Wright's inherent sense of harmony, were those of the first story of the Drum Tower in Pekin, which was erected in 1273. At the rear was the usual massive Wrightian chimney, and a romantic polygonal stair tower. Again, there was no question as to the location of the front door. In the McArthur house this aperture occurred halfway down the side of the house facing the Blossom property; but Mr. Winslow could march directly into his mansion from the street. Chicago architects were impressed with the Winslow job, although those with a critical professional eye might observe that the mass of the building got away from its designer in the back. Nevertheless, Daniel Burnham affirmed that it was "a gentleman's house from grade to coping." Burnham was so favorably impressed that he called Wright to the attention of the prosperous real-estate promoter, James B. Waller, who was one of those Chicagoans who heeded the axiom about making big plans. Waller, who was later to order several of the largest projects drawn by Wright, and to see one or two of them to completion, now offered to subsidize the young architect for four years of study in Paris and Rome, including all the expenses of his family. Wright turned down this princely offer, saying, "Thank you both. I know how obstinate and egotistical you think me, but I am going on as I've started."

He was going in a direction that appealed as strongly to

some people as it failed to charm and attract certain others. Generally speaking, the Wright client of the great period that now began would be progressive in politics and liberal in religion. Universalists and Unitarians were perhaps more likely to come to Wright's atelier than strict Presbyterians or high-church members of the Anglican faith.

One of Wright's friends was Jane Addams, the prototype of all dedicated social workers, who was starting her career of service at Hull House and shared his suspicion that the big interests were not those of the working man. Incidentally, Wright's hero William Morris had formed a socialist cadre, and did not give up hope for the immediate arrival of the revolution in England until the late 1880's. Morris had appeared on the streets of Hammersmith clad in a Biblical robe and playing on a rebeck to attract attention to his teachings. He had also delighted the ungodly by not understanding why there was a coolness among the comrades after he remarked, at a Socialist picnic, "I was brought up a gentleman and now as you see can associate with all sorts." When this notable poet and art propagandist died in 1896, his doctrines were widely spread in the United States.

Ideas could circulate with amazing rapidity throughout the republic even before the blessings of radio and TV. The carriers were the hundreds of leaflets and weekly, monthly, and quarterly magazines that circulated in the cheap, prompt, and frequent mail of those days. The handmade paper of the *Bibelot*, for example, carried the advertising text of a Chicago publication that was read in Wright's circle, called *To-Morrow*, "a monthly handbook of the changing order." This magazine, published by the People's Industrial College on Calumet Avenue, laid "special stress on the new values dominating our social, industrial and intellectual progress." In an unconscious parody of the

Indiana humorist George Ade, the editor of *The Papyrus* ("A Magazine of Individuality") stated that his product was for people who wanted to "get away from the Eternal Trite—who are sick and tired of Canned Literature—who demand Thinking that is born of the Red Corpuscle." From Philadelphia, editor Horace Traubel promised that *The Conservator* would carry "virile writings," with a "revolutionary summons to social faith." During the same period in the nineties *The Reader* scheduled a sequel to William Allen White's famous essay "What's the Matter With Kansas?" in which he inveighed against "the iniquities of an unrestrained competitive system," and discussed "the wider significance of the struggle for industrial independence." Now the Society of Arts and Crafts was formed, to promulgate "the strong and wholesome principles that must necessarily underlie permanent success in genuine handicraft." Into the field, within a few years after the founding of the parent body, came the society's magazine, *Handicraft*.

But this should not be confused with *The Craftsman*, published by Gustav Stickley at Syracuse, New York, nor with *The Artsman*, a magazine that carried the views of members of a society of artificers called the Rose Valley Association, in Delaware County, Pennsylvania. Indeed, *The Craftsman* was a publication of considerable importance, devoted as it was to the arts, the workman, and the home. Every month the subscribers were offered complete plans for a house, with the services of the magazine's architectural department available to the building contractor. These Craftsman houses had a great deal of influence, and whether or not they exercised any on Wright, they helped to prepare a public for many of his central ideas.

This magazine proposed to make art and architecture

recognized and important factors in worth-while daily life. Thoughtful men and women would find in its pages the rules for something called Simple Living, which would take place in beautiful homes built in "the Simple, Structural Style, in which every architectural detail serves a well-defined constructive use." The houses could be built for from two to fifteen thousand dollars, and many of the plans came up to what Stickley promised. Stickley seemed to be an inheritor of the plan-books that had been popular in the seventies and eighties, one of the most popular being that of the Englishman Charles Locke Eastlake, whose "cottage style" was well known, and whose general building philosophy was a popularization of Ruskin and Morris. The plan books also had a powerful echo in the pages of the *Ladies' Home Journal*, whose editor Edward Bok was to have an important meeting with Frank Lloyd Wright within a few years.

Wright's clients, in the main, were readers of all such publications, and also of the purely literary experimental journals that had begun to appear, the only one of permanent stature being Harriet Monroe's *Poetry: the Magazine of Verse*.

A less famous publisher than Miss Monroe was Chauncey Lawrence Williams, of Way & Williams, whose River Forest mansion was perhaps Wright's greatest opportunity of 1895. Here there appeared again an arched entrance with Sullivanesque ornament, flanked with mounds of boulders gathered by architect and clients from the bed of the Des Plaines River to symbolize the period when glaciers ground the surface of the prairie. There was a steeply pitched roof, a feature soon to disappear from Wright's designs, but most pleasing nevertheless, with the great geometric form of the chimney cutting through, and a low overhang beneath.

Admirable though this might be, it had no effect on a strong-minded Oak Park lawyer, Nathan G. Moore. He came to the architect in that same year with his own notions thoroughly in mind. "Wright, I want you to do me a house," said Moore, "but I'm hanged if I'll take a back street to the morning train to avoid being laughed at. I want it black and white—half-timbered—the Tudor sort of thing, you understand?" Evidently Mr. Moore was a descendant of the man who told Mr. Pickwick he didn't care for originality, and didn't see any need for it. Moore may not have wished to go so far as those who referred to Wright's works as "the dress reform houses" in reference to Amelia Jenks Bloomer, still living at the time, who had affronted the decencies by advocating the elimination of the skirt from women's wardrobes. The general idea of unorthodoxy, and not any resemblance to the garment associated with Mrs. Bloomer's name, caused the unconverted onlookers to speak of Wright's houses in this manner; but in any event, Mr. Moore was having none of it.

It was natural enough that a man like Nathan Moore would give definite instructions to an architect. Wright's acquiescence was considerably more startling. He liked to say he did not insist that clients take exactly what he offered, but that "The client shows he wants my work when he comes to me." Wright later explained that when Moore approached him, he suddenly thought of his children's needs, and agreed to carry out the order. The resulting house was a popular success, and caused a number of requests for "another design just like the one you did for Mr. Moore," all of which Wright refused.

One of those who did not demand a reprise of the Moore house, or who was talked out of it if he did, was Isidor Heller of the South Side, owner of substantial property that

included a narrow lot on Woodlawn Avenue. The house
that Wright completed for this client in 1897 is worthy of
note. At that time in American cities, and most especially in
Chicago, the residential districts showed a riot of architectural imagination—a carnival of strange and curious shapes,
many of which remain to this day to gladden the eye of the
observer. Experimental or fantastic roof forms were part of
the game, and Mr. Heller could not complain that Wright
had failed him here. What he got for the third floor of his
long brick house was actually a sort of loggia, with a vaguely
Moorish look, from which he might have addressed multi-
tudes of subjects had he been an Oriental monarch instead
of a Chicago citizen. With this third story removed, the
Heller house might be vaguely reminiscent of the Charnley
house set with its side to the street. The entrance was
easily to be found in the middle of the south elevation of
the house; engaged Romanesque columns set off this
aperture, while above it there rose a porch, crowned by a
row of small decorated terra cotta columns. This was the
kind of eclecticism that Wright was soon to be denouncing
in most measured tones; but to less serious persons it was
architectural entertainment of a high order, and showed the
element of fantasy that would reappear from time to time
in some of Wright's best work, still lying in the future.
Indeed, the whole question of Wright's words as opposed
to his works is one which will probably attract the attention
of scholars for many a day. It is possible to theorize that he
wrought as his daemon commanded, and then, like Sullivan,
constructed what he took to be a philosophy of life and
esthetics to subsume his personal artistic product. It may
be that in discovering his philosophy, Wright's thinking was
like that of Sherlock Holmes when he found the wax
vesta at the scene of John Straker's death. It will be recalled

that the Inspector indignantly remarked, "I cannot think how I came to overlook it"—and that Holmes calmly answered, "It was invisible, buried in the mud. I only saw it because I was looking for it."

We shall have to give further thought to this question as the story of Wright's life and work unfolds; but at the time the Heller house was finished, Wright was still quite young, and had not yet completely stated his architectural thesis, nor fully formed his personality. It is true that he had begun to make speeches, his first public address having been delivered to a group in Evanston in 1894. Less culturally inclined, but of considerably more value to Wright, were the members of a River Forest group who entrusted him with the plans for a golf club, the year after the Heller house was completed. This club was a marvel: it stood low to the ground, with horizontality most powerfully expressed in the trim of its low-lying wooden parapets, sheltering the entrance in a manner that Wright would repeat again and again. The main room was octagonal, with two massive fireplaces, and was placed at the end of a foyer that featured an equally substantial double fireplace between locker room and dining room, each opening on a terrace. Wright got the prime feeling of shelter here, and the essential notion of a club, perhaps reprehensible but entirely human, as a fortification against nonmembers. In this the comparatively modest building in the Middle West shared a certain basic motivation with the Italianate stone palaces that McKim, Mead, and White constructed for New York clubs. Wright did not preach his Whitmanesque democracy to these clients, nor to the members of the River Forest Tennis Club, for whom he built an equally snug and appropriate home a few years later.

Business conditions now began to improve; with his

campaign managed by the political strategist Mark Hanna,
the Republican William McKinley had entered the White
House on a gold-standard platform, promising a full dinner
pail for the working man and proportionate benefits for
those who stood on the professional rungs of the economic
ladder. In the same year that Wright designed the Golf
Club volunteers were marching into the staging areas to set
sail for Cuba and war with Spain. As a heavily burdened
family man, Wright gave only momentary thought, if any,
to military service. As he saw it, he already had a continual
battle at the Studio to stay out of creditors' hands; on one
occasion a sheriff camped in the drafting room all night
over a bill for a mere eighty-five dollars. Next day the
money was raised, but it represented only a shift in the
structure of debt, not an advance toward solvency. Loyal
though she was, Catherine found this sort of living hard to
endure.

The new century, Wright said, would bring new opportunities to all forward-looking persons; so far as architecture
was concerned, he would formulate a gospel, preach it far
and wide, and build for the enlightened clients who would
hear his message throughout the land. Even this early, he
was beginning to get practical support: before the new
century was six months old, his Chicago colleague Robert
C. Spencer, Jr. contributed an article, "The Work of Frank
Lloyd Wright" to the *Architectural Record* of New York.
Spencer was one of a group of like-minded men who
lunched at Kinsley's, where Wright took a leading part in
the conversation, and who shared quarters at various times
in various downtown office buildings. On the whole, they
were the nucleus of what would come to be called the
Chicago school.

As the capital city of a rich heartland, Chicago supplied

the specializing professionals for the prospering high bour-
geoisie of solid towns as far away as Joliet and Galesburg—
supplied the surgeons, big-case lawyers, and architects. So it
was that B. Harley Bradley of Kankakee, whose comfortable
inherited fortune was derived from farm machinery, looked
for a Chicago man when the time came for him to build a
sizable house in his home territory. Much has been said and
written about the Bradley house; most of all, perhaps, it
expressed what Wright later said he was trying to achieve
in the interior of Oak Park's Unity Temple—"the sense
of a happy cloudless day." Near the banks of the Kankakee
River, Bradley's house rose to a height of two stories under
low, wide gables with splendidly projecting eaves. The
main entrance receded under a porte-cochere, and the feeling of privacy and shelter was enhanced by a terrace behind
a substantial parapet. From some angles there was a suggestion of the Swiss in this delightful house, but whatever
its total impact on the viewer, it seemed to belong to the
earth from which it sprang: looking at the harmonious
structure, it was impossible to think that there had ever
been a time when it had not been there. In this early performance, Wright was demonstrating one of his greatest
gifts, and one that he consciously and quite properly ex-
ploited—his sense of site. His reputation for brilliant siting
grew great, and justly so; but it might have caused embarrassment on the occasion many years later when an expert
visited a small Wright house and dilated at length on its
remarkable visual relation to the land on which it stood—
only Wright could have placed it so fitly, said the learned
man. The owner did not have the heart to tell him that the
house had been moved from its original situation, half a mile
away. But nothing would move the Bradley house, nor the
similar house that Wright put up nearby for a brother-in-

law, Warren Hickox. These houses were wholly successful; perhaps because of their quality of serenity—they were new, yet they belonged where they were as surely as if built by pioneers.

The new century was only a little more than a year old when Wright received an opportunity to reach the forward-looking elements of Chicago under the best of auspices, those of Jane Addams at Hull House, where on a chilly evening in March Wright delivered to the Arts and Crafts Society an eloquent address called "The Art and Craft of the Machine." His preaching blood stood him in good stead as he rose to speak after Miss Addams' introduction, and at once got the sympathy of the audience with his handsome face, confident carriage, and the Welsh music in his voice. For all of the immediate charm of his presence, his hearers knew that he was addressing not only them, but the nation, and indeed, the whole world.

"The machine is here to stay," said Wright. "It is the forerunner of the democracy that is our dearest hope." The fact that Wright's point was not always easy to grasp did not in the least disturb his enchanted hearers. They followed him willingly as he played them a series of verbal fugues on such subjects as the false Renaissance dawn (referring to his boyhood reading of Victor Hugo), architecture as the universal writing of humanity down to the invention of printing, and the idea that the "engine, the motor, and the battleship" were "the works of art of the century." But the "magnificent resource of machine and material" had brought a dreadful degradation "a pandemonium of tin masks, huddled deformities, and decayed methods: quarreling, lying and cheating, with hands at each other's throats—or in each other's pockets; and none of the people who do these things, who pay for them or use them, know what they mean . . ."

What Wright meant was that historical styles should be abandoned, since in large public buildings an envelope of stone concealed the true nature of a skeleton of steel. Techniques had outrun design, as he saw it. A "simple, sincere clothing of plastic material" was what the steel frame called for. After some further rhetoric that partially obscured what he was getting at, Wright came to "the Decorative Arts—the immense middle-ground of all art now mortally sickened by the Machine . . ." Here there was a deadly perversion, "the magnificent prowess of the machine bombarding the civilized world with the mangled corpses of strenuous horrors that once stood for cultivated luxury— standing now for a species of fatty degeneration simply vulgar." He may have been referring to over-decorated machine-turned furniture here; at any rate, his next point was that machines, when used to make objects of common use, should produce in a simple style—and suddenly came a significant statement: "The beauty of wood lies first in its qualities as wood." Presently Wright got into his own principal field of domestic architecture (where considerations of a steel frame were not apposite), and said that concrete might make a "simple, modestly beautiful robe" for a house, and that there was no need for any architect to drag in "five different kinds of material to compose one little cottage." Concrete had been in use as a building material for more than seventy-five years at the time Wright delivered this address, but whether or not he was aware of that, he now sailed on through some remarks on electro-glazing and pictorial reproduction, with a reference to Whistler, and then took off on a long passage in which he spoke of Morris, Ruskin, and Tolstoy, and defined an Arts and Crafts movement in which artists might "make some good impression on the Machine." Today the tools of the artist are "processes and machines where they were once a hammer and a gouge." And so it went till Wright rose to a Kiplingesque peroration in which he invited his audience to "be gently lifted at nightfall to the top of a great downtown office building"—obviously in recollection of the evenings with Sullivan—from which to survey "this thing we call a city." A thousand words of vivid description followed in a final effort to define "the texture of the tissue of this great thing . . . the Machine . . ." into which the forces of art were "to breathe the thrill of ideality—A SOUL!"

"The Art and Craft of the Machine" earned its author immediate notice in the Chicago papers, and there came a request to deliver the address before the Western Society of Engineers, and then to permit publication of a printed version in the catalog of the fourteenth annual exhibition of the Chicago Architectural Club. Three years later he delivered the speech before a convention of the Daughters of the American Revolution, and as late as 1930 he used it as a source of material for lectures at Princeton University. Two eminently sound notions were that "the Machine," if one might take that term to mean modern technology in general, would greatly increase the leisure hours available to the average man; the other was that architectural modules of various kinds and sizes might be manufactured in quantity and assembled at the building site.

Few people at the time Wright enunciated "The Art and Craft of the Machine" were inclined to criticize him and most of those who heard or read the essay felt that he had stated important truths, in illuminating terms. One of those who were so impressed was Ward Willits, for whom Wright built what well may be his most successful house. A rising executive in the railway supply firm of Adams and Westlake, Willits took Wright to a lot in Highland Park, a North Shore suburb, and asked him what he thought would be suitable as a family residence there. As he walked over the ground, Wright saw the complete house before his inward eye. Again it was a composition in wood and stucco, like the houses at Kankakee; again he achieved serenity, and the feeling of a cloudless day. During this period, Wright was asked by colleagues, "Do you hypnotize your clients?" He had no need of exercising such powers on the Willitses, for he gave them a house that was as easy to live in as it was pleasing to look at, with its simple but flexible plan that featured a large living room with a broad and deep fireplace. The dining room, principal area in the other element of the cross-shaped plan, was ready of access, and beautifully lighted by its bands of casement windows.

The spacious main rooms of the Willits mansion were not divided by narrow doorways, and their ease of entrance and exit led to a curious neologism, indulged in by many critics who wished to praise the house and similar products of its designer. They spoke of something they called "the flow of space"—as if space itself, and not its occupants, could move. The ambiguous language merely meant that persons who were fortunate enough to be able to afford large rooms found them roomy; an ample sheltered area in which to turn around has always been a blessing to mankind. But the habit of applying moral terms to architecture was beginning to bring on a rather similar habit of applying the language of theoretical mathematics to structures with perfectly understandable floors, walls, windows and roofs. A quarter of a century before, Professor William Kingdon Clifford of Cambridge, who said "I am above all and before all a geometer," had suggested that matter is a type of curvature of space, thus foreshadowing much of twentieth-century physics. Clifford wrote that the commonly accepted laws of geometry do not apply to certain portions of space, which may be said to be distorted or dislocated. This movement in mathematical philosophy doubtless contributed to the doctrine of the Cubists, who painted more than one aspect of a given object in the same picture. Cubism established an artistic logic, but there may be some question as to the wisdom of using its vocabulary when speaking of architecture. Whether "interpenetration of space" is more readily understandable than saying "a glass wall," or "a deep porch" may be debatable. Indeed, there have been descriptions of modern houses, from the time of the Bradley and Willits commissions to the present day, that unhappily remind the reader of the man in the parody of "Hiawatha" who attempted to put the outside inside. But there can be no question that within the Willits house, something new, and perhaps pure gold, was noticeable on the Chicago architectural scene.

This was what became known as the Prairie style. Some students have said that it was "perhaps not *a* style, but that it was *Wright's* style." In any event, these houses by Wright had in common an open plan, wide roofs with a decided projection, "T-square" ornamentation, and careful connection between structure and site—and always at the heart of the house, an enormous fireplace that breathed with the throat of a great solid chimney. Wright was concerned that the houses should appear to be natural growths from the flat ground of northern Illinois. He had already begun to talk of "abolishing the box"—the meagre and severely cubical house that was sometimes produced in the American vernacular, with cramped rooms. As it turned out, Wright himself designed hundreds of boxes, in the small bedrooms of many houses, and uncommonly snug and convenient boxes they were, sometimes putting one in mind of the cabins on ocean liners. But this was not what he meant by a bad box, a choking and unpleasant box: his idea was to save on sleeping quarters and use the extra space in the living areas. This was the assault on the box as interior; on the outside, he reduced the severity of walls by extending his great eaves and making the roof itself a reassuring shelter. And as a final touch, he set around these suburban houses long parapets equipped with concealed earth pockets from which vines grew to soften the edges of hard masonry.

Anyone looking at the low-lying houses, that seemed at evening almost to dissolve into the landscape, could agree that they might be said to make a direct expression of the prairie. The great flat spaces of mid-America had long been felt as an influence; Washington Irving visited Oklahoma as early as 1832, and William Cullen Bryant had composed an ode called "The Prairies" in which he found them "Fitting floor/For this magnificent temple called the sky." Perhaps not so well known was the fact that Wright's mother's favorite philosopher had written that the true American art and genius—something that had not yet appeared in the sage's lifetime—might be connected with the "sea-wide, sky-skirted prairie." Indeed, Emerson had recorded his hope that some day an architect would provide the pleasure of viewing an uninterrupted line, by remarking, "I know not why in real architecture the hunger of the eye for length of line is so rarely gratified."[1]

[1] Emerson had met Horatio Greenough, the American sculptor who lived in Italy, and had found that in Greenough's paper on architecture, published in 1843, the American had "announced in advance the leading thoughts of Mr. Ruskin on the *morality* in architecture." Greenough sent Emerson a letter in which he said, "Here is my theory of structure: A scientific arrangement of spaces and forms to function and to site; an

All of this would find agreement with two clients who now came to Wright with the claims of blood relationship to add to their approval of his work. These were his aunts Nell and Jane Lloyd-Jones, who had retired from eminent official positions in the teaching profession, to found the Hillside Home School near Spring Green, an institution where boys and girls would be educated in a relaxed family atmosphere. By 1902, they were ready to have fairly extensive buildings erected to bear the motto "Truth Against the World." Seven years before, the sisters had called on Wright to design for the school farm "a pretty windmill tower" which they preferred to the steel towers they had seen. Wright's farmer uncles, who were much in evidence around the school as the kindly familiar spirits of the place, counseled caution. And the eminent Uncle Jenkin, who happened to be at Spring Green when this question came up, ruled that anything but a practical and cheap steel structure would be nonsense. However, the sisters meant to set their tower on a hill that could be seen from all the nearby valleys, and they decided that Frank should have the commission.

Accordingly, Frank prepared a sketch that was duly inspected by the uncles who now cried out in alarm, as did a local contractor and engineer. The thing would never stand up, they said. Aunt Nell sent a telegram to Chicago

---

emphasis of features proportioned to their *gradated* importance in function: color and ornament to be decided and arranged and varied by strictly organic laws, having a distinct reason for each decision; the entire and immediate banishment of all make-shift and make-believe." In England Emerson had seen "comfort and splendor" in the work of landscape planners, and that of the architects Inigo Jones and Christopher Wren, and the woodcarver and sculptor Grinling Gibbons, who had handed on much magnificence to an age of owners. The philosopher saw that "man serves himself" with metals, wood, stone and glass, and in the process "honors himself" with architecture. (In these two quotations, the emphasis is that of the original authors.)

asking for reassurance. Frank sent back the words "BUILD
IT." The structure proved completely practical and was also
a charming piece of design: from a stone base rose an
octagonal wooden structure, into which was built a
diamond-shaped oaken spine that supported the heavy, fan-
bearing wheel at the summit. The projecting edge of this
diamond-shaped element protruded in the direction from
which came the prevailing winds, and Wright called it the
"storm prow." He was to make further use of this idea of a
tower with a central core; but as it first stood, it was the
object of a prophecy of doom by the five grey-bearded
uncles. They said it would not survive the first big wind;
and for years, after every storm, the uncles would come
to their doors and peer over to the tower hill—and there it
would be, its wheel turning with the movement of the air.
In fact, the famous "Romeo and Juliet" tower, as Wright
named it, was destined to survive both its critics and its
architect.

With this example before them, the sisters did not hesitate
to set Wright to work on their enlarged school plant in
1902. Though Wright did not realize it, he was designing
for himself as well as his aunts; almost a third of a century
later he was to use the school buildings for an educational
project of his own. Now he took advantage of a site on the
side of a hill to compose two connected buildings of great
suitability to their purpose. Working from a base of local
stone laid up in ashlar, he made a basically simple pattern
of pavilions and bays with many an unexpected turn and
angle to keep the boys and girls from growing tired of their
combined home, school, and workshop. A Biblical text was
placed prominently on view in the lettering around the
balcony of the two-story assembly area that was organized
beside the mighty fireplace. It was from fortieth Isaiah,

Wright's old memory task, the concluding verse, having to do with mounting on wings like eagles, and running without feeling the pull of weariness. From the roadway outside, the school buildings were a natural part of the landscape; like all Wright's most successful work, they seemed to have been eternally there.

This same year, the Chicago Architectural Club gave Wright a singular honor by devoting more than half the catalogue of its annual exhibition to his work. That must inevitably have led many to think that Chicago architecture of the time consisted first of Frank Lloyd Wright; and second, all the rest. His work seemed to bear this out; at any rate, there was liberal published recognition of Wright's accomplishments, for Spencer's article in the professional press had already been followed by Wright's appearance, in 1901, in the *Ladies' Home Journal*, whose editor Edward Bok had announced that he intended to eliminate the American parlor. What Mr. Bok had in mind was to persuade American women to abandon the custom of shutting off one room—frequently the best in the house—from ordinary use. He could not have found a more enthusiastic man than Wright to aid him in this; Wright's first *Ladies' Home Journal* plan, that of a thoroughbred Prairie house, had its library, living room and dining room in one long axis. Next came "A Small House with 'Lots of Room In It'" —plus text that mentioned the crisp outlines of the two-story building, and the way the plan took advantage of "light, air, and prospect, the enjoyable things one goes to the suburbs to secure." For once Wright would not be able to perform his wizardry in suiting structure to site, for as it turned out, no one ever built this small house with plenty of room, even though Bok appended a note: "As a guarantee that the plan of this house is practicable and that the estimates for cost are conservative, the architect is ready to accept the commission of preparing the working plans and specifications for this house to cost $5835.00, provided that the building site selected is within reasonable distance of a base of supplies where material and labor may be had at the standard rates."

The *Journal* houses, with their scale of costs not higher than $7500 for residences including servants' rooms, indicate the range of building prices just after the turn of the century. The fee for an architect's services was from 6 to 8 per cent of the total building cost, though Wright said on various occasions that he charged from 10 to 15 per cent. This will give some idea of the earnings of architects from domestic work, and explains why most practitioners then as now welcomed commissions for business premises, churches, public buildings, and schools, though the expense of preparing drawings for a large job is of course very great. It should also be borne in mind that the dollar of 1901 was five times as large in purchasing power as that in circulation sixty years later—and the Federal income tax was not proclaimed as law until 1913.

Few if any of Wright's fascinated clients begrudged him his fee; and most of them seem to have enjoyed the exclamations of wonder or even of disapproval that his houses brought forth. An especially fine Prairie house, though it was near the heart of Oak Park, was the residence of Mr. and Mrs. Frank Thomas on Forest Avenue, that had been commissioned by Thomas's father-in-law, James Rogers. Perhaps because its entrance is approached by a walled pathway, and its capacious porch is raised above a blank wall, one observer nicknamed this tranquil structure "The Harem House." Mr. and Mrs. Thomas may well have been amused, and even pleased, by this notice of their home.

Some years later, a lady occupying a Wright-designed house in Cincinnati remarked in all seriousness that she "used their house to find out who their real friends were," apparently feeling that persons not truly like-minded would be unable to pretend understanding for the architect's work. Another lady testified that she considered it a rare privilege to live and bring up a family in a house that Wright designed. Thus he seemed able with many clients to put an additional dimension, a moral and ethical consideration, into drawings that he submitted.

"You'll live like a king and queen!" was an expression Wright liked to use, especially when costs began to exceed estimates, or if clients winced noticeably at his command of "Tear it out!" when he saw something amiss with the building. Thus it was that clients to whom expense was little object found it especially stimulating and bracing to deal with him. Such a substantial client was the banker Arthur Heurtley, for whom Wright did a remarkably fine house in 1902, a little further out Forest Avenue from the Thomas place. Here the arched entrance was still to be seen, framing the front door in a manner reminiscent of the Williams house. But the Heurtley house was long and low where the design for the Williamses had gloried in high peaked roofs; the Heurtleys had their second-floor living room behind an uninterrupted row of casements, looking out over a terrace, and giving on an elevated porch. As one approached the house, the flattened urn, a Wrightian trademark that had been introduced as long ago as the Winslow house, was to be seen. Summer and winter, this tawny house stood handsome and self-possessed, being especially effective when the silver spears of icicles hung from the generous eaves of its broad roof.

One of the next important commissions came from downstate, in Springfield, where the old Italianate mansion of the pioneer Lawrence family was surrounded, after two years of building, by a Wrightian Prairie structure in his finest manner. Susan Dana, old Mrs. Lawrence's daughter, was a woman who looked for cultural horizons much as Sinclair Lewis's mid-western heroine Carol Kennicott was to seek them, twenty years or so later. But where the fictional lady was hampered by lack of money and the scarcity of congenial company in an utterly provincial village, Mrs. Dana lived in the capital of Illinois and had ample funds and access to Chicago, where many progressive persons were talking of the brilliant new young architect Frank Lloyd Wright. Architect and client clothed the old house with the entire wardrobe of Wright's style—the long roofs, the terraces, the low parapets, the bands of decorated casements, even the flattened urn near the main entrance. It was a great success, except for some of the furniture. Wright could design excellent couches, chairs and tables, but sometimes, especially in the case of chairs, the architectonic quality in furniture would get the better of him. A notable failure, for example, was the high-backed dining room chair in which the slender slats of the back ran straight up from the floor like the piers of a skyscraper. The result, as Wright himself realized, was not only uncomfortable, but much too structural in appearance, yet he clung to such chairs all his life and frequently put them in a place of honor. At its worst, Wright's furniture is an interesting failure. At its best, it can live quite happily beside good Grand Rapids reproductions of Hepplewhite and Phyfe—or, indeed, beside the real thing. With highly uncharacteristic self-denigration, Wright would on occasion cry out, "Oh, *why* can't I design a decent piece of furniture?" Perhaps he was willing to say this because he knew that his successes far outnumbered his misfortunes in this line.

The Oak Park house that Wright designed in 1903 for W. E. Martin of the Martin and Martin Stove Polish Company, though not outstanding in itself, led to some of Wright's best work. This came about when the Chicago Martin's brother, Darwin D. Martin of Buffalo, came west on a visit and met the architect. "Mr. Wright, I think you're the man for me!" said Darwin Martin, and proved that he could back his own judgment by becoming a lifelong friend and supporter of Frank Lloyd Wright. Martin had plenty of challenging work to offer. The largest commission was the administration building for the Larkin Soap Company in Buffalo, of which Martin was head. In carrying out this assignment Wright erected a building that was world-famous, though later destroyed—a cliff of brick with such features as air conditioning, uniform metal furniture, and a central well where office workers sat surrounded by tiers of balconies from which executives looked down, somewhat after the manner of those in Charlie Chaplin's movie, *Modern Times*. Though Martin was pleased, Wright thought the members of the Larkin family were rather uneasy over their building. They also committed the heinous offence of having their homes designed, by fashionable and conservative architects, in the Georgian style.

But Darwin Martin made up for this by giving Wright the commission for a large residence in Buffalo in addition to the office block. Completed in 1904, the year the Larkin Building was started, the Martin house was altogether splendid. No financial limitations hampered the architect, and the place attained grandeur as a striking composition of planes and angles that was at the same time restful to the eye. In its horizontality, emphasized in the handsome per-

6. Residence of Darwin D. Martin, Buffalo, New York, 1904

7. Larkin Building, Buffalo, New York, 1904

8. Residence of Frederick C. Robie, Chicago, Illinois, 1909

9. Dining Room, Residence of Frederick C. Robie, Chicago, Illinois, 1909

10. Residence of B. Harley Bradley, Kankakee, Illinois, 1900

11. Unity Church, Oak Park, Illinois, 1906

12. Residence of Ward W. Willitts, Highland Park, Illinois, 1902

13. Residence of Susan Lawrence Dana, Springfield, Illinois, 1903

gola that led to the conservatory, this was one of the Prairie houses, though situated on a Buffalo boulevard. Nearby was a secondary house of equally happy composition for the family of Darwin Martin's brother-in-law, George Barton. Unusually enough for one of Wright's great houses, the Martin mansion was left unoccupied for a time in the middle nineteen-fifties, subsequent to its owner's death, and made a melancholy though romantic spectacle in its weed-grown neglect. Fortunately, a new owner took over in 1956.

At the time Wright was building these houses and the soap firm's offices, Martin introduced him to one of the Larkin company's founders, in the person of Elbert Hubbard, the remarkable writer, printer, and advertising expert who had achieved a large circulation for an argumentative magazine that was called, in ironic reference to Matthew Arnold, *The Philistine*. What impressed Wright most about Hubbard was the center of activity he presided over at East Aurora, near Buffalo. The Roycrofters, as the place was called, was a successful combination of school, hotel, publishing house, medieval guild, and art-goods factory. Years later Wright was to be principal of a somewhat similar concern.

Hubbard's outward aspect announced the practitioner of the arts even more insistently than Wright's—his hair was longer, his necktie more curiously arranged. Sometimes while writing his popular studies of great men Hubbard would wear the traditional painter's smock and velvet Tam-o'-Shanter, symbolizing an artist of the pen before his verbal palette. But for all this Hubbard was a by no means contemptible essayist, while at the same time enjoying the careers of businessman and master salesman. The way Hubbard made a go of things unquestionably fascinated Wright. Years later his son John Lloyd recalled how Hubbard told Wright that modesty was nothing but egotism in reverse. "I am an orator, a great orator!" cried Hubbard. "I have health, gesture, imagination, voice, vocabulary, taste, ideas—I acknowledge it myself. What I lack in shape I make up in nerve . . ." In reply, Wright here first made his celebrated remark about intending to become the greatest of all architects, and added, with a flourish, "And I do hereunto affix the 'red square.' " (This geometric figure, usually with a sprawling signature added, was Wright's personal chop.) It is conceivable that at the time they met Hubbard was the more impressive figure; but his life was to end with the sinking of the *Lusitania* in 1915, and he is remembered mostly for his editorial "A Message to Garcia."

Though not on a par for general industry with Hubbard's establishment, the Studio was now busy throughout the day and night. In fact, Wright could just barely crowd all his activities into twenty-four hours a day. W. E. Martin entrusted him with the design of the E-Z Polish plant on the West Side, a lucrative contract in which Wright made his first extensive use of reinforced concrete. But the building of houses was not neglected: Wright made his first appearance in Racine, Wisconsin, with the South Main Street residence of W. P. Hardy, a performance that showed him at his incomparable best. A hillside site overlooking Lake Michigan challenged Wright; at the street level, he gave the house an elegant but noncommittal public façade. In the rear was a balanced composition of three stories with two wings overlooking a terrace that crowned the steep gradation down to the lake. Wright could never surpass this moderate-sized house—and he was entitled to the additional value he got from the setting, since he took such shrewd advantage of it.

He worked at white heat, and put down his ideas very rapidly, usually in finished form, or close to it. Never forgetting that Sullivan had told him he drew the elevation of the Wainwright Building in three minutes, having turned the whole idea over so thoroughly in his mind that when he came to his paper all he needed to do was draw a building which in a sense was already there, Wright kept his own ideas constantly turning in his mind. In his old age he would say, with a twinkle, that he "rolled them out of his sleeve." It looked like wizardry, but actually was the skimming from a pot that was always on the boil. Similarly, in the Studio days, Wright was constantly thinking in three dimensions, as indeed all architects must, and so when the clients came, he already had ideas in mind that he could adapt to specific needs and uses. The myth had begun to grow that he bullied clients, marshalled them into line, and ordered them to burn their favorite easy chairs and ancestral portraits. But this was not the fact, any more than the hypnotism that some of Wright's colleagues thought he exercised. Wright stated, "No client *must* take anything he doesn't want," which discredits the legend that he could order grown men and women—successful businessmen in a self-confident age, and their frequently opinionated wives —to do what they did not want to do, pay for what they did not like, and live in surroundings that would remind them every day of a lost battle of wills against an architect. No, it was entirely different from that; the Wright clients were like-minded with the designer, and in a sense his followers when they came to him. If a client wanted something that struck Wright as bad design, he might denounce the idea in strong terms. But if he saw the client's heart was set on it, he immediately turned to his persuasive vein, saying, "Let me show you how you can have the same thing—only so very much better."

Many of the plans submitted, and the details decided on later, were drawn at night or in the early hours of the morning, when the clamor of the children was stilled. Wright found an enormous satisfaction in the sight of blank paper under the direct white light in the drafting-room, with plenty of freshly sharpened colored pencils at hand. Perhaps he could smell his favorite baked onions in preparation for a late supper, while Catherine played Bach to heighten his creative mood; then to paper and pencil, and suddenly it would be light outside. There were two Negro servants, one the cook whose hand was evident in the baked onions, the other a houseman who could keep the Studio fireplace going in winter, or provide a supply of iced lemonade during the hot months. In a way, everything revolved around the master's convenience, with his great talent recognized as the central fact of house and working quarters. And yet the situation was not ideal. There were stresses and strains in the crowded domestic life, and there were emotional demands by wife and children who seemed to need more than Wright had to give after the exhaustion of his night-long labors. Friends thought that Catherine loved Wright with "an almost bitter love"—in any event, bitter were the conflicts that often arose between them. In some quarters, people murmured that perhaps this was another case of a brilliant man marrying in extreme youth a wife who couldn't keep up with him. This was unjust to a woman made of good stuff, who was in every human and ordinary way her husband's equal, if not his superior. But Catherine, though the mother of six children, was not creative. Who had designed the Hardy house, and crowned

the Heller mansion with that amusing loggia? Not Catherine, obviously. Thinking it over some thirty years later,
Wright concluded that family life in Oak Park "conspired
against the freedom" to which he felt every soul was entitled. The conspirators may have seen it another way; such
problems are insoluble. Nor could Wright be accused of
failing to make an effort to live as a family man and a husband; in 1905, for example, he took Catherine on a trip to
Japan, along with Mr. and Mrs. Willits.

This journey not only demonstrated the progress Wright
was making as an architect in order to be able to spend the
necessary money and time, which included thirty days each
way on the steamer, but also was the foundation of his lifelong admiration for Japanese art and architecture. Wearing
native costume, Wright went on happy print-buying excur-
sions, beginning the great collections he was later to sell in
times of financial stress. Wright became an expert on Japanese art, and could with perfect confidence write catalogues
on the subject, and discourse on Hokusai and Hiroshige.
He became a great enough expert to admit it when he had
made a mistake; at one time he was fooled by the work of
a faker, and when later research showed the goods were
counterfeit, he promptly reimbursed the officials of the
Metropolitan Museum, to whom he had sold the prints, with
a selection of impeccable and genuine work from his private
collection. But this episode lay far in the future on the first
Japanese trip, when Wright was enchanted by the people
and their background, made up as it was by a landscape
that seemed to compose itself into a picture wherever one
looked, setting off the fascinating mystery of the cities and
towns.

It is possible that on this first journey to the Orient
Wright was introduced to the Japanese paper-folding game

called Origami. The pastime calls for high mental precision, and the ability to materialize a solid object from a conception of its dimensions as it lies flattened into one plane. There are chairs at Taliesin, the Wisconsin estate that Wright began to build some five or six years after his introduction to Japan, that look very much like Origami exercises, with their flat arms folded out from the central mass. However, the talk of Japanese influence in Wright's work can easily be carried too far. The truth seems to be that he was directly influenced by the Japanese in just about the proportion that he truly understood their character—in other words, very little. Like many travelers, Wright made oracular statements about the Japanese. One was to the effect that they would never attack the West. Because of his enthusiasm for their light and airy houses of wood and paper, Wright failed to see certain important facets in the Japanese character: the cruelty lurking under the neatly folded surfaces, the sentimentality that existed beside serene beauty, the arrogance and contempt too often masked by courteous docility.

But with Pearl Harbor no more to be imagined than the tragedies that would overtake Wright himself, he returned to Oak Park after this first trip out of his native country much refreshed, and ready to bring his first artistic period to a thrilling close. The Studio hummed with activity, apparently to a rhythm that Wright found as simple as it was insistent. He expressed his feelings about the Studio schedule by composing a set of "T Square and Triangle verses" that gave the reader somewhat the effect of a ride in an Irish jaunting car: "I'll live as I work as I am," the verses sang, "I'll think as I act as I am/Nor for fame e'er man made/ Sheathe the naked white blade/My act as beseemeth a man." There was more on the same line, to the alarm of Richard

Watson Gilder, editor of *The Century*, who returned the verses with the admonishment, "The rhythm of the drum, Mr. Wright, can hardly be translated into poetry." Although Vachel Lindsay's *The Congo* might prove Gilder wrong in one instance, the fact is that Wright's "Work Song" is doggerel of the most appalling sort; which would not be worth recording were it not for the light it throws on his character, when we consider that these verses were later set to music, and sung by Wright's students at his Wisconsin headquarters, where they are still written large on the wall near the main drafting-room, so that all who pass may read them. This shows that the fairies who bestow genius do not always put self-criticism in the cradle.

Wright lived in an atmosphere from which overt criticism was noticeably absent. He cast a spell over clients, friends, and even over his associates and employees. And where the magic of his personality failed to function, or was for some reason not brought to bear, there was nearly always a solid respect on the part of those who knew him. Barry Byrne was an example of an employee who felt honest admiration where others were worked upon by charm alone. The youth had volunteered for the job of office boy in order to get his start in architecture, and felt that it was a good bargain, for he had the impression that it was his privilege to watch an astonishingly competent professional at work. To those who could profit by it, this was a form of teaching. It may be that some of the professional associates had an even higher opinion of Wright's abilities than the clients—they were in a position to understand his virtuosity, whereas the patrons could only be amazed. At any rate, there was no doubt that the most warmly expressed admiration for Wright came from among his clients, and that among the clients, the most uncritical adulation was that expressed by certain of the women. There was, for example, Mamah (pronounced "May-mah") Borthwick Cheney, the college-educated wife of an Oak Park manufacturer of electrical equipment. This Mr. Edwin H. Cheney had a romantic heart. As a suitor, he made countless visits to the small Michigan town where the young woman was working in the public library. After many rejections, Cheney at last persuaded Mamah to marry him, and brought her to Oak Park, where he was happy to please her by commissioning the interesting architect, Frank Lloyd Wright, to design their home. So far as architecture was concerned, Cheney made no mistake, for the house was one of Wright's best small designs. With its one-story balanced plan, it had an air of mystery behind its low brick garden walls; Mrs. Cheney was delighted, eagerly becoming one of Wright's enthusiastic supporters.

There was nothing to turn Wright's head in the fact that he won Mrs. Cheney's friendly interest. Cordiality from lady clients was a familiar story; several years before meeting the Cheneys, for example, Wright had a woman friend among his patrons who made a habit of furnishing flowers for his downtown office. A Japanese draftsman made a disrespectful remark about this lady, and was unlucky enough to be overheard by Wright, who kicked him halfway downstairs for his impudence. Next day, Wright found the man still hanging around the premises, and this time booted him all the way down. The Japanese complained to Uncle Jenkin, but failed to get satisfaction, as Wright refused to give him back his job.

Probably the Reverend Dr. Jenkin Lloyd-Jones was the worst intermediary in Chicago to send to Wright on any errand. As an architect, Wright felt that he had achieved the same standing that his uncle claimed as minister and public personage, and sooner or later, they were bound to clash. It could have been predicted, as though by feeding data into a mechanical brain, that this falling out would occur when Dr. Lloyd-Jones commissioned Wright to design a large building to house the activities of his church, to be called the Abraham Lincoln Center. It was to include an auditorium, and rooms for various sorts of gatherings, along with a library, gymnasium, and kitchen. There would be little or nothing about it to suggest religion in the usually accepted sense. No architect in town could have been more sympathetic to this point of view than the pastor's nephew, and his first suggestion was for a tall building that looked like the Wainwright, without ornamentation. This was modified to a design for five stories, but with the same treatment of the roof and corner piers. Wright thought enough of this version to exhibit it as a plaster model in a Chicago Architectural Club show.

In spite of the favorable notice that the plaster Lincoln Center received, client and architect could not get to final plans; many more drawings had come out of the Studio, where it was obvious that a disproportionate amount of time was going to the Lloyd-Jones project. The pastor kept talking about a "four-square building for a four-square gospel," thus foreshadowing Aimee Semple McPherson. It was, indeed, unusual that Wright put up with this recalcitrant client as long as he did. One reason was, of course, that he was anxious to do a big church, especially so if it did not look like a church. Also, he evidently wanted somehow to prevail over his uncle, or at least equal him in argument, as would be made evident if they could agree on plans and specifications. Yet, incredible as it may seem, Wright put five years into the project without getting final approval of the work. At last he stopped trying to do business with Uncle Jenkin, and called in Dwight H. Perkins, an architect of high gifts who thought along much the same lines as those laid down in the Studio. But Perkins also had to give up, and wrote on a blueprint "bldg. completed over protest of architect" before walking out. The Center, satisfactory to Dr. Lloyd-Jones at least, was finally erected in 1905.

More than fifty years later a Chicago clergyman, the Rev. Mr. Robert M. Rice, was inspecting the Doge's Palace in Venice. "This is one of the two greatest buildings in the world," said the guide. "The other is a church near Chicago in the Western Hemisphere." "Yes, I know," said Mr. Rice. "I'm the pastor of that church." Indeed, the minister was so often called upon to act as a guide on his home grounds that he sometimes wondered whether he was a preacher or a lecturer on architecture. Pilgrims from all over the world came to visit the building over which he presided, for it was Unity Temple, opened in 1907, and one of the most remarkable and widely known of all the works of Frank Lloyd Wright.

A fire that destroyed the old church gave Wright his opportunity to build for the forward-looking Unitarians of Oak Park. This happened in June of 1904, and Wright was at work on plans for the new church building within two months. The pastor, Dr. Arthur Johonnot, who had succeeded Miss Chapin, originally had in mind something along the lines of a New England meeting house. He was persuaded to accept Wright's revolutionary ideas by the arguments of Charles E. Roberts, a member of the building committee who was an engineer and had a high respect for Wright's abilities. Even for a Unitarian church, Wright's design was breath-taking in its absolute lack of iconography. In fact, it would take a theologian who was also an architectural scholar to find any evidence from the building that Christian worship was to be carried on there. It can be theorized that the main element, the auditorium, is built as a Greek cross within the square of enclosing walls. It is also true that in working for Unitarians, Wright confronted a much simpler task than that which faced the architects who labored to build the cathedral at Chartres. His explanation of the religious meaning in the work was that the room itself was a complete entity, so symbolizing the unity of God and man, which was enough to satisfy his patrons. This main architectural element of the church is an impressive Egyptoid mass of pebbly, elephant-gray concrete, as seen from the outside, but marvelously light and spacious within. The auditorium is reached by ramps running behind and under the pulpit, and when one enters the sky-lighted room from either of these dark and narrow passages, there is an undeniable lifting of the heart. Wright's magic was working well in this meeting place, and in the smaller mass that housed the parish house and a fellowship lounge in the rear, connected to the main church by a wide hallway with glass walls that gave on a courtyard to the east. Norman Bel Geddes, the theatrical designer, saw the merits of the composition, but annoyed Wright with his first reaction, and may have caused a momentary doubt in his mind. This occurred as Wright led Geddes along Lake Street from the west, toward Kenilworth Avenue, and the gray walls rose into view.

"It looks fine, Frank," said Geddes. "What is it—a library?"

Geddes knew better, of course. His question was an example of the urge that various people felt, at times, to plunge a needle into Wright's self-confidence. But Geddes' joke came long after Unity Temple was known throughout the world, and after Wright had made up his mind as to what he had accomplished in this building. He said of the Temple that it was, so far as he knew, "the first concrete monolith to come from the forms as architecture completely finished."[2]

Wright had used concrete on the Unity commission primarily because the cost of a comparable structure in stone would have gone far beyond the $35,000 to which he was limited in the contract. Prescient though he was, and deeply concerned with the philosophy of his profession, he had no way of foreseeing that concrete would be employed most effectively in an architecture of pure motion—the interweaving highways of the motor age—rather than in such static monumentality as he attained in Unity Temple.

The first service in the main room of Unity Temple was held in 1908, with the official dedication on Sunday, the 26th of September in the following year, with Dr. Johonnot preaching on the text, "Except the Lord build the house, they labor in vain that build it," and at the evening service reading with the congregation from Psalm 84, "How lovely are thy dwellings, O Lord of Hosts! My soul longeth, even fainteth for the courts of the Lord." The Oriental imagery was considerably cooled by the serene lighting of the auditorium, and the church's Committee on Plans felt obliged

---

[2] William Ward completed a house made entirely of reinforced concrete, at Port Chester, a few years after Wright was born. In 1837, a similarly named builder, Mr. G. A. Ward, the New York merchant, erected a house of precast cement blocks laid up in mortar at New Brighton, Staten Island. In 1889, the engineer Ernest L. Ransome finished the California Academy of Sciences, the entire building in concrete except for the iron columns around its central court. In 1895, the San Francisco Ferry Terminal presented a series of groined vaults cast as a continuous structure of reinforced concrete; but the most famous concrete building in the world at the time Unity Temple opened its doors was the apartment house on the Rue Franklin, in Paris, designed and built by the Swiss architect Auguste Perret.

to issue a large amount of explanatory matter. This was of great benefit to Wright, stressing as it did the quiet surfaces, unbroken lines, and restful interiors, shielded from the noise of Lake Street, that characterized both the Temple and the connected structure, Unity House. The fame of this mid-western church penetrated to the study of the learned and distinguished Englishman, Banister Fletcher, whose *History of Architecture on the Comparative Method* was and is a standard treatise. "Unity Temple," said Sir Banister, a trifle austerely perhaps, "is remarkable for its avoidance of historical precedent." Wright would have agreed; he said to a group of architects some years later, "After this building of Unity Temple I thought I had the great thing well in hand. I was feeling somewhat as I imagine a great prophet might. I often thought, well, at least here is an essentially new birth of thought, feeling and opportunity in this machine age. This is the modern means. *I* had made it come true. Naturally, I well remember, I became less tolerant, and I suppose, intolerable. Arrogant, I imagine, was the proper word. I have heard it enough."

Wright heard no such reproaches, however, from Mrs. Avery Coonley, a lady from the substantial suburb of Riverside. Upon meeting the architect, Mrs. Coonley said, "Mr. Wright, I see in your work the countenance of principle," and quickly commissioned him to build a large house. An ideal client, this lady was rich, a graduate of Vassar, and a leader in the fight for women's suffrage. The terraced mansion that Wright conjured up for the Coonleys was hailed by the discerning as the sort of architectural master-piece that can only be created when a liberal patron meets a great designer and there is perfect confidence between them.

Like Harley Bradley of Kankakee, Mr. Coonley had inherited a fortune that came from farm machinery, and so, indirectly, from the rich Illinois soil. Thus local talent served indigenous wealth, and brilliantly demonstrated that native elegance could exist in the State of Illinois. Wright built this grand house on a key-shaped plan, the big living-room and the service wing forming the handle, the family bedrooms the shaft, and the guest wing the crosspiece. As in many of Wright's fine houses, all the important rooms were on the second floor, the living-room being poised at the end of a reflecting pool. In this great sky-lighted room, Wright's lamps and furniture were an unqualified success, the whole harmoniously blended in his favorite tones of autumnal tan, gold, and green. Inside and out, a decorative module could be traced: a stylized geometrical tulip made up in pink and white squares of differing sizes. Set off by thin rectangular shapes, the flower appeared in such varied materials as concrete and bronze, ceramic tile, wrought iron, and electroplated glass. Together with a reed frond motif, this decoration gave the Coonley mansion a richness that was never insistent. Wright later said that their house was one of his favorites, and it obviously belongs among his great ones.

Chicago and its tributary towns and suburbs now had a population of over 2,000,000 people, and within the city limits there stood 475 buildings that were at least ten stories high. By this year of 1909, Wright's share of the architectural business of the great town had him working so hard that some friends wondered how he did it; but to his clients he presented the aspect of one whose fund of ideas was as inexhaustible as his supply of natural energy. One patron who had special reason to be delighted with Wright was Frederick Carleton Robie, who came to the architect when the Coonley house was nearing completion. "Mr.

Wright," said Robie, "I want a fireproof, reasonably priced house to live in—not a conglomeration of doodads." The lot at Fifty-Seventh Street and Woodlawn Avenue, near the University of Chicago campus, cost Mr. Robie $14,000. The house was to cost $35,000, with $10,000 more for furniture either designed or selected by Wright. All this came within the definition of a reasonable sum to the client, a native Chicagoan who had gained a fortune from his Excelsior Motor Supply Company at Twenty-Second and Halsted Streets. The resulting house is perhaps the most widely and consistently celebrated of all Wright's works; whereas the Coonley house was a suburban villa, and not easily reached for inspection, the Robie house is a city stronghold, and any visitor to Chicago may quickly make the trip to the South Side and observe at least the outward aspect of this clean-cut brick structure, as confident of its virtues today, in a neighborhood where many styles of building may be seen, as it was fifty years ago. Professor Carroll L. V. Meeks of Yale, who has written with authority and understanding on railroad stations, calls the Robie house "one of the great monuments of American architectural history." The *Architectural Record* says it was "one of the seven most notable residences ever built in America." Wright himself, with that readiness to praise his own work that was a noticeable foible in his personality, compared this house to a fine piece of sculpture or a beautiful painting. As sculpture, it might be considered an abstract composition in lines and planes; as a picture, it pleases the eye with the tawny brick of its walls and the dove-colored concrete trim of the parapets that give it an air of fortification and security. Inside, Mr. and Mrs. Robie enjoyed the sensation of extra privacy that came from having the principal rooms raised one story above the ground; the first floor of this house was actually a raised basement, and the entrance was tucked away along the north wall halfway down the long axis of the lot. The attached garage was another novel feature of this house—perhaps the first example of something now so common as to be taken for granted, but a remarkable step in a time when the garage had not yet fully divorced itself from the stable, which retired a certain distance from any gentleman's dwelling for obvious reasons. It is not possible to sum up the Robie house in a few words, or perhaps in any words, but many critics have been most impressed, on first seeing this building, by a sense of precision from its long lines, sharp angles, and the clean and crisp connection of its elements. The continuous lines extending over the void of the raised basement and the emphasis given the massive central pylon of the chimney led some observers to fancy they saw in this house a resemblance to a ship. This gave rise to a legend, typical of many about Wright and his relations with his clients, that Mr. Robie had asked for "a house like a steamship" in memory of a happy wedding trip aboard such a vessel. Equally absurd is the tale that Wright instructed Mrs. Robie to wear dresses made from cloth with horizontal stripes, to harmonize with the lines of the house, offering to design the fabrics for her, as he was also supposed to have done for Mrs. Coonley. Wright could and did design fabrics, and, in the case of his wife Catherine, even designed dresses. But he felt that an architect's duty to his clients was fulfilled when their house was sited, designed, built, and furnished. The Robie house, of course, was a great triumph—perhaps the climax of the Prairie style. After some years of residence, Robie sold the house to Marshall D. Wilber, head of the Wilber Mercantile Agency, and by the late 1950's, the building was in the hands of the Chicago Theological

Seminary. This institution made use of the famous house as a residential hall, but finding it impractical to maintain, put it up for sale and almost certain destruction. Meanwhile, the city commission on Chicago's architectural heritage had marked the Robie house as an official landmark. Unfortunately, the commission was merely an advisory body, without funds to buy and set aside buildings it listed.[3] At this point the world-wide fame of the house, and its still living architect, caused a discussion in the newspapers. Wright himself appeared on the scene, and pronounced the house in good shape, merely in need of proper maintenance to last indefinitely. His Phi Delta Theta fraternity brothers accompanied him on a tour of inspection, and suggested a scheme to exchange their property two doors north on Woodlawn Avenue for the Robie house, while the Seminary was to trade the Phi Delta Theta property with still another fraternity, and so come out of the intricate deal with something approximating what was required as the site for a new faculty apartment house. Though all parties negotiated in good faith, this plan proved too complicated, and word went out that the Robie house was doomed, even though Wright's friend Carl Sandburg said that "To tear it down would be an irretrievable loss, like smoke on the horizon with wind blowing it away never to have it again." But in 1959, just when it seemed that the Robie house would vanish over the horizon of history, the real-estate developer William Zeckendorf stepped in and bought it. For the present, it was announced, the Zeckendorf firm would use the house as office space, and it would not be destroyed.

[3] As was demonstrated in 1961 when Louis Sullivan's Schiller Building, more recently known as the Garrick Theater, went down before the iron ball of the wreckers.

At the time the Robie house was completed, Wright's problems were far removed from the question of preserving his work. What he needed was the nervous energy to continue producing it, in the face of the emotional troubles that permeated the house and studio in Oak Park. He gave all the classic symptoms of nervous breakdown: shortness of temper, insomnia, chronic fatigue (to which he felt he must not cater by taking a vacation), and the general feeling of being "up against a dead wall." Mamah Cheney understood him, he thought; and being near her was a kind of rest. Otherwise, he felt broken and empty, condemned to find peace only in work, and more work, that could only end in artistic exhaustion and emotional disaster.

It cannot be said, however, that Wright lacked professional encouragement during these tense and unhappy days. A distinguished visitor at the Studio in 1908, for example, was Dr. Kuno Francke, Professor of the History of German Culture at Harvard. Though an American citizen, and a member of the Harvard faculty since 1884, Francke communicated an air of European approval to Wright, since he had been born at Kiel, and his doctorate was from the University of Munich. Not long after he first received Francke's encouragement, Wright got word that the eminent German art publisher, Ernst Wasmuth of Berlin, wished to bring out an elephant-folio illustrated monograph on the work that Wright had done in the American Middle West. Wright was glad to give permission for this publication, which was to have a great influence on European architecture; but he felt that he could not get away from Chicago and go to Berlin to oversee preparation of the monograph. In later years, Wright liked to say he thought it was Francke's recommendation that caused Wasmuth to embark on publication. There is no question that Wright received the most enlightened kind of sympathy from the professor, and through him, the endorsement of worlds beyond Oak Park; but one wonders if Wright's memory was correct when he said that Francke told him it would be fifty or even one hundred years before Wright's countrymen became ready for what he was doing and could give it proper appreciation. If so, both Wright and Francke overlooked the fact that it was a number of their countrymen who had commissioned the world-famous work.

Another encouragement came during this period in the form of what appeared to be the opportunity of a lifetime—the chance to design a family seat for the Harold Mc-Cormicks. If the McCormick clan was not the first family of Chicago, it was certain that no family took precedence over them; and their fortune had been started in the traditional Chicago way. The founder of the line, Cyrus McCormick of Virginia, had been poor as dirt; then he invented a reaping machine, and from the vast wealth that accrued, many a solemn palace was to spring. In fact, an area around Rush and Ontario Streets in what is now called the near North Side had so many of this family's stately mansions by the early 1900's that it was known as Mc-Cormickville. Cyrus married Nettie Fowler, of Clayton, New York, who was to outdo all other communicants in benefactions to the Presbyterian Church. His son Harold married Edith Rockefeller of Cleveland, daughter of John D. Rockefeller. This lady was long referred to as the richest woman in Chicago, and was generally acknowledged as the town's social leader after the famous Mrs. Potter Palmer abdicated that position by continuing absences from the city. Mrs. Harold McCormick was to absent herself more and more frequently, too, in later life, spending several years under the tutelage of the Swiss psychiatrist, Dr. Carl

Gustav Jung, and at one time unsuccessfully attempting to persuade James Joyce to submit to psychoanalysis. But at the time this wealthy woman met Frank Lloyd Wright, her base of operations was Chicago, and her home an immense mansion at 1000 Lake Shore Drive. Unlike many Chicago magnates of their rank, the Harold McCormicks had bought their house from a previous owner rather than having it built to order. However, the place was the work of Solon Beman, who well knew how to please such patrons. He had designed the massive pile for Nathaniel S. Jones, who came to Chicago in 1875 and founded the commission firm of Jones, Kennet, and Hopkins. The house had another owner before the McCormicks in General Joseph T. Torrence of the Illinois National Guard. Torrence had come to town as engineer in charge of the furnaces at the Chicago Iron Works, and also had a share in the "belt-line" railroading operations that served the city's factories. He thus became wealthy enough to establish himself for a time at 1000 Lake Shore Drive, behind the ornamental iron gate and the arched entrance that was reached by wide stone steps under the command of a high, many-turreted roof. Although they acquired this enormous place to set up as Chicago housekeepers, Edith Rockefeller and Harold McCormick were married in New York, thus betraying a certain distrust in the stature of the home city that could sometimes be observed in Chicagoans, though impossible to explain when one considered Chicago's vitality and magnificence. This lack of complete faith in the Middle West was to have its effect on the career of Frank Lloyd Wright, as we shall shortly see; but at the time the McCormicks put him to work on drawings and plans, the sky was the limit—and it was the infinitely promising sky above Lake Michigan. They offered the architect a magnificent site on a bluff looking out over the water at Lake Forest, about thirty miles north of town. Here Wright could perform as he had in the Hardy house at Racine, but on a grand scale. After preliminary interviews with his clients, and a survey of the dramatic site, Wright planned a marvel of a house—or rather, a complex of connecting houses—with the bluffs reinforced by retaining walls to make a running base for the entire composition of pavilions and galleries. There was magic and wonder in his conception—one can imagine how it would have looked from the lake at night. And no imagination is needed, when looking at Wright's drawings, to see how his galleries would have framed the changing vistas of the lake. But Mrs. McCormick apparently succumbed, as the Coonleys and Bradleys had not, to that haunting doubt which sent Chicagoans to New York, as it sent New Yorkers to Europe, to the lifelong interest of Mr. Henry James. Whatever demon of indecision got into the lady—for it seems clear that she rather than her husband was responsible—Edith Rockefeller McCormick at the last moment decided not to approve Wright's plans. Instead, she went to New York and engaged Charles Adams Platt, an accomplished designer in the Palladian style. The resulting Villa Turicum, though correct and elegant, and handsomely set in formal gardens, has long since been torn down.

Had he known that the house his patron finally commissioned would not survive—or even that Mrs. McCormick herself would at last die in relative poverty, after divorcing her husband, and losing her own fortune by speculation—it would have given little satisfaction to Wright. For financial and emotional reasons, he needed the McCormick commission then and there; the major disappointment of seeing his plans put aside could not have come at a worse time. Overwork on the professional and artistic side of his life was accompanied by increasing lack of harmony on the personal side, where his marriage was no longer an even remotely satisfactory thing. The disagreement between Wright and Catherine had grown like an evil plant; now he had come to the place where he wanted an end of it. And there was no use trying to conceal what Catherine called the infatuation with Mrs. Cheney. Wright replied, and apparently correctly, that it was much more than this. He told Catherine, as he has recorded, that his feeling for Mrs. Cheney would be a permanent part of his life. Unless Catherine could accept this, Wright said, there would have to be a divorce. He thought the whole thing through in his orderly mind, and produced three main generalities. The first was that marriage must be mutual, and when it is not, it is no more than slavery. Second, "Love is not property." This meant that people could not own each other. Third, there was no such thing as an illegitimate child; but there could be illegitimate parents. From these three principles, he deduced three conclusions as to the legal aspect of the matter. He stated as the first conclusion that legal marriage is only a civil contract, governing property and the provision for children. Sexual relations in marriage, however, should be voluntary and not part of the contract. Secondly, he concluded that "Love, so far as laws can go to protect it, is entitled to the benefit of hands-off and the benefit of the doubt." And third, that it is the duty of the State to enact laws to protect children, but that the most important thing a child can have is the love of its parents—and this cannot be a concern of the laws.

So far, so good, as Wright saw it. But this reasoning did not have the effect he could have wished on Catherine. She still loved her husband, and wished their marriage to continue. It might be true that "love was not property"—but somewhere there seemed to be a fallacy in the reasoning, at least from Catherine's point of view. At any rate, Wright's request for a divorce came at about the time of the McCormick disappointment, in the late summer of 1908. The only suggestion that Catherine would make was that Wright wait for a year; then, as he recalled the circumstance in writing his memoirs at a later date, Catherine was to grant the divorce if he still wanted it.

Disappointed, exhausted, harried with debt, and sometimes trailed by bill-collectors, Wright continued to find sympathy and understanding with Mrs. Cheney. He was by now not only well known but highly noticeable, and his association with Mrs. Cheney was observed, even by casual passersby, marked as it was by frequent rides with the lady in a low seated, chugging Stoddard-Dayton through Oak Park streets. But nobody in Chicago, much less in conservative Oak Park, was prepared for the front-page news of Sunday morning, November 7, 1909—Frank Lloyd Wright and Mrs. Cheney had eloped.

Chapter Four

TRAGEDY AT TALIESIN

MANY ODD INCIDENTS occurred as a result of the wide and copious variety of work that Frank Lloyd Wright accomplished in his long life. One day in the 1950's, for example, a woman in California, who thought she was alone in her house, walked from her bathroom to the kitchen wearing a large towel. Looking into her living room, she was displeased to see an unknown young man frowning at her fireplace. The intruder had no criminal intent, but was merely one of the large number of persons who considered a house like this lady's to be part of the public domain, since it was designed by the world's most imaginative architect—the great and famous Frank Lloyd Wright.

Through the years, owners of Wright houses could tell many stories like this one, involving men and women who behaved as though inspecting public monuments. An especially startling invasion took place at a house near Chicago when a Volkswagen bus rolled into the courtyard and a seemingly endless procession of bearded Englishmen began to emerge. Advancing on the door in a phalanx, they told the lady of the house they were emissaries of some national foundation or other; evidently they were under the impression that this outfit could grant them free admission to all houses planned by Wright, and they did not appear to grasp the idea that the lady who greeted them was no caretaker, but the owner.

It happened that the lady was giving a dinner party for which the guests would arrive within an hour, and she was on her way to pick up the ice cream. It would be all right, she said, if the tourists took a few pictures, but they must be gone by the time she got back. One can picture the lady's consternation when on her return she found that Englishmen had spread through the house like termites, had moved the table out of the dining area, and filled the hallways with reflectors and other photographic gear. But what seared her memory was the injured tone in which the leader remarked, as she drove the intruders out, that she was "a most unsympathetic occupant for a house by Mr. Wright."

Less appalling persons, such as journalists, architects, and architectural historians, who telephone for appointments, also appear from time to time, but some dwellers in Wright houses have understandably adopted a policy of "Keep Out —This Means You." They feel that a house is still a castle even when it happens to be a work of art. Owners in this frame of mind have resorted to wire fences, locked gates, and fierce dogs, and have removed their names from mailboxes in an effort to preserve privacy.

Such measures are understandable in the light of the experience of a lady for whom Wright designed a house on the Arizona desert. Relaxing one afternoon in her bedroom, she began to have the feeling that someone was looking at her. Glancing at the long band of characteristic Wrightian windows, she saw that this was actually the case, for a lady and gentleman had ridden up on horseback and were staring into the room. Seeing that the occupant had noticed them, the rubbernecks struck up a conversation along the lines that it must be a privilege to live in a house designed by Mr. Wright.

"Oh, yes, indeed—a great privilege," the owner replied. Next came the question, were there any disadvantages to living in such a house? The householder then said, between clenched teeth, "Yes, there is one frightful disadvantage—

awful people ride up on horses and look through your bedroom windows."

Peering intruders, however, are not the only difficulties
of houses designed by Frank Lloyd Wright. A minor an-
noyance comes from his habit of scaling the width of
passageways and the height of lintels to his own trim five-
foot-eight-and-one-half-inch body, which causes persons of
greater bulk to have some slight trouble in getting through.
In this connection it might be noted that the modest-sized
Sir Christopher Wren did the same thing, to the inconvenience of his royal patron, who was too great a gentleman to
protest. Moreover, the main rooms of Wright's houses,
though commodious, occasionally have brought on a
feeling of psychic pressure. This caused Professor Otto
Vulckers of Stuttgart to remark that in some of Wright's
rooms one heard incessant voices calling, "Here I am, the
chimney; and I have been laid up naturally of stone taken
from out of the earth . . . Here I am, the ceiling; and I am
coming right down at you!"

Something like that must have overcome the lady who
reported that, after buying a Wright house from its original owners, she found it so disturbing that it put her in
a hospital with a nervous breakdown. But she resolved "not
to let the house conquer her," went back and got used to it,
and found that living there gave her feelings of satisfaction
and joy. A similar difficulty was dealt with in another way
by a lady who found that her Wright house "asked too
much of her." She moved to Washington, D. C., had a
fashionable architect build her a house "in pure copybook
Georgian," and lived happily ever after.

So it would seem that the demands of Wright houses are
outweighed, on the whole, by the delight of living with
one's own special version of the artist's sense of proportion

and color; and if there are difficulties, they are mostly those that also might occur in lesser houses, where the compensations of Wright's genius are not to be found. But in the year 1909, there arose a special disadvantage, keenly felt by some owners of Wright houses, that has now completely passed away. This discomfort came from the householders' fears that they might share in the heavy public reproach that was directed against their architect because he had run away to Europe with a client's wife. There had been something epic in the scale of desertion achieved by Wright and Mamah Borthwick Cheney—between them, they had abandoned eight children, as well as two worthy and respectable mates. Moreover, if Wright had conducted months of research to find the exact spot in the United States where such an episode would evoke the severest censure, he could not have improved on conservative Oak Park. And he topped the performance by announcing, "I am no woman's property."

In leaving his home at Oak Park, Wright was doing what his father had done nearly a quarter of a century before at Madison. Wright's departure, as sudden and anguished as that of Christian taking off for the Celestial City—it will be recalled that he also left wife and family—occurred in early October. At that time, Mrs. Cheney and her two children, a seven-year-old girl and a boy of five, were at a Colorado mountain resort. Wright was a busy man on the day he left; he rushed around Chicago selling his collection of Japanese prints, taking money from the bank, and handing over the plans on the Studio drawing boards to an architect named Hermann von Holst. Though competent, von Holst had not been close to Wright, and presumably knew little or nothing about his work; sensibly enough, he got the help of Wright's associates Marion Mahony and

Walter Burley Griffin in finishing the designs and seeing them to construction. Meanwhile, Wright arrived in New York, and met Mrs. Cheney, who had come on from Colorado, leaving the children in her sister's care. Wright and Mrs. Cheney sailed together for Europe the following day.

All this was known—and thoroughly talked over—in church and social circles in Oak Park, but some weeks went by before anything became known that a newspaper could print. The publicity of November 9 was based on the discovery by the *Tribune*'s Berlin correspondent that cablegrams and mail addressed to Mrs. E. Cheney were handed to the lady who was represented by the words "and wife" after the signature of Frank Lloyd Wright on the Adlon Hotel register. The same reporter came upon a postcard addressed to Wright at the Wasmuth offices, 35 Markgrafen Strasse, and cabled a copy to Chicago. "O. P., October 20," said the postcard. "My Dear: We think of you often and hope you are well and enjoying life, as you have so longed to. From the children and your wife, Catherine L. Wright." The other side of the card was a photograph of Unity Temple.

With this lead in hand, a large party of reporters set out at once for Oak Park, their editors justifying the concentration of forces, and the inspection of hotel registers and mail, by pointing to Wright's international reputation as an architect. Supported by a clergyman, Catherine Wright met the press and made what now seems to have been a regrettable gesture by issuing a long statement that not only did not end the story, but did a great deal to keep it alive.

"My heart is with him now," said Mrs. Wright. "He will come back as soon as he can. I have a faith in Frank Lloyd Wright that passeth understanding, perhaps, but I know him as no one else knows him. In this instance, he is as

innocent of wrongdoing as I am. These cablegrams and bits
of verification do not change my position in the least, nor
alter my feelings. Why, this is simply the publicity part of
a struggle that has been going on for a long time." Mrs.
Wright continued in this vein for a while, and then a reporter asked what she thought of Wright's manner of signing the Adlon register. Catherine replied with a question:
"If he were an ordinary rake, do you think he would have
done that?" She then went on, "He is honest in everything
he does. A moment's insincerity tortures him more than
anything in this world. Frank Wright never has deceived
me in all his life." After pausing for a moment to reflect on
nearly twenty years of marriage, Mrs. Wright continued,
"His whole life has been a struggle. When he came here
as a young architect, he had to fight against every existing
idea in architecture. He did fight, year after year, against
obstacles that would have downed an ordinary man. He
has fought the most tremendous battles. He is fighting one
now. I know he will win."

The reporters then asked if Wright would be compelled
to add a court action to his other struggles. Catherine answered, "Whatever I am as a woman, aside from my good
birth, I owe to the example of my husband. I do not hesitate
to confess it. Is it likely then that I should want to commence
court action? I shall make no appeal whatever to the courts.
I stand by my husband right at this moment. I am his wife.
He loves his children tenderly and has the greatest anxiety
for their welfare. My heart is with him now. I feel certain
that he will come back when he has reached a certain decision with himself. When he comes back, all will be as it
has been."

When Mrs. Wright made that remark, the reporters, with
professional hardihood, immediately asked her, "When Mr.

Wright comes back, how will Mrs. Cheney fit into the picture?" Mrs. Wright's reply was, "With regard to Mrs. Cheney, I have striven to put her out of my thoughts. It is simply a force against which we have had to contend. I never felt that I breathed the same air with her. It was simply a case of a vampire—you have heard of such things. Why must the children suffer for things they are unaccountable for? They cannot think of a separation. They worship their father and love their mother. If I could only protect them now, I would care for nothing else. My life—" Here Mrs. Wright broke off, then added, "I could write a wonderful story."

The story of Mrs. Wright's interview filled several columns the following day, but its candor failed to keep the newspapers from applying to her husband and his fellow traveler the words "affinity" and "soul mate." Meanwhile, the other deserted partner, Edwin Cheney, gave Catherine an example of a different kind of press relations when reporters approached him during a concert intermission outside Orchestra Hall. They asked, "Will you seek a divorce?" and Cheney replied, "I have nothing to say." "Did you suspect that your wife was with Wright when you sent letters to the Wasmuth office?" "I don't care to talk about the matter at all," said Mr. Cheney, and walked back to his seat at the concert.

But a great many other people in Chicago, whether or not they had anything to do with Frank Lloyd Wright, discussed the matter freely. The city's preachers, for example, were prompt in pointing out the error of taking up with a soul mate. This was more than a nine days' wonder; some time after the first excitement, the question was still on one prominent pastor's mind, and a full house crowded the pews of Pilgrim Congregational Church when the Rev. Dr. Frederick E. Hopkins rose to speak on the subject, "Affinity Fools."

The minister depicted for his hearers a married woman who "tries to make herself think she understands a lot of gab from the platform of her club about the larger, the fuller life and her sphere. Along happens a knave. Together they begin to think and talk about how they understand each other and breathe deep, like an old setting hen. What wonderful things they discover together, and how different the world looks through each other's eyes. Thus they proceed through weeks and months of slush until one day there is a splash, and both have tumbled into the same old hog pen where thousands have tumbled before them."

Then the pastor told of the husband who leaves a good wife for a woman "made by milliners, dressmakers, dancing academies, and the devil." A note of horror came into the peroration when Dr. Hopkins said, "If you have gone down into the refrigerating rooms of a big packing house and looked at a row of pigs' faces hanging on their hooks, you have seen a perfect picture of affinity fools unmasked."

Not realizing that he could be the subject of such eloquent preaching, Wright continued his stay in Berlin, consulting with the Wasmuth people about the monograph on his work. It was reasonable indeed that he should visit Ernst Wasmuth while this important publication was being prepared; but it was emotional pressure that finally dislodged Wright from his suburban workshop and brought him to Berlin; less than a year before, he had been saying it was altogether impossible for him to get away. While in Berlin, Wright could have seen little if anything in the way of architecture to make him have the slightest doubt of his own creations. He undoubtedly inspected the royal museum, an imposing edifice on the northeast side of the Lustgarten,

facing the royal palace. This structure had been completed
in 1830 by Karl Friedrich Schinkel, the eminent classicist,
at the order of Frederick Wilhelm III. There was authentic
majesty in the portico supported by eighteen colossal Ionic
columns, rising and lengthening as one mounted the wide
stone steps. But Wright had little to learn from Schinkel
when it came to obtaining an architectural effect; nor was
he likely to see many buildings that he would consider to
have any distinction elsewhere in the city, though he was
impressed by Alfred Messel's huge department store.

Wright and Mrs. Cheney soon traveled to Florence and
other Italian cities. He gave careful and sensitive study to
the Florentine painters, sculptors, and architects—many of
them, of course, were all three—and came to the conclusion
that no truly Italian building can seem ill at ease on its site.
He looked at humble structures as well as palaces, and saw
that they were rendered directly, and with natural feeling.
In all Italy he felt an "ineffable charm," close to the earth;
and to enjoy it at leisure, he and Mrs. Cheney took up residence in a small villa at Fiesole, among the olive-tan Tuscan
hills. He inspected the Roman theater and baths (perhaps
recalling that the Roman touch in Wales had been light),
marveled at the paintings of Fra Angelico at the nearby
Church of San Domenico, and strolled in the villa's high-
walled garden, breathing the odor of flowers and pines.
Whatever the world might think of his departure from Oak
Park, Wright did have sore need of rest and a change of
scene, for even his great energies were exhausted. To say
nothing of the emotional stresses he had inflicted on himself
and his family, he had put in years of unremitting toil at
what may well be, next to the doctor's, the most demanding
of all professions.

Over and above the physical and mental exhaustion, of

course, was Wright's belief that he was arrayed in mortal combat against forces of artistic reaction. Wright did not hold this belief alone; when Catherine told it to the reporters, she was expressing what all his friends and disciples held as an article of faith—that he had a battle flag, and it carried the Lloyd-Jones motto, "Truth Against the World." But up to this time, the world had scarcely mistreated Wright, for it had given him international critical recognition and more work than he could do. The real struggle on Wright's hands in 1909 and immediately thereafter was not to compel recognition of his professional merits, but to regain a place in conventional society. And the way he went about it was not only characteristic, but certain to postpone his social rehabilitation for an indefinite time. Wright proposed nothing less than to compel the public to admit that everything he had done was fully justified.

With this end in view, he left Mrs. Cheney in Europe and came back to the United States toward the close of 1910. During his absence the newspapers had coined the grinding phrase "spiritual hegira" to describe Wright's travels, and these words were ringing in his ears when he returned to his Oak Park home. He told Catherine he was willing to meet his obligations, and to live at the Studio—but he would still act as Mrs. Cheney's protector. Catherine would not accept this arrangement, nor would she agree to a divorce.

"Very well," said Frank Lloyd Wright, showing his remarkable ability to adjust to the inevitable, "I shall accept a worm's-eye view of society." At this time, encouragement of a sort came from Wright's mother, who gave him the two hundred acres of farm land she had inherited as her portion of the family lands near Spring Green, in the southern Wisconsin hills. Here he began to build the house Taliesin, taking its name from that of a Welsh bard, literally trans-

lated, "Shining Brow." Much was summed up in Taliesin:
first of all, perhaps, Wright's natural desire to put down
roots where he had passed the happiest days of his boyhood,
and learned to love the land with its rich burden of grain,
its apple and cherry trees, and the never-failing views of
distant purple hills that framed the valleys. Here he would
set the ideal country home and farm, something on the high
order of Henry James's Great Good Place, with a touch
of fantasy in house design and landscape architecture like
that which Poe described in "The Domain of Arnheim." A
symbol as well as a house, and never quite completed because of Wright's ceaseless alterations and additions, Taliesin
is perhaps his greatest work. With characteristic feeling for
terrain, he put it just below the crest of a hill from which
there spread a magnificent prospect down the valley and
across a countryside similar to that from which his Welsh
ancestors came.

"No house should be on a hill," said Wright. "It should
be *of* the hill." He thus echoed his maxim that decoration
should be an organic part of a structure's surface. But Taliesin was far more than mere decoration. Part of the hill it
was indeed, with its connecting courts built of the fawn-
colored local stone, so that they looked like a natural out-
cropping. It all struck the enchanted viewer as a splendid
working out of Wright's organic theories, along with a suggestion of the outlaws' lair in *Lorna Doone*.

While the walls of the magical house were rising, important things took place in the lives of Wright and those
close to him. Among these significant events was the awarding of a divorce to Edwin Cheney, in August of 1911, on
grounds of desertion. He retained the children, though they
were to be allowed to visit their mother from time to time.
Again Cheney resisted any temptation he may have felt to

discuss his affairs with reporters, and several months went by without newspaper mention of Frank Lloyd Wright. Then it became known, just before Christmas, that Mrs. Cheney had returned from Europe and was permanently established at Taliesin. This was the announcement of Frank Lloyd Wright himself, given to an invited audience of reporters. They found him standing before the great fireplace at Taliesin, wearing a crimson robe. Nearby sat Mamah Borthwick Cheney in an Oriental gown, listening while Wright read the statement.

"Let there be no misunderstanding," he began. "A Mrs. E. H. Cheney never existed for me, and now is no more in fact. But Mamah Borthwick is here, and I intend to take care of her. To answer a specific question would be of no value. The solution of this case will be individual, and worked out by honest living, not by patching broken conventions, nursing wounded sensibilities, or hiding behind expediencies. No one will suffer owing to my neglect of any rational obligation, economic or otherwise. Meantime, the public will be asked for nothing but the opportunity to work exactly as before, which is likely to be denied, for that matter tore close to the social fabric in a rotten spot."

Following the axiom that the best defense is an attack, Wright then shifted into the admonitory tone which was one of his lifelong characteristics. "A written contract does not make a marriage nor keep it holy," he said. "We depend too much on outward forms and are careless of the spirit beneath them. Integrity of life means unity of thought and feeling and action, and therefore a struggle to square one's life with one's self. Every man of ideals and a work to do is elevated by the vision in his soul and consumed by the desire to see it come true."

Having delivered this Emersonian homily, Wright turned

to the actors in the drama as he continued, "Here were four people, who had each, according to his or her ability, assumed earlier in life the responsibilities of marriage. Then the thing happened which has happened to men and women since time began—the inevitable. As soon as their situation became apparent to them, there was the struggle with the conscience, the concession to duty, but not the clandestine relation furtively continued to save the face of the public— not the usual suits and countersuits, quarrels and vilifications, or shirkings of responsibility. On the contrary, as soon as the situation developed its inevitable character, a frank avowal to those whose lives were to be affected by a readjustment to meet the new conditions was made." In making these statements, Wright had unfortunately forgotten another architect, Pecksniff by name, for in Wrightian language, all he was saying was that he and Mamah Borthwick had announced they were going to leave. He went on to explain that they waited a year before walking out, but since he "neglected to inform the Chicago newspapers" it was "said that he had eloped." Of course that was exactly what he had done, and the wrong of the intrusive newspapers did not make it right. But he achieved a certain dignity, and spoke in a tone more worthy of him as artist and man when he concluded, "Thus may be written the drama that is played now in countless places behind the curtain, so that honest souls may profit. And most may find in it the triumph of selfishness. I cannot care. Perhaps the veritable in the final analysis is not much more than the selfishness of nature . . . And now that all have worn their hearts for daws to peck at, may not the matter be left in privacy to those whose concern it chiefly is?"

As if this statement were not enough to explain his position and that of Mamah Cheney, Wright followed it up within a week by issuing a written account of the entire affair. His document described the troubles of four people, "a wife and a man and a husband and a woman." The wife was Catherine, and according to Wright, she "characterized the matter as mere infatuation that would pass." Consultations were held "between the wife and the husband, the mother and friends." But this did no good, for "Both the wife and the husband declared that anything they could do to break up the new relationship they would do, each in his or her own way, with plenty of friendly assistance." And so the statement continued, very much along the lines of what Wright had read to the reporters when they came to Taliesin; the manifesto, apparently issued to clarify the first statement, was something of a redundancy, as can be seen. Today its greatest interest is its curious resemblance to the continuity of a silent movie, an art form then at its height, in which characters labelled The Boy, The Girl, The Father, The Husband, and so on, capered through flickering ballets that still have fascinating power. Perhaps Wright wished to be thought an actor in a drama of which he was also the author; in any event, no comment is needed on the need for explanation and justification that these statements showed.

If Wright was to some extent acting a part—as indeed everyone must—it is not difficult to identify some of the elements from which he assembled the role. To begin with, people were quite willing to regard an architect as a romantic figure: such a man might be expected to have the tendency not to conform to general standards that was associated with artists, and yet might have a hard and practical side, for after all, an architect did have to see to it that solid houses came into being. Thus the architect was a convenient figure by which literature and the drama could state the eternal problem of the artist. In the early nineties, to take a conspicuous example, Henrik Ibsen created a stir with his play, *The Master Builder,* in which the hero, Halvard Solness, a married man in love with a young girl, had his life further complicated by lack of public sympathy with his artistic aims. A significant passage has the girl Hilda asking, "Why don't you call yourself an architect like the others?" with the answer, "I have not been systematically enough taught for that. Most of what I know I found out for myself." Solness wants to "build homes for human beings . . . Cozy, comfortable, bright homes, where father and mother and the whole troop of children can live in safety and gladness, feeling what a happy thing it is to be alive in the world . . ." This sounds remarkably like Wright extolling the virtues of the Coonley mansion, but it should be recalled that Ibsen ended his play by having Solness climb a steeple and fall to his death. Hilda's final speech is: "But he mounted right to the top. And I heard harps in the air."

In the light of all this, one may ask, did Wright think of himself as a full-fledged genius at the time he took up with Mrs. Cheney? It is evident that though he made his mistakes, he never fell into the error of failing to take himself with sufficient seriousness; but he had need of genuine self-confidence when he spoke of his willingness to look at society from "a worm's-eye view." An accurate measure of how Wright viewed the state of his achievements during his first great notoriety may be gained from the paper entitled "In the Cause of Architecture" that he contributed to the magazine *Architectural Record* in 1908. Here he spoke of what he had done so far as "the work," or "this work," and made it clear that he felt he was dealing in ethical and philosophical values as well as in brick, timber and concrete. For centuries, he wrote, architectural practice had been to turn away from nature, where he saw the essential forms of building find their original life; now he was turning to "the elemental law and order inherent in all great architecture." When he started out, he had few sympathizers, as he saw it, though inspiration was burning within him and he longed for professional comrades who would understand his message. These he found, in men like Myron Hunt and Dwight Perkins, but with the passage of only a few years, he became too busy to see them as often as he would like. But a middle western school had been formed which stood, above all, for integrity. He had seen many "fantastic abortions" in American domestic architecture, but the ideals of the new school were making progress. Things were not so bad as they had been, now that clients were to be found with "unspoiled instincts and untainted ideals." Though mostly men of business, these people were capable of encouraging "this work" because they saw the logical and rational qualities of it.

But in order to reach these clients, Wright recorded, he had been compelled to make himself the enemy of the entire established industrial order, which was no light matter. He had persevered, however, to establish a pure and simple grammar of building, with his schemes "conceived in three dimensions as organic entities, let the picturesque perspective fall where it will." But the art of architecture, on the whole, was moribund; the old structural forms were decayed. "These ideals," Wright said, referring to his own doctrines, "take the buildings out of school and marry them to the ground." This would seem to be true, allowing for a touch of hyperbole; but Wright went on to say that in the exteriors of his houses there was a democratic character that had earned them the enmity of persons evilly disposed. He then took up the subject of the assistants who had worked with him at Oak Park, mentioning a number of them including Byrne and Griffin. Speaking of these employees as a group, Wright said, "It is urged against the more loyal that they are sacrificing their individuality to that which has dominated this work; but it is too soon to impeach a single understudy on this basis, for, although they will inevitably repeat for years the methods, forms, and habits of thought, even the mannerisms of the present work, if there is virtue in the principles behind it that virtue will stay with them through the preliminary stages of their own practice until their own individualities truly develop independently. I have noticed that those who have made the most fuss about their 'individuality' in early stages, those who took themselves seriously in that regard, were inevitably those who had least." Wright went on to say that he allowed his helpers to meet his clients, a privilege that in the hands of "selfishly ambitious or overconfident assistants" would soon wreck his system. One individual—Wright himself—formed the central concept of everything that was done in his drafting room; and that same man determined "the character of every detail in the sum total, even to the size and shape of the pieces of glass in the windows, the arrangement and profile of the most insignificant of the architectural members . . ." As for the future, Wright said "the work" was to grow more simple, more expressive; and be idealized "with the cleanest, most virile stroke I can imagine." Moreover, this work would itself idealize the characters of those who were surrounded by it—in a sense it would become an atmosphere as pure and elevating as that of nature herself.

Much of this manifesto by Wright to the architectural profession defies analysis; and much of it seems entirely admirable. It is hard to quarrel with his doctrine that one man should be responsible for the total effect, if the building is to be a work of art. Committee art and architecture was never for Frank Lloyd Wright. Though he did not mention it, an apt illustration for his feeling about an architect's responsibility might be the medieval custom that singled out the master builder when a cathedral was completed. He and he alone stood underneath the stone roof when the last of the wooden centering was knocked away—if it fell, it fell on him.[1] But his remarks about his associates are somehow embarrassing, and his conclusion as to the effect of "this work" has the supreme self-confidence that only a genius can show. In his early forties, as he stood in the ruins of conventional esteem, Wright had good reason to take a solid stand on professional pride. In fact, if he had never designed another building, the work described in the Wasmuth monograph—and spread beneath his native Middle Western sky—would have assured him a permanent lease on a seat of high architectural honor. But whether he could enjoy that eminence as a member of the social community was quite another thing.

Frank Lloyd Wright settled down, if the term may be used, to a life divided between his drafting room at Taliesin, an office at Orchestra Hall, and a small apartment at 25 East Cedar Street on the near North Side. He tried to spend every weekend at Taliesin, and was a familiar sight on the train between Chicago and Madison, usually reading from a volume of Shakespeare or Whitman to while away the journey. Mrs. Cheney, or Mamah Borthwick as she was now legally named, had settled in as the lady of the house at Taliesin. From time to time she had her young son and daughter at her side, though they stayed mostly with their father,

[1] Wright's representatives made a somewhat similar demonstration to convince workmen that a house at Cincinnati in the 1940's was properly constructed.

who had remarried a year after his divorce. Since her days
were not altogether taken up by the duties of motherhood,
Mamah Borthwick was able to indulge in various intellectual
pursuits. It was this side of Mamah's personality that made
her so attractive to Wright. He was delighted to join his
"loyal comrade" not only in strolling through the Taliesin
gardens, and driving along the back roads in the spring
wagon behind the farm horses Darby and Joan, but in trans-
lating a work on free love by the Swiss feminist Ellen Key,
and in making plans to buy the weekly *Spring Green Republican* and convert it into an organ of enlightenment
with Mamah as editor.

Wright was also pleased that his second son, John Lloyd,
joined his office at this time to learn architecture. Always
sympathetic with his father, John found nothing to complain
of except a difficulty in collecting his pay. One trouble was
the Wright's great allies had been women; now they had
reason to look on him with caution as one who would put
aside the conventions provided for the protection of their
marriages and their children. As a result, commissions for
houses, once so plentiful in Wright's office, became noticeably scarce; and while Wright's income dropped, his expenses rose. In fact, the support of two families, together
with the building and furnishing of Taliesin, subjected
Wright's bank account to intolerable strains, and he was
compelled to put extreme demands on what economists call
the credit cycle. Financially speaking, Wright was now in
the predicament of a juggler who has to keep tossing Indian clubs into the air to avoid being hit on the head by
those coming down.

Wright met these embarrassments with a bold face that
never faltered. He was capable, for example, of inviting a
group of colleagues to supper at a restaurant and passing

the hat among them for the bill with perfect composure when he discovered he was short of money. Thus he gathered the thanks due a host while at the same time enjoying the practical advantages of a Dutch-treat party.

His fearlessness in the presence of bailiffs and creditors was exemplified when a sheriff's man appeared at the Orchestra Hall atelier with an order to lock the place and seal its contents in judgment for a $1500 debt. Wright coolly asked for thirty minutes' grace, saying to John, "Show him what we have here," as he hurried out. While the man marveled at the drawings John spread before him, Wright went to a friendly client and obtained a $10,000 advance. He came back just under the deadline, took the bailiff to the bank, got the money for the check, and handed him $1500 in cash. The officer withdrew most respectfully, with many apologies for having disturbed Mr. Wright. But here was the pleasant sum of $8500 left, and Wright said, "Let's go shopping, John." On the ensuing excursion through the Loop, Wright bought a fur-lined overcoat, a dozen chairs for Taliesin, various objects of art, and two grand pianos. Then he returned to his office, apparently happy to be broke again.

In the year 1912, Wright worked out the drawings for a skyscraper in San Francisco, but the sheer-rising structure, with its extended roofline, was not built; more than a third of a century would pass before Wright was represented in San Francisco. He was much pleased when a large commission in Chicago came along, toward the close of 1913, apparently just in time to avert disaster. This was the contract to design the Midway Gardens on the South Side for young Edward Waller, whose father had once offered to finance Wright on a tour of European study. The son now proposed to erect on Cottage Grove Avenue opposite Washington Park "the most beautiful and complete concert garden in the world." And he succeeded in doing so, though the Gardens were destined to financial failure. But they were an unforgettable island of civilization in the few years before Prohibition tore them down.

When this conception was laid before Wright, he instantly understood what Waller had in mind. As his colored pencils flew over the paper, he showed the promoter where patrons would enjoy themselves in beautifully proportioned rooms, or outdoors along lantern-lighted walks and flowering terraces. A stage took form before Waller's eyes—that was where Max Bendix of the Chicago National Symphony would lead a concert orchestra, and the ballet dancers would perform, and the highest class of vaudevillians sing and caper. And over here, in a roomy pavilion, would be the "opera chairs" for those who wanted only to see the show and hear the music, and not be urged to order food and drink. But on the other side, a private clubhouse would be placed, for the limited but highly desirable class of customers to whom the expense of an evening's entertainment was no object. The Federal graduated income tax had just been adopted, and neither architect nor promoter dreamed of a day when an expense-account economy would raise its problems both for the prudent patron and the civilized host. As it was, Waller announced a $10 season ticket as an excellent investment for "any regular patrons of Midway Gardens—above all, for the fortunate owners of automobiles." His announcement added, "If you want to reduce this to simple arithmetic, multiply the regular admission fee of 25 cents by the number of times the hospitable automobile owner is likely to drop in at Midway Gardens, bringing several friends."

No one got rich from Midway Gardens, but the buildings

were begun in an atmosphere of great hope and high purpose. Although the architecture of the Garden's walls and balconies was based on geometric forms, like all Wright's designs up to that time, and was in that sense a work of abstract art, the architect decided to adorn the composition with sculpture based on the human figure. He found perhaps the one man who could do this for him in Alfonso Iannelli, a sculptor who had gained a fine reputation by his contributions to the San Diego Exposition. Working in a shack that Wright and his colleagues called "the black and silver studio" because of the effect of shiny nailheads against its tar paper, Iannelli produced the famous sprites of the Midway Gardens, figures that somehow combined plane surfaces into gracefully posed young women with hauntingly enigmatic smiles.

This brilliant solution of an aesthetic problem by a colleague was typical of the way things went at the Midway Gardens. Everything turned out well: John Lloyd Wright distinguished himself on an abstract mural in the bar; Waller brought in one of the city's leading caterers, John S. Vogelsang, to take charge of the food and service; and even the union goons who blackmailed the project were somehow satisfied. It was a period of serene and encouraging achievement; but it presaged an unimaginable storm, both in the world at large, on which the war in Europe was about to burst, and in Wright's own life.

The Fourth of July 1914 found Wright working hard at the Gardens, while most Chicagoans were relaxing in various ways. Some took in the matinee performance of Barney Bernard and Alexander Carr in *Potash and Perlmutter*, or viewed the sensational screen drama, *Traffic in Souls*, with its bold exposure of commercialized vice. Others, like Edwin Cheney in Oak Park, passed a quiet day in preparation for taking the children to see the fireworks in the evening. At the end of the month, Cheney planned to send the girl, twelve-year-old Martha, and her ten-year-old brother John to their mother at Taliesin, and he wanted to enjoy their company while he could.

The children brought good reports from Spring Green, where there were horses to ride, streams to fish, and many fascinating things to be seen in the drafting room or around the building projects that were constantly going on. By all accounts, Cheney reflected, Wright must have made things comfortable up there, as he had a butler and cook, in addition to farm help. And it was good for the children to be with their mother.

The Taliesin servants were Julian Carleton, a Barbadian Negro, and his wife Gertrude. Wright had engaged them on the recommendation of his catering associate, John Vogelsang, who certainly should know what he was talking about when it came to butlers and cooks. Carleton seemed unusually bright and well educated. His wife was a courteous and willing worker, and together they were an important part of the generally satisfactory setting in which Frank Lloyd Wright was now playing his role. In fact, Mamah and Wright agreed that the couple, in their third month of service, were "almost too good to be true."

All in all, though money was scarce, these were good days, with work on the Midway Gardens going so well; of course, when Wright had time to read a newspaper, he was disturbed by the developments in Europe, where terrible consequences were following the assassination of the Austrian archduke. Many Chicagoans, Wright noticed, were hurrying home, among them Mrs. Samuel Insull and her son. Arthur Meeker, a leading Chicagoan, stated that he would fit out a yacht to bring Americans home if the State Depart-

ment bungled the job, and on the first of August, when
Germany declared war against Russia, the papers published
long lists of Chicagoans still stranded abroad, while assuring
their anxious kin that there was no cause for alarm. Next
day, a German army mobilized on the borders of Belgium,
and John and Martha Cheney left Chicago for Spring
Green.

Nothing could appear more normal than what the children found when they got back to Taliesin. Mamah Borthwick, as always, was delighted to see them; their friends
among the draftsmen and farm people were still there; and
the Carletons functioned in their usual quiet and efficient
manner. But in the kitchen, during the next two weeks,
Gertrude sent frequent apprehensive glances toward her
husband. No one had made any remark, but Gertrude
knew he had been acting in a strange way, and more than
once she heard him mutter that certain people were picking
on him. Sometimes at night Gertrude would start up suddenly, her sleep interruptetd by the sound of someone shift-
ing in a chair, to find Julian sitting at the window, staring
into the darkness with wakeful eyes. Perhaps this odd
behavior was due to the war talk, or the heat that filled the
valley in the afternoon, beneath the fat clouds in the August
sky. At any rate, Gertrude was pleased when Julian ordered her to tell "the Wrights" that life at Taliesin was too
lonely for city servants, and that after lunch on the fifteenth,
he and his wife were going back to town.

On this day, with Wright in Chicago, six employees
gathered for lunch in the staff dining room at Taliesin. They
were William Weston, skilled carpenter and trusted foreman of the farm; his son Ernest, a boy of thirteen who did
chores and studied architectural drawing; Emil Brodelle

and Herbert Fritz, draftsmen; and two handy men, Thomas
Brunker and David Lindblom.

Carleton placed soup before the employees, then served
Mamah Borthwick and the children on a table overlooking
the pond, and returned to his kitchen. Herbert Fritz finished
his soup and became aware of a slight delay. Glancing
around the room, he noticed a film of grayish liquid, with
clusters of bubbles on its surface, flowing from under the
kitchen door. He assumed that Carleton had accidentally
upset some liquid soap—but the material was gasoline, which
the butler was carefully pouring from buckets in the
kitchen. Carleton had been at work with the swift efficiency
of a Commando raider, locking the door from the dining
room to the courtyard, and arming himself with a hatchet.
He now opened the kitchen door and tossed a lighted match
into the dining room. As the gasoline exploded, the five men
and the boy rushed against the locked door. While they
were trying to break it down, Carleton ran to the terrace,
where he killed Mamah Borthwick and John Cheney before
they could get up from their chairs. Martha was running
when Carleton caught up with her in the courtyard. He left
her dead on the flagstones. Meanwhile the powerful William
Weston had broken down the dining room door, and he
came staggering into the courtyard, helping his son Ernest
along. Carleton sprang at them, knocked Weston down
with a glancing blow, and killed the boy and David Lindblom, whose clothes were on fire.

With their clothes also in flames, Brodelle, Brunker, and
Fritz had jumped through the dining room window. Now
Fritz looked up to see Carleton come around the corner of
the house and kill Brodelle. Though shaken and dazed,
Fritz had the presence of mind to roll downhill and put
out the fire in his clothes. Before running out of sight, Carle-

ton knocked Brunker unconscious. He lay there with his clothes blazing: three days later he died of the burns. That night Fritz sent his mother a telegram that was a model of brevity—"Our house burned. I am all right." But at the moment, he pluckily ran back up the hill toward the burning building, unable to believe the facts of the waking nightmare—in about two minutes, Carleton had killed or fatally injured seven people.

A column of smoke rose into the sky, and the bell in the Lloyd-Jones family chapel, at the foot of Taliesin's hill, began to sound the alarm. Neighboring farmers, many of them related to Wright, hurried to fight the fire; some ran home for weapons and started through the fields in search of Carleton after they heard what he had done and saw his work. The Rev. Dr. Jenkin Lloyd-Jones, the Chicago uncle, who happened to be in Spring Green, rode out at the head of a posse, while sheriff J. T. Williams summoned deputies to see that Gertrude was safely transferred to the Dodgeville jail, from which she was later released. The murderer could not be found.

In Chicago, Wright had finished lunch with his son John in the uncompleted bar of the Midway Gardens. They were discussing their work, as usual, when a telephone call came in. "Mr. Wright?" he heard a voice say. "This is Frank Roth in Madison. Be prepared for a shock. Your wife— that is, Mrs. Cheney—" and after that it became incredible. Wright replaced the receiver and said to John, "I must go to Spring Green at once."

While Wright's train rolled from flat to hilly country on the way to Madison, the volunteer firemen were controlling the flames at Spring Green. But only a third of the house remained, and what the fire had not destroyed was ruined by smoke. Meanwhile, the search for Carleton continued, and as the sheriff picked his way through the ruins, he heard a noise in the boiler of the central heating system. He opened the door and dragged Carleton out. The man's thin lips were burned, but not by the fire; he whispered one word—"Acid." After the massacre, he had swallowed a muriatic cleaning fluid from the household stores. This was the last word Carleton spoke; they took him to the Dodgeville jail, where he died from the effects of the poison.

When Wright got to Spring Green later that day, deputies and armed countrymen brought him to the house he had designed for his brother-in-law, Andrew T. Porter, where the hacked and burned bodies lay. Sympathy for Wright was tempered by a strong though irrational feeling that the tragedy was somehow his fault. In the shock of horror, Wright said that a funeral service for Mamah Borthwick "could only be a mockery" and he ordered a deep grave dug in the family chapel grounds. At this point Edwin Cheney appeared. Leaving the Porter house, he encountered Wright, who tried to express his grief and remorse.

"It's all right, Frank," said Cheney.

"Thank you, Ed."

"Good-by, Frank," said Cheney, and continued on his way.

Wright told the Taliesin carpenters to make a plain box from newly cut white pine. When this was ready next day, he filled it with flowers from Mamah Borthwick's garden. Helped by his son, he lifted the body and, as he recorded the event, "let it down to rest among the flowers that had grown and bloomed for her." The faithful little sorrel horses, Darby and Joan, were waiting at the spring wagon, and to this conveyance the workmen carried the coffin. Walking beside the wheels, and followed by John and two young Lloyd-Jones cousins, Wright went slowly down the hill to the churchyard. The August sun was setting as they lowered the pine box. Wright asked them to leave him. He filled the grave, stood there until darkness fell, then walked back to Taliesin.

A studio workshop had escaped destruction, and Wright tried to sleep there on a cot. He remembered long afterward how despair paralyzed him and he could not close his eyes. He got up and walked around the ruins, where a sentry was posted because of rumors that Carleton had confederates nearby. But Wright felt no fear—only anguish and desolation. The gaping black hole left by the fire on the hillside, he later recorded, was a charred and ugly scar upon his life.

Chapter Five

AND THEN TOKYO

FRANK LLOYD WRIGHT stood close to final defeat at the end of August in 1914. The massacre by the mad West Indian was equal in blood and violence to any classic catastrophe ever visited on those who angered the gods with too much pride; and after so shocking and sensational a tragedy, some of Wright's contemporaries took it for granted that he would never be heard from again. But Wright's amazing qualities of endurance were not even yet fully tested. Half his life lay ahead, to be marked by the same sort of intense effort and achievement, struggle and victory, foolishness and grandeur, as had gone before.

Sufficiently dreadful to command newspaper space in competition with the First World War, which had just broken out, the Taliesin tragedy attracted the attention of preachers, some of whom had referred to Wright before in discourse from the pulpit. To the ministers' way of thinking, the great flaw in the arrangements at Taliesin was that although Mamah Borthwick was divorced from her husband, she was not married to Frank Lloyd Wright. This caused some pastors to regard the destruction at Taliesin as a substantial installment on sin's payroll, though they could not explain why six unoffending persons were included and not Wright himself.

On his part, Wright made the by now characteristic gesture of issuing a manifesto, in the form of a public letter to the Spring Green neighbors who had helped put out the Taliesin fire. "To you who have rallied so bravely and well to our assistance," Wright's letter began, "to you who have been invariably kind to us all—I would say something to defend a brave and lovely woman from the pestilential touch of stories made by the press for the man in the street, even now with the loyal fellows lying dead beside her, any one of whom would have given his life to defend her." Mamah Borthwick, Wright went on to say, was a noble and soulful woman whose ideals were so high that she had been forced to "crucify all that society holds sacred and essential—in name" to maintain them. Then he got down to what had goaded him—the newspaper statement that Mamah Borthwick had left her children. On the contrary, Wright said, Mamah was much interested in her children and had them with her a great deal of the time. No one could understand how it escaped Wright's notice that this point, at least, had been established by the children's terrible fate. But he plunged on: "She felt that she did more for her children by holding high above them the womanhood of their mother than by sacrificing it to them." Without giving his readers time to analyze that statement, Wright now turned again to the matter of the publicity surrounding his life. "The circumstances before and after we came here to live among you have been falsified and vulgarized," he went on, "and it is no use now to try to set them straight." That, of course, was just what Wright was trying to do; but he probably failed to creep into the public's heart when he turned, near the end, to his hortatory manner: "You wives with your certificates for loving—pray that you may love as much and be loved as well as was Mamah Borthwick! You mothers and fathers with daughters—be satisfied if what life you have invested in them works out upon as high a plane as it has done in the life of this lovely woman." Then, after a passage of revolting sentimentality about the location of Mamah Borthwick's grave, Wright once again redeemed himself, as he invariably did somewhere in these long statements, by a

moment of genuine dignity. He spoke of Taliesin, the
blackened ruin. Taliesin would rise again. "Little by little,"
he said, "I shall replace it as nearly as may be done. I shall
set it all up again for the spirit of the mortal that lived in it
and loved it—will live in it still. My home will still be
there."

For the rebuilding, Frank Lloyd Wright ordered wood cut
and stone quarried; several months went by in this work and
the completion of Midway Gardens. There was no need for
draftsmen at Taliesin now, and Herbert Fritz, much shaken
by his experience, but still clinging to the violin on which
he had often played for Wright, appeared at the Minneapolis
office of George Grant Elmslie, Wright's old ally of Adler
and Sullivan days. Elmslie was in partnership now with
William Gray Purcell, and between them they were to build
many a church, business structure, and dwelling house
throughout the Middle West in their distinctive manner.
Now they were happy to employ the gifted and competent Fritz, who came to Purcell and Elmslie only two days
after the tragedy at Taliesin. His new employers and his
office mates respected his evident desire to be asked no questions about the terrible experience. He later enjoyed a long
and productive career as an architect on his own account.
Wright may have been pleased that one of his surviving
Taliesin employees had found a good berth, but probably
devoted little thought to it, for his anguish of soul was increased by the strange stories that followed the Taliesin mur-
ders and found their way into print. One such tale had it
that a telegram signed with Mamah Borthwick's initials had
reached Wright a few hours before Carleton ran amok.
"Come at once," this message was supposed to have said,
"we are in great danger." An investigation showed that there
was no record of this telegram having been dispatched

from either Spring Garden or Madison, the reason being, of course, that there was no such telegram. The truth is that the state editor of a metropolitan newspaper, who had charge of the country correspondents, would print wild rumor, and even fiction, to keep a good out-of-town story alive. Even in the present day a rural murder story will generally be decked out with mysterious strangers, women in black, and astonishing statements attributed to local officials. One of the latter, especially unsavory in its reference to Wright, which received prominent space in some of the papers, announced that law enforcement officers around Spring Green were looking into the possibility that the Taliesin massacre was the result of a plot on the part of Wright's "enemies." But who these enemies could be or why they would commit such dreadful deeds was never specified.

As he lived through these days, Wright's face was tired and drawn and he had little to say. Hundreds of letters came to him; he tied them in a big package and burned the lot. But in order not to destroy the letters of friends, he had his correspondence screened by various assistants, including David Robinson, office manager at the Chicago working quarters in Orchestra Hall. Hoping to cheer Wright up, Robinson would sometimes show him an especially sympathetic or well-phrased letter from a stranger. One of these was from a woman signing herself Miriam Noel, who said she too was an artist, and so could truly understand Wright's suffering. These words gave momentary comfort, and Wright acknowledged the note. Soon afterward, Robinson said, "Say, boss—here's another letter from that Noel woman. Shall I throw it away?" Wright said, "No, I'd like to see it."

The second letter from Miriam Noel brought the suggestion that Wright grant her an interview, for she was not only an artist, but had known great sorrow, and might be able to give him helpful advice. He replied by setting an appointment, and a few days later Miriam Noel sat opposite Wright's desk as the afternoon sun came through his office windows. He saw a woman who was obviously no ordinary person, and who retained much of what had evidently been great youthful beauty. Richly dressed, with a sealskin cape, she had a pale complexion contrasting with her heavy dark red hair. A monocle hung by a silk cord from her neck, and the general effect was that of a cross between Elinor Glyn and Theda Bara in *A Fool There Was*. Mrs. Noel settled herself and took out a dainty cigarette case, then handed Wright a limp black book: *Science and Health, With a Key to the Scriptures,* by Mary Baker Eddy. A slight but continuous trembling of her fine hands indicated some nervous disorder, but Mrs. Noel's voice was controlled and pleasant.

"How do you like me?" Miriam Noel asked.

"I've never seen anyone remotely resembling you," said Wright.

Mrs. Noel then informed him that she was a sculptress, living in Paris and forced to return to America by the war. She was divorced, had two married daughters, a grown son, and nowhere to go and no desires. Her health had been broken, she said, by an ill-fated love affair somewhat like Wright's with Mrs. Cheney, and after reading of the Taliesin tragedy, she had thought about it until finally the conviction came that it was in her power to offer help. Wright did not know it, but for all her exotic exterior, this lady had been born in the Fox River Valley, thirty-five miles from where they sat.

This would have made no difference, however, for the visitor's sympathy, rather than her sophistication, was what attracted Wright. He later said that as he looked at Miriam Noel he believed himself to be in the presence of an enlightened comradeship, a rescuing understanding, and "something to see by." This was a mistake of majestic proportions. Nevertheless, within a few months of the tragedy at Spring Green, Mrs. Noel and Wright set up a household, and he announced to the world that she was to be the chatelaine of Taliesin II. Needless to say, Wright expended time and emotion in justifying this move, with remarks about voluntary and open intimacies between independent men and women having high ideals and self-respect.

Wright had good reason to believe that his personal life was being judged along with his professional achievements when the *Western Architect*, an influential magazine, proposed public recognition of great contemporary designers. John Wellborn Root, Dankmar Adler, Wright's beloved master Louis Sullivan, and Solon S. Beman of the Prairie Avenue palaces were there, but Frank Lloyd Wright was not even a doorkeeper in this architectural hall of fame. Wright also felt the disapproval of Albert Nelson Marquis, the proprietor of *Who's Who in America*. Though he conferred the honors of print on thousands of nonentities, Marquis omitted Wright from his reference work for many years, and was pleased with himself for doing so. Thus Frank Lloyd Wright was more than ever convinced, as his forty-seventh birthday came in sight, that he was engaged in a struggle of truth against the world.

Neglect by such weathervanes of respectability as A. N. Marquis may or may not have done Wright harm; but there could be no question that he seemed to attract the malevolence of emotional and unbalanced persons as a lightning rod draws charges of electricity, and this did have a most unfortunate effect on his ability to work and produce. For

example, there was Nellie Breen, a former housekeeper at
the Cedar Street apartment, who saw Mrs. Noel there, heard
that this lady also was established at Taliesin in Wisconsin,
and wrote to the District Attorney to demand that Wright
be prosecuted under the Mann Act, a piece of legislation that
established penalties for transporting women across state
lines for immoral purposes. This Act, which stands as a
monument to Wright's old Oak Park neighbor, Representative James Robert Mann, was aimed at certain commercialized activities that were regarded as a national menace at
the time. But the law could also be invoked in the harassment of private citizens.

As it turned out, the Breen letters deprived Wright of his
peace of mind rather than his liberty. Accompanied by the
famous attorney Clarence Darrow, Wright visited U. S.
District Attorney Michael L. Igoe and Federal Bureau of
Investigation district chief Hinton G. Clabaugh, and explained his relationship to Miriam Noel. Darrow then announced that the officials were inclined to accept the arguments that Wright should not be prosecuted. If a greater
humiliation was ever inflicted on an American artist, there
is no record of it. But Wright could not leave it alone.
Within two days he was back in his usual form with a public
statement, in which he said that in the last six years he had
been allowed no private life. "What was most precious to
me has been stolen, stripped, or whipped from me—flung
under foot to satisfy the man in the street. Law has been
made the tool of spite and hatred, which meddles in matters
that can only be shown right or wrong by the hearts and
consciences of those to whom they are sacred." Here again
the self-serving note was not apparent to Wright, and most
readers felt he was on more understandable ground when he
made angry reference to "a blackmailing, venal, scandal-

mongering domestic." If that was severe, we can at least be certain at this distance in time that if Nellie Breen had good qualities that Wright overlooked, the prime virtue of minding one's own business was not among them.

With this comment on an unpleasant affair, Wright would have been well advised to retire from public view for an indefinite period. Unfortunately, Miriam Noel now took occasion to show that she had become infected with Wright's mania for public utterance, along with a touch of his literary style, by issuing a manifesto of her own. Newspaper editors throughout the land were delighted to print a statement in which Mrs. Noel declared, "Because I love Frank Lloyd Wright and admire him more than all men, and honor the life he has lived, I am here at Taliesin, the beautiful country home. I understand and deeply sympathize with the struggles and terrible trials his life and his great work have passed through. Now, because of my deep love for him, he is again persecuted." Mrs. Noel then introduced an ominous note by stating that her real faith in Wright was in good repair, but "in attempting to have him understand my ideals I have at times belittled him, have been unfair and impatient in my criticism of him, as he has been unfair and unkind in his criticism of me." This sounded quite different from enlightened comradeship and rescuing understanding. Nevertheless, Mrs. Noel was able to conclude by saying, "Frank Wright and I care nothing for what the world may think. We are as capable of making laws for ourselves as were the dead men who made the laws by which they hoped to rule the generations after them. There is perfect harmony between me and Mr. Wright."

There was some question as to the perfection of the harmony between Wright and Mrs. Noel even this early in a relationship that was to include marriage and divorce.

The truth was in a letter Wright sent to his son John in a moment of despondency during the period referred to by Mrs. Noel. "A relation that was a disinterested one for me seems to have been a calculated one for her," Wright wrote. "She has made my life a living hell off and on during the months I have known her . . . I must take the consequences of not caring much what became of me at a time when I was all ready to die for the sake of dying. She caught me in that mood and has taken advantage of it ever since."

In spite of this unenthusiastic private estimate of Mrs. Noel's character and intentions, Wright remained loyal to the odd and neurasthenic woman who had invited herself into his life. He was grateful for the help she offered, no matter from what motives. Wright needed emotional support, for what he took to be misunderstanding sprang up on every hand. In the spring of 1917, for example, an organization called the Gamut Club held a dinner at which Wright was called on to speak, and it was noticed that when he touched on the Midway Gardens, and those connected with it, he made no mention of the sculptor, Alfonso Iannelli. Shortly afterward a magazine called *The Studio* devoted an illustrated article to the Midway Gardens. When Iannelli read the piece, he was surprised to see that the magazine gave him credit only for executing the sculpture, and listed Wright as the designer. Wright sought to head off Iannelli's protest by writing him a letter in which he devoted the opening paragraph to thanking Iannelli for introductions in California. Then he continued that he had seen an article in *The Studio* mentioning Iannelli as "executing" the Midway sculpture, and he hoped there would be no feeling about the matter on Iannelli's part. Wright assured the sculptor that he never had picked other people's brains or taken their

credit, and never intended to, and there he would like to
see the matter rest.

If this letter was supposed to make the sculptor happy, it
was a signal failure. Iannelli was, to begin with, perhaps the
most gifted artist ever to collaborate with Wright, and a man
of great originality, talent, and stature in his own field.[1]
After reading Wright's letter, he sat down in Los Angeles
to write a reply in the mood of an outraged man determined
to have his say as forcefully as courtesy would permit. He
began

> "First—my profound respect for you as a great
> Architect, and one to whom I owe much of my
> point of view, which to me is invaluable and be-
> yond words of expression, and which I hope I
> shall not lose sight of in my analysis of this situa-
> tion.
>
> "The article in the 'Studio' came much as a
> shock to me; I mean the statement that the work
> was 'designed' by *you* and executed by me, and
> not the statement that John designed, etc., be-
> cause I do not know that situation excepting as
> John in one of his letters casually mentions the
> fact that he executed the mural from your sketch,
> and also because I have much regard for John's
> ability. There is, however, something of a com-
> parative contrast which helps to intensify the
> situation. But the part I hate most is the fact that
> I should be placed in a position where I am to
> ascertain or to dictate to you the way in which
> credit due me should be expressed. . . .

[1] He has performed in more than one field. Alfonso Iannelli is today a
painter, industrial designer, and architect as well as sculptor. Some of
his finest statuary is in churches by Barry Byrne, once a junior associate
at Wright's Oak Park studio.

"In regard to the figures in the article, circle, triangle, etc.,—you suggested the idea of the geometric forms to be used in these groups. I designed these groups in pencil and showed them to you and you approved of them, and they were carried through hardly without a change. In these groups there has entered an idea never before accomplished to my knowledge, and that is, the usage of the architectural form through the human figure, which goes far in making them the result they are—such as they are—and which to me offers the only solution to the problem of the adaptability of sculpture to architecture, where one is the outgrowth of the other. As you know, I did this. . . .

"My suggestion would be, that you consider the truth in this matter and that I be given the credit due me as such only. The way seems clear: 'Frank Lloyd Wright, Architect—A. Iannelli, Sculptor,' is all right, just as you had it in the folder which announced your exhibition in the Art Museum of May, 1914, or, as you gave credit to Mr. Bock in your German Book—and not the explicit untruth in the Studio article, which error should be righted to accord with the facts. Of course the work must necessarily be criticized by you in the harmony of your building and have the necessary feeling, but that does not make you the designer of the sculpture.

"The one thing which is hard for me to understand, is that you above all others, should allow such a mistake or such a misunderstanding of the actual conditions; and the part which hurts me the most is the terrible blow to my conception of you as a man, if this is true. . . .

"I do not accuse you of picking my brains to your advantage, as that would be ridiculous, for it would not be very long before such a thing would prove itself in the work. The disposition of the human animal is dependent upon the degree of evolvement of each individual, and each one from his state of being picks the way which seems to him best.

"I hope I have made myself clear in this unfortunate incident.

"Yours with great respect,
"Alfonso Iannelli."

Wright answered promptly, and at some length, suggesting that their relationship might be analogous to that of Beethoven and Paderewski—creator and interpreter. However, Wright said he would agree to have the official credit stand as Wright, Architect, and Iannelli, Sculptor; indeed, it would have been so printed in the magazine article had Wright not been preoccupied with other matters when he looked at the captions before they appeared in print. On the reception of this, Iannelli may have been pleased to be compared with Paderewski, but as Wright had said, the question of who created and who interpreted was at the heart of the dispute about the Midway Gardens sculpture. There was a question of fact involved; and hoping to settle the whole matter, Iannelli replied at length:

"While I find many interesting thoughts in your recent kind letter, yet, so far as our affair is concerned, the following is my summing up of the whole situation.

"The square, octagon, triangle and circle suggestions in pencil, were given by you; the further suggestion of masculine and feminine was NOT given by you; neither was the suggestion that each figure partake of the form characterized. You did not suggest to me the idea of conventionalizing the flesh in this particular, nor in any other instance. . . .

"According to my knowledge of my own life, the idea of using geometric forms came to me much before my advent in Chicago; also the using of one form in each creation throughout, so that one nature of movement would be the result.

"One instance regarding the conventionalizing of the figure, is the first time you visited the little studio where these groups were carried out, and the first exterior pier sculpture was first in progress—John mentioned the fact to you that I had something which he wanted you to consider to see if you approved of it; and I tried to explain to you how I wanted to do this conventionalizing of the figure, which had not had time to develop in the large figure up to that time, and you said that the best way to see and express your opinion would be after I had worked it out.

"Another instance following this one, which John may remember, was one afternoon when an argument was carried on between John and me, lasting quite a while—his side being that my way of conventionalizing was not as good as a more realistic expression.

"Summing up these and similar occasions, it seems to me I not only had the 'idea' from the start, *but that I had to fight to put it through!* . . .

"Your comparison of Beethoven and the pianist is not a correct comparison at all under the circumstances, because the music in this case happens to have been written and composed by me, and only suggested in part by you, and not at all to the extent which you state in your letter. . . .

"Your suggestion in your note of this matter not being of interest to any but ourselves, to me is wrong. If you are in earnest in your statements I should think this is a fine chance to prove once and for all, the real connection between artists and architects in this country, and the relative credits due them, if such a thing can be determined.

"The idea of this sculpture, considered as a detail and outgrowth of the architectural scheme and connected with the building, is yours—but the idea of the sculpture in itself, is mine.

"My suggestion to you would be, that when you need any more sculpture, you want to pick out the man who is capable of doing it; let him furnish you with designs, and when the designs have been accepted, then leave the sculptor absolutely alone until he is through and the work is ready for you to see; the results then, I believe, would be more successful in every way. Of course a sculptor must be enlightened as to the general movement of composition required by you.

"I hope I do not convey the impression to you through these frank statements that I do not appreciate the tremendous help you have been to me in general, my gratitude for which I shall hope to prove.

"Respectfully and sincerely yours,
"Alfonso Iannelli."

Wright did not answer this letter, and Iannelli let the correspondence drop. Certainly he had stated his position plainly, and delivered some penetrating observations about sculpture in collaboration with architecture. On his part, Wright made little or no use of sculpture as such after this in his major works. The houses and buildings might be said to have a sculptural quality in themselves; but as we have seen, their designer could not work happily with any creative person who did not acknowledge his prior inspiration and complete control. Needless to say, Wright never again offered to collaborate with Alfonso Iannelli.

At this period, some of those who were close to Wright wondered why he did not get rid of Miriam Noel, whose frequently expressed sympathy did not entirely make up for the fact that she also just as frequently got on his nerves. Wright's many uncharitable critics formed the theory that he had managed to put his private life into such a public framework that there was no way to eliminate Mrs. Noel without letting the world know he was backing down from his principles; meanwhile, the divorce from Catherine Wright seemed as remote as ever. In these circumstances Wright was pleased when a splendid opportunity to leave the country came his way, in the commission to design and build the great new hotel in Tokyo that was to be named in honor of the divine and sublime personage who ruled Japan.

Wright had first heard of this on a trip to New York in the previous year, when a Japanese delegation had waited on him in Suite 223 of the Plaza. They had been brought together by the New York art dealer, Mr. Yanaka, with whom Wright had done business. Some of these emissaries thought "Wrieto-San" was an architect in the manner of Charles A. Platt, or McKim, Mead, and White, who had put their lordly mark on New York City in many a handsome Italianate structure. Accordingly, Wright did not consider the Imperial commission assured until the fall of 1915, when the hotel manager, Aisaku Hayashi, came to Taliesin and looked at the sketches Wright had prepared. The Oriental feeling in Wright's drawings, and in Taliesin itself, was highly satisfactory to Hayashi, and early the following year, Frank Lloyd Wright and Miriam Noel set out for Tokyo.

Here they were provided with an apartment, where a staff of servants was on call. Sometimes these employees heard the sound of violent disagreement between the lady of the house and Wrieto-San. He was involved night and day with his plans, and though he had the loyal help of his son John, it was very difficult to convey Wright's ideas to Japanese engineers and workmen across the language bar. Therefore it was sometimes a trial for Wright to endure the insistent conversation of Miriam Noel, and to go out into general social life, in addition to his exhausting work.

His energy never flagged, but he found it fatiguing to attend a dinner party and be told afterward by Miriam that his efforts to talk in an interesting way had been ridiculous, if not repulsive, and that she had barely managed to save him from disgrace by diverting attention from his more outrageous errors. The fact was nearly the exact reverse. It was noted in the Russian, English, and American official and business colonies, where Wright and Mrs. Noel were well known, that Miriam seldom took her eyes from his face when they were out together; and her constant interruptions were a nuisance to those who wanted to hear Wright talk. It was all most unfortunate, for the unconventional nature of their union need have caused no embarrassment in Toyko —the Americans and Europeans disregarded it; the Japanese didn't care. In spite of this favorable social and ethical climate, it seemed to Wright that the brilliant, self-sacrificing Miriam was steadily losing her hold on reality.

Meanwhile the cavernous "Impeho" was taking shape, a broad-winged, lion-colored structure of lava and brick. Appropriately Wright had put on paper a touch of his Oriental sympathies, and now they took form, with the entrance at the end of the garden, for example, recalling the marble gateway over the main street in Weihsien, Shantung. But more than decoration was involved; down in the sea beneath Japan there was a dragon who lifted his back from time to time and caused death-dealing earthquakes on the land. Circumventing this beast was Wright's particular object, and to this end he devised a way to absorb shocks by sinking the central supports into soft earth, to hold up the floor slabs "as a waiter balances a tray on his fingers."

Wright gave lavish praise to his own engineering in his reports on the Imperial Hotel, and undoubtedly it was sound and well conceived. He had seen the railroad stations and office buildings of Chicago supported on piers penetrating the sludgy soil that lay beneath the Loop; there was no question in his mind that the Imperial required similar foundations. From that time to this, engineers have been somewhat impatient when told of the waiter carrying his tray, and the rest of the circumstances surrounding the underpinning of the Imperial Hotel. As recently as January, 1961, a correspondent wrote to the magazine *Architectural Record*, "What the man did was drive piles. It's as simple as that." At any rate, no matter how the Imperial was seated on its supports, there was no question that here was a remarkable building, a masterpiece from a great master of romance.

The source of the magic was not always clear to those who

clung to the idea that a building must have an historical or
at least a regional style. In spite of the Oriental spirit of the
main entrance, many of these people would murmur, "I
see—Mexican," or, "Aztec," at their first sight of the
Imperial. This gave rise to a persistent story that Wright
had designed the hotel some years before for clients in
Mexico City, and after that deal fell through, had sold the
same plans to his unsuspecting Japanese clients. But this
was not true: in every surface and angle, the Imperial was
planned for its royal site in Tokyo. A cultivated American
remarked of it, "Fascinating, ingenious and unique are the
words that leap to the mind; the same are probably equally
applicable to a rabbit warren." It was true that one could
lose the sense of direction after leaving the balconied main
lobby of the Imperial, and entering the huge banqueting
hall for the first time was an emotional experience somewhat
like that experienced by Mr. Mole and Mr. Water Rat when
they were ushered into Mr. Badger's subterranean home in
The Wind in the Willows. This was intentional, the work
of a magician consciously weaving a spell; so was the
treatment of the windows, placed high on the walls of the
sleeping chambers, so that a businessman from Tennessee
remarked, "I never in my life paid so much money for a
room I couldn't see out of."

Though all this was new and strange, no one doubted
Wright's engineering or architectural competence during
the construction of the hotel. It was the business side of the
project that caused alarm to spread among the sponsors.
This was apparent as it became known that the emperor's
interest in the new hotel was more than that of nomen-
clature. It also extended to the hotel's profits as a going
concern, for a cut of the money was to be handed to the
chamberlain of the imperial household after each day's take

had been tallied. With this in mind, some members of the building syndicate began to worry for fear the Wrightian structure might lack the element of commercial success. If the imperial household suffered a financial pinch, face would be lost. It also appeared that the original estimates had been too low, and more money must be raised.

At this crisis a meeting was called, attended by Wright and under the chairmanship of Baron Okura, who had impressed the architect by the fact that he had jet black hair and was still fathering children at the age of eighty. The baron called for order, looked round the table at the nine or ten syndicate members present and asked them to state their views. Wright later recorded the scene in detail, noting how the magnates expressed their high respect for him and their equally great doubt that his plans could be completed, especially in view of the additional money required. Soon they were all talking at once, and the interpreter stopped trying to keep up with them.

Hesitating clients were an old story to Wright, but he could hardly do himself justice with the few words of Japanese at his command. The hotel was now saved by Baron Okura, who had approved the plans and considered his honor involved. His lower lip projecting and quivering —a sure sign that he was in a rage—the baron jumped to his feet and began to pound the table with both fists. He also began hissing, in a more menacing and sibilant manner than Wright had ever heard—and at his peroration, the others fell backward as though a cyclone had struck. Afterward the interpreter told Wright that Okura had said money would be found to complete the building, that he would guarantee the imperial household against loss, and that they could all go to hell, with his compliments. Thinking over the events of the day, Wright asked himself if Pericles might not have

played some such role as the baron's in connection with the
Athenian economy and the architectural firm of Ictinus and
Callicrates, when the Parthenon was built.

The backers were angry with Wright for causing them
to lose face before Okura, and he worked under difficulties
until the hotel was substantially completed in 1922. From
time to time, Wright got relief from the pressure by going
back to the United States, hoping to establish a practice in
California. One of the architectural influences on California
at the time was the construction of the enormous outdoor
set for the Babylonian sequence in D. W. Griffith's absurd
but powerful motion picture epic, *Intolerance*. The great
mass of this screen setting, and its architectonic sculpture,
recalled the art of ancient times in which a building could
be as mighty as a mountain or as angry as a bull. No one
has suggested that Wright was directly influenced by the
Intolerance set (or by the sheer walls of the castle in
Douglas Fairbanks' *Robin Hood*), but the currents of
romantic thought that caused Griffith to call for the Feast
of Belshazzar also acted on Wright. Each of these American
masters was hunting for something beyond the contemporary scene. Wright had already shown his interest in
primitive masses by designing a warehouse for his home
town of Richland Center that resembled a Mayan temple.[2]
And in his most important California assignment, the house
in Los Angeles for the oil heiress Aline Barnsdall, it is easy
to see suggestions of Mayan rather than North American
shapes.

[2] In *A Testament* (1957) Wright said: "As a boy, primitive American
architecture stirred my wonder. Great American abstractions, earth-
architectures all: gigantic masses of masonry planned as mountains; a
vast plateau in itself or a range of mountains." In another part of this
book he added: "As for the Incas, the Mayans, even the Japanese—all
were to me but splendid confirmation."

This job was made interesting for Wright by the circumstance that the rich Miss Barnsdall had never been subjected
to the inconvenience of failing to get her own way, and in
addition, was something of a parlor radical. Wright was able
to handle Miss Barnsdall by exerting all the force of his
talent and his personality, but he nearly came to grief against
her corps of paid and unpaid advisors. Here Wright had an
ally in another man of talent and perhaps of genius. This
was Norman Bel Geddes, a Middle Westerner like Wright,
whose ideas in staging and theater design had attracted
Miss Barnsdall's attention. Geddes had an air of authority
and competence to match Wright's own, but he deferred
to the older man even in the matter of designing a theater
which was to be a companion piece to Miss Barnsdall's
house, and the home of Geddes's productions. As it turned
out, this theater was never built—only the house, which
Geddes thought "looked more like a miniature palace of
some ancient civilization than a contemporary private
home." Geddes may not have been fully aware of the difficulties Wright faced in persuading California contractors
and workmen that his plans for the big concrete structure—
called Hollyhock House after the motif of its stylized
decoration—were feasible. But he shared with Wright the
growing conviction that Richard Ordynski, a graduate of
Max Reinhardt's European theater, had more influence with
Aline Barnsdall than either of the Americans. Miss Barnsdall
had once studied acting under Eleanora Duse, who had
tactfully suggested that her greatest service to the theater
might be as patron rather than performer, and Ordynski's
European background seemed to outweigh what Wright
and Geddes had to offer. But at last Ordynski wore out his
welcome. "As a personal kindness to me," Miss Barnsdall
said to her friends and followers, "never mention Ordynski's

name again." After a four-year relationship of client and architect, Wright finished the Barnsdall house, on Olive Hill at the intersection of Sunset and Hollywood Boulevards, in 1920. By degrees, the theater project had been abandoned; Geddes became resigned to this as he saw that the plans Wright had made would not be satisfactory to him. Years later, Wright would construct a theater in Dallas that was a producer's and director's dream—it allowed for the technical aspect of stagecraft in a way that Wright had brushed aside during the Barnsdall episode, as Geddes saw it. But at least a formal friendship was maintained after the younger man, disappointed on the Barnsdall project, came east to make a start on his brilliant career, with the help of Otto Kahn. For years afterward, Wright would motor from Taliesin to New York when a Geddes production was in work, attend rehearsals, and discuss problems of theatrical procedure and architecture far into the night. Perhaps some of this discussion bore fruit in Dallas. But for all of the surface cordiality, Geddes felt that Wright never took the Barnsdall theater project farther than four façades. After many years Geddes still felt unhappy about it, as is shown in a melancholy passage from his autobiography, *Miracle in the Evening*:

> "The tragedy was that, in spite of Aline's doing everything possible to appease [Wright], their relationship terminated unhappily. She had selected the finest architect she knew of, and had written into his contract an expression of confidence and faith few other clients had ever done. In return, he treated her with a total lack of appreciation; felt in fact that she was the one lacking in appreciation. As for cooperation, she gave him everything he asked for, while he, though em-

ployee, granted no request involving a difference
of opinion. His stubbornness in return for her
generosity had a discouraging effect upon her
regard for all creative people. After five years of
trying to get her theater, she finally gave up all
her hopes and plans. The house was, indeed,
finished, but it recalled for her so many unpleasant moments that she lived in it for only short
periods over a few years and then gave the entire
hilltop property to the city as a park. Frank
Lloyd Wright, by behaving as he did, was responsible in my eyes for thwarting what might
well have been the greatest creative theater organization this century had ever seen, or ever
will see."

At the time Hollyhock House was brought to completion,
Wright would have said with perfect sincerity that he, if
anyone, was being thwarted. "This is worse than Japan,"
he said, as he struggled against what he felt was a downright conspiracy of contractors, plus much voluntary advice
from the sidelines where the members of Miss Barnsdall's
entourage were ranged as critics. It is true that Aline
Barnsdall did not enjoy Hollyhock House for lengthy
periods, but contrary to what Geddes thought, this may
be more plausibly explained as an expression of her restless
temperament than as the result of a grudge against the
architect or the house. She died in Los Angeles, on the 18th
of December, 1946. It is true that Hollyhock House had
not been altogether peaceful; twice in the years between
its completion and its owner's death Miss Barnsdall
had been called to court to pay for injuries inflicted by
the pack of twenty-two savage spaniels she maintained on
the property. Five thousand dollars of her $3,500,000 estate

was left for the care of these creatures; the grounds are now called Barnsdall Park in memory of her father, and the house itself, with an addition that Wright designed in 1956, is an art museum for the use and pleasure of the people of Los Angeles.

No matter how Wright may have suffered in his struggles to build the Barnsdall mansion, his trials were mild in comparison with what lay in store for him in the construction of another famous California house, La Miniatura, in Pasadena. Here for the first time he used an invention of precast hollow concrete blocks fastened together on steel cables and filled with poured concrete. The blocks could be cast with geometric patterns that gave a highly pleasing surface texture. Mrs. George Madison Millard of Chicago was the owner of La Miniatura; Wright had built one of the first Prairie houses for this lady before the death of her husband, a Chicago bookstore executive. Setting up a new life in a new state, Mrs. Millard was an ideal Wright client in her generous trust and enthusiasm. But neither Mrs. Millard nor her architect were gladdened by the sight of a house their contractor was building for himself, while the costs on La Miniatura grew and grew. Here a porch would sprout on the contractor's house, there a second-floor addition, then a grand piano in the parlor. Legal difficulties arose, court proceedings ensued—and still La Miniatura was not finished.

But at last the beautiful house stood complete, by virtue of semi-professional labor—and was nearly washed away by a California cloudburst. La Miniatura's site, cunningly selected like most of those on which Wright houses stood, was in a ravine that turned into a river bed when the big rain fell. One thing was fortunate, as Wright was able to point out to Alice Millard: there was no basement to be

14. Residence of Thomas P. Hardy, Racine, Wisconsin, 1905

15. Midway Gardens, Chicago, Illinois 1914

16. Imperial Hotel, Tokyo, Japan, 1915-22

17. Main Lobby, Imperial Hotel, Tokyo, Japan, 1915-22

18. "Hollyhock House," Residence of Miss Aline Barnsdall, Hollywood, California, 1920

19. Residence of Mrs. George Madison Millard, Pasadena, California, 1923

20. Studio, Taliesin East, Spring Green, Wisconsin, 1925-59

21. Taliesin East, Spring Green, Wisconsin, 1925-59

22. Taliesin West, Scottsdale, Arizona, 1938-59

23. Living Room, Taliesin West, Scottsdale, Arizona, 1938-59

24. Residence of Richard Lloyd-Jones, Tulsa, Oklahoma, 1929

25. Residence of Richard Lloyd-Jones, Tulsa, Oklahoma, 1929

26. "Falling Water," Residence of
    Edgar J. Kaufmann,
    Bear Run, Pennsylvania, 1936

27. *Above, right:*
    Living Room, "Falling Water,"
    Residence of
    Edgar J. Kaufmann,
    Bear Run, Pennsylvania, 1936

28. "Falling Water," Residence of Edgar J. Kaufman,

ar Run, Pennsylvania, 1936

29. Interior, V. C. Morris Store, San Francisco, California, 1949

30. V. C. Morris Store, San Francisco, California, 1949

flooded. And the loyal client did not blame Wright at the next downpour, when the roof began to leak as though an automatic sprinkler system had been turned on. In this the architect was not to blame, as he discovered while remedying the defect, which was caused by substandard waterproofing rather than any structural flaw. La Miniatura stands today as a small masterpiece—still occupied, and the probable source of the hundreds of stories about leaking roofs and Frank Lloyd Wright.

Traveling back and forth between Japan and California, and meeting architectural problems at both ends of the line, put Wright in trim to finish the Imperial Hotel on July 1, 1922. Guests were accomodated for the first time on July 4 of that year, at a reception for Japanese and foreign dignitaries. Before this date, an insoluble personal difficulty arose when Wright's mother, past eighty but filled with energy, came for a visit in Japan. Baron Okura and the other magnates were charmed by Madame Wright, and made much of her; but Miriam Noel resented her appearance and departed for California in great indignation. Wright's distress was temporarily relieved when the backers of the hotel, in a genial mood at the completion of the tremendous task, joined Okura in getting drunk on champagne at a lunch in the architect's honor. Wearing a pith helmet, Wright made his last inspection of the Imperial's courtyards, while the workmen stood cheering by, and then sixty foremen accompanied him at their own expense to the docks eighteen miles away at Yokohama, to see him up the gangplank with cries of "Banzai, Wrieto-San, banzai!"

After the rest and relaxation of the voyage, Wright was in an expansive mood when he arrived in Chicago on his way to Spring Green. Reporters interviewed him at the Congress Hotel, and he told them, "I shall rest at Taliesin, and decide whether to make the headquarters of my work in Los Angeles or Chicago." When asked about Japan, Wright replied, "The Japanese are very much afraid of us. They look upon us as a great giant which can crush them if it wants to. And they are anxious to be friendly. There is among the Japanese nothing of the animosity that a great portion of the American press would have the people believe." A reporter asked what Wright thought about the increasing size of the Japanese navy, and was told, "The Japanese have taken the steps they have because they feel they must protect themselves if possible. They know that the white man had swept other races from his path at will—that the Japanese and Chinese are left—and that they may be the next to become extinct."

In Tokyo, the owners of the Imperial Hotel ruefully wondered if their bank accounts were to become extinct, for they figured that the structure had cost them three times the original estimate of ¥3,000,000. On the last day of August, 1923, the hotel was given an especially careful polishing by a crew under the direction of Assistant Manager Tetsuzo Inumaru, who would succeed in due time to the head managership, and the presidency of the company. Now he was anxious to provide perfect service at a large lunch party scheduled for the following day. Up early on September 1, Inumaru was busy all morning, and took the opportunity to relax for a moment in his office just before the lunch guests were due to arrive. He felt the building quiver, and knew that an earthquake had struck. His first thought was for the kitchen, and when he arrived there, he was horrified to see the boiling fat in the pans leap out and explode on the electric ranges, some of which fell over. Inumaru immediately sent a messenger to the electrician, telling him to cut off all power, and hurried to the Peacock

Room, where the party was to be held. As he entered this fantastic chamber, the earthquake struck again. Covered with chairs, plates and silverware designed by Frank Lloyd Wright, the floor rocked as though a long rolling wave was rising beneath it. But the walls and ceiling held; nothing fell except the electric fans on the balconies, which landed at Inumaru's feet with a series of metallic thuds. The earthquake-making dragon had met his match in the architect of the Imperial Hotel. A few days later, a radio message from Tokyo arrived at Taliesin.

HOTEL STANDS UNDAMAGED AS MONU-
MENT OF YOUR GENIUS. HUNDREDS OF
HOMELESS PROVIDED BY PERFECTLY
MAINTAINED SERVICE.

CONGRATULATIONS.

OKURA

The publication of this message in the newspapers was the start of the widely believed and printed myth that the Imperial Hotel was the only building in Tokyo to withstand the earthquake. This, however, was far from the truth. Among the notable buildings in Tokyo that also stood up throughout the catastrophe were the head office of the Mitsubishi Bank, the Mitsubishi Renting Office Buildings, the Mitsukoshi Department Store, the Bank of Japan, the head office of the Teokoku Seima Company, the Daiichi-Seimei Mutual Life Insurance Building, the Ministry of Justice, and the Supreme Court. In Tokyo as a whole, hundreds of thousands of buildings and houses remained standing even after the fire; the quake, as distinct from the fire, destroyed only 1 per cent of the buildings in Tokyo, including flimsy shacks that were expected to fall down in anything more than a strong puff of wind. After the earth-quake, the associated insurance underwriters published a detailed report of the damage. In this they listed five categories: Number 1 was undamaged; Number 2 was a small amount of damage; Number 3 was moderate, Number 4 was severe, and Number 5 total destruction. On this scale, the underwriters listed the Imperial Hotel in Category Number 2.

Wright was anxious for the durability of the "Impeho" to be widely known, because he believed he was now the object of studied neglect by other members of his profession. The appearance of no less than seven issues of the Dutch art magazine *Wendingen*, entirely devoted to his work, with an article by Louis Sullivan praising the Imperial Hotel, did nothing to make Wright feel better about the attitude of his other American colleagues. Europeans of stature were represented in these pages, paying their respects to Wright and admitting his influence; Hendrik Berlage, the Dutch-man, spoke of his "exquisitely sensitive taste," and J. J. P. Oud said that Wright's work "convinced on sight." But unanimous American applause for his achievement was lack-ing, though Wright felt that even the best of the Americans owed him something, and that he should still be recognized as their leader, as he had been recognized nearly a quarter of a century before when the Chicago Architectural Club gave more than half its annual exhibition to his work.

The article on the Imperial was Sullivan's last gesture in support of Wright. Reconciled since 1914, the two met from time to time, Sullivan now at last calling Wright by his first name. By the early 1920's, Sullivan was a discouraged man; as always, he gave Wright an example, but this time it was of something to avoid—a loss of tone, a disillusion-ment so deep as to inhibit action. Broken in health, the 'beloved master' lived in a modest hotel and spent most of his time in his customary chair at the mellow Cliff Dwellers Club overlooking the lake and Michigan Avenue. Here kind friends had seen to it that Sullivan had permanent membership, and the courteous scarlet-coated Negro doorman greeted him nearly every day. A table in the writing room was Sullivan's by common consent, and there he wrote many pages of his autobiography, and various essays on architecture and art. Perhaps Sullivan's failure to keep up his practice in his later years can be explained not by the evil of the times (as he saw it) but very simply by the failure of his health. But whatever the true state of affairs, Wright felt that Sullivan was raising a plain warning: never give up—for if you once surrender, the end is near. Wright's health was excellent, his face still had youthful curves, his abundant hair was scarcely touched with gray. When he visited Sullivan he tried to cheer him up, and even rubbed his back, as though he might somehow contribute a share of his vitality to the failing man. Was he not the good pencil that had once been so reliable in the master's hand? That was true, but when Sullivan died in 1924, the managers of the funeral put Wright in a back row, and another hand designed the Graceland Cemetery Memorial.

The question of selecting between Chicago and Los Angeles as Wright's architectural headquarters had been answered by now. The choice, of course, fell on Chicago, which was really Wright's home city—the metropolitan center of the area of which Richland Center was a part. Wright's California practice of the 1920's resulted in very few completed commissions. One might suppose that the California of that period, with its increasing population of mature and prosperous former Middle Westerners, would have been the happiest of hunting grounds for a Frank Lloyd

Wright in search of clients. He reacted strongly and favorably to the state's mountains and deserts, and to the tawny foothills surrounding its towns. His feeling for California sunlight, then untainted by smog, should have run from client to client like the idea of the Prairie houses during the great days in Oak Park. Indeed, Wright had such hopes for business that he maintained a Los Angeles office while the Imperial Hotel was going up. In charge was R. M. Schindler, a brilliant Viennese who had been one of Wright's assistants at Taliesin and in the Chicago office. Schindler was to put his own mark on California, along with William Wurster, Bernard Maybeck, the brothers Charles and Henry Greene, and Irving Gill, who had worked for Adler and Sullivan. But aside from Aline Barnsdall and Mrs. Millard, only three clients saw work go through to completion in Wright's California office during the 1920's. All of southern California was on the verge of a boom, and the explanation of why Wright did not have a greater part of it may lie in his frequent absences. Wright's work would doubtless have had a larger place had he himself been consistently on the Los Angeles scene. Certainly he had the personal showmanship to obtain and hold the attention of this community where showmen of various sorts performed so ably. But in his heart he did not want Los Angeles to be his home; Taliesin was calling, and there he would go, to try to organize his life. His greatest triumphs in California and the Southwest waited in the future.

In Chicago, a curious commission soon was presented when Nathan Moore's Tudor mansion burned to the ground. Wright accepted the responsibility of rebuilding it, and loyally provided his client with the strikingly handsome house that one sees today in Oak Park at the corner of Forest Avenue and Superior Street. Impossible to describe in words, a Wrightian feeling comes through the Tudor dress of this great mansion, whose air of mystery and romance casts a powerful spell on many who see it, and encourages speculation as to the remarkable effects Wright would have obtained had he cared to work in derived styles. But this, in Wright's view, would have been to practice charlatanism. However he may have felt about the rebuilding of the Moore house, there was news in Oak Park that would have a profound effect on his life and career—perhaps as deep an effect as any single occurrence in his life, short of his meeting with Mamah Cheney. The news was that Catherine had at last decided to permit a divorce, on grounds of voluntary separation, so that Wright was free to mary Miriam Noel.

He had felt that he was permitted to make no gesture to the memory of Sullivan; now he was able to make a supremely important one to show his loyalty to the woman who had tried to bring him comfort in the time of anguish after the tragedy at Taliesin. The divorce was granted and, as a result, a ceremony was held at the exact center of a bridge over the Wisconsin River on a chilly midnight in November, 1923, making Miriam Noel the wife of Frank Lloyd Wright. They chose this odd ritual to symbolize the bridging of all difficulties between them; but a more unfortunately wedded couple could not have been found in the length and breadth of the United States.

Chapter Six

TIME OF TROUBLE

MIRIAM SEEMED TO BE burning up with an inward flame, but not the sort that gave light or warmth to those around her. Wright was so greatly troubled that he arranged for his wife to see a Chicago psychiatrist. After three interviews, the doctor said that Miriam's neurasthenia was far advanced and that it would be dangerous to oppose her in anything. In a few months Miriam went to Los Angeles to "live a life of her own." She said to Wright that there would have to be a divorce, and a financial settlement, for had she not given him her best years, and under the most trying conditions a sensitive woman could endure? Worn and tired, Wright agreed that lawyers should be instructed to work things out.

Wright now found it necessary to drive himself to the drawing board. As so often in his life, a providential turn for the better came with the appearance of a sympathetic and generous client, this time in the person of Albert M. Johnson, president of the National Life Insurance Co., who laid out $20,000 for studies of a new sort of skyscraper, to be built on Water Tower Square in Chicago's near North Side. "I want a virgin, Mr. Wright—a virgin!" cried Johnson, and the architect found his relationship with this client as stimulating as his manner of speech.

Johnson resembled his contemporary, J. Pierpont Morgan, in his fondness for the company of clergymen, perhaps because he had been moved to conversion after hearing a sermon by the famous evangelist, Billy Sunday. Though he refused for years to admit it, Johnson was backer for the eccentric known as Death Valley Scotty, and once drove

Wright clear across the country in a Dodge touring car to visit Scotty at his lair in the badlands of Grapevine Canyon in Death Valley, California. Scotty told Wright his story of having found a lost gold mine somewhere out in the wilderness, from which he derived unlimited wealth. As proof of this, he could point to two barnlike buildings that were rising out of the alkaline rock. "Scotty has brought his castle in the air down to earth," Johnson would say, looking at Wright and Walter Edward Scott with his hooded eyes. The lean cold moneyman had a hidden taste for human oddity, and may have paired Scotty and Wright in his queer bookkeeping mind. Johnson kept a precise record of his whereabouts at every minute of the day, and by referring to files could tell you exactly where he was, and how occupied, at a given moment twenty or thirty years before. Now he expressed admiration for the imported panelling and tapestry in the castle, and for the great chandelier in the main hall, where he would sit tapping his foot appreciatively as Scotty played "The Whistler and His Dog" on an electric organ.

Wright would later show in Arizona what he might have done in Death Valley if his odd client's whims had turned in that direction. He certainly guessed the true relationship between Scott and Johnson, for on the return trip he said to his patron, "I believe *you* are the hidden gold mine Scotty is always talking about." All Johnson would say in reply was, "If that is so, I've been more than paid off in laughs."

Aside from his curious notion of humor, Johnson had one good reason for erecting Scott's fantastic desert headquarters. The only person Johnson loved and respected was his wife, born Bessie Morris Penniman, who was a graduate of Stanford, and a person of deep spiritual convictions. When completed, the palace in the badlands was to be a center for Bessie's religious activities, under the title of the Gospel Foundation of California, and to some extent Scotty earned his keep by acting as paymaster and superintendent of the building activities. It is evident that Wright might have been useful here, for Bessie disliked the "warehousy look" of the two big buildings, and called in M. R. Thompson, of the Stanford engineering department, to do what he could. The structures were linked, so that they formed an H, with a wide tiled patio between the two wings. The builders closed off one end of the H with low Roman arches, and erected a bell tower, connecting its carillon to the organ's keyboard, so the "The Whistler" could be enjoyed for miles around by snakes and lizards. Johnson lost interest in the Gospel Foundation after his wife's death in a traffic accident in 1943. Two years before, he had turned on Scott, and obtained an uncollectable judgment against him for $243,291, for money advanced over a period of thirty-six years.

Johnson's management of the insurance company was subjected to criticism and investigation, and he told Wright that the depression cost him a heavy sum. He also said that he was compelled to write a check for $14,000,000 in 1932 to clear his skirts when the public utilities empire of Samuel Insull collapsed in widespread ruin. All of this makes it understandable why Albert Mussey Johnson, in spite of his enthusiasm, never got around to building the great National Insurance skyscraper. Had he done so, that part of Chicago would now be dominated by opalescent copperbound glass, instead of the stone piers of the Palmolive Building. The complete plans of Wright's wonderful structure lie today in the vaults of Taliesin; a public benefactor could render no greater service than to see that this building at long last takes form on its original site, or on Park Avenue in New York, where it would indeed be a sight for sore eyes.

As he gradually realized that Johnson would go no farther than expressing admiration for the plans, Wright was deeply disappointed. It was not that he felt frustrated in the act of creation—with Wright, that was always completed when he finished the work on paper. What hurt was the loss of public achievement—the legitimate advertisement of a fine building on Michigan Avenue. Though Wright usually condemned tall buildings, calling them Molochs, he designed a number of skyscrapers during his career, and would cheerfully have rebuilt the entire Chicago Loop with such structures if anyone had asked him to. As it was, the National Life Insurance Company's glittering home shone only in its creator's mind; and an intense depression began to fasten on the life and spirit of Frank Lloyd Wright.

He was never alone—there were assistants at Taliesin, as always. They included Richard Neutra, who was to become well known, and who had recommended R. M. Schindler. In the evenings Wright would sit benignly among the young men, some of whom had with them their young wives; chamber music soothed him, and there was talk of art and life. And such visitors as Carl Sandburg, Edna St. Vincent Millay, and Ring Lardner sometimes entertained the residents of Taliesin with their conversation. But in spite of these refreshing interludes Wright recorded in private that "Taliesin no longer seemed to know how to live. Dissension and discord had shamed the place, outraged its friendly walls and lifting ceilings. A hope only lived there, wishing as always to bring back happiness."

This hope was realized by a chance meeting of the sort that fiction writers dare not use. One afternoon, Wright and his artist friend Jerome Blum booked two balcony seats for the matinee of the Russian dancers at the Auditorium. A third seat in the box was empty. Just as Karsavina's performance began, a woman was quietly ushered to this vacant place. Blum and Wright noted with approval that she was slender and elegant, wearing no hat, with her dark hair parted in the middle and smoothed over her ears. Foreign, they thought—maybe French?—or Russian? On her part, the lady saw that her neighbors were obviously gentlemen, obviously connected with the arts. During the intermission Blum said, "Pardon me, Madame—I believe we have met somewhere before. Was it in New York, at Waldo Frank's, perhaps?" The lady did know Mrs. Frank, as it happened; Blum mentioned a few more names she recognized, then introduced his friend, "Frank Lloyd Wright, the noted architect." The charming stranger had never heard of him, but graciously acknowledged the introduction in a low, musical voice. With equal grace she accepted Wright's invitation to tea after the performance at the nearby Congress Hotel.

Over the teacups Wright learned that this lady was a Montenegrin named Olga Iovanovna Lazovich Milanoff Hinzenberg, in Chicago to confer with her husband, from whom she was divorced. She had a young daughter named Svetlana. She herself was generally called Olgivanna, a combination of her first two names. Her next two names were those of her father and grandfather—one a chief justice, the other a general who had been a hero in Montenegro's fight for independence from Russia. Soon she was going back to France to continue her studies with Gurdjieff, the noted Asiatic savant who had founded an institute for the harmonious development of man. Anything like this, of course, was fascinating to Frank Lloyd Wright;

and before he rose from the tea table, he was in love with the fascinating Olgivanna.

This time he was making no mistake. Olgivanna—in her country the nickname was a respectful form of address—was not only attractive but shrewd, durable, sensible, and smart. No wonder Wright was enchanted—no two better suited people ever met. Almost from that day, until his death, Olgivanna was to stay at his side; but the years that immediately followed were to be extraordinarily trying, both for Wright and his Montenegrin lady.

It must be granted that the flouting of convention, no matter how well intentioned one may be, is sure to lead to trouble, or at least to the discomfort that goes with social disapproval. Even so, many of the things that happened to Wright and Olgivanna seem inordinately severe. Their afflictions centered on one maddening difficulty: Miriam held up the divorce proceedings that she herself had asked for. Reporters began to trail Miriam everywhere, and to encourage her to make appalling statements about Wright and his doings. Flocks of writs, attachments, and unpleasant legal papers of every sort began to fly through the air. The distracted Miriam would agree to a settlement through her legal representative, then change her mind and make another attack on Wright as a person. At last her lawyer, Arthur D. Cloud, gave up the case because she turned down three successive settlements he arranged. Cloud made an interesting statement in parting from his client: "I wanted to be a lawyer, and Mrs. Wright wanted me to be an avenging angel. So I got out. Mrs. Wright is without funds. The first thing to do is get her some money by a temporary but definite adjustment pending a final disposition of the case. But every time I suggested this to her, Mrs. Wright turned it down and demanded that I go out and punish Mr. Wright.

I am an attorney, not an instrument of vengeance." Miriam
Noel disregarded the free advice of her departing counselor,
and appointed a heavy-faced young man named Harold
Jackson to take his place.

There were three years of this strange warfare; and
during the unhappy time, Miriam often would charge that
Wright and Olgivanna were misdemeanants against the
public order of Wisconsin. Yet somehow, when officers
were prodded into visiting Taliesin to execute the warrants,
they would find neither Wright nor Olgivanna at home.
This showed that common sense had not died out at the
county and village level—though why the unhappy and
obviously unbalanced woman was not restrained remains a
puzzle. The misery of Miriam's bitterness can be felt today
by anyone who studies the case—it was hopeless, agonizing,
and destructive, with Miriam herself bearing the heaviest
burden of shame and pain.

To get an idea of the embarrassment and chagrin that
was heaped upon Wright and Olgivanna, we should bear
in mind that the raids were sometimes led by Miriam
in person. One of the most distressing of these scenes
occurred at Spring Green toward the end of the open
warfare, on a beautiful day in June. At this time Miriam
Noel appeared, urging on Constable Henry Pengally, whose
name showed him to be a descendant of the Welsh settlers
in the neighborhood. A troop of reporters brought up the
rear. Miriam was stopped at the Taliesin gate, and William
Weston, now the estate foreman, came out to parley. He
said that Mr. Wright was not in, and so could not be arrested on something called a peace warrant that Miriam was
waving in the air. Miriam now ordered Pengally to break
down the gate, but he said he really couldn't go that far. At
this point Mrs. Frances Cupply, one of Wright's handsome

daughters by his first wife, came from the house and tried to calm Miriam as she tore down a NO VISITORS sign and smashed the glass pane on another sign with a rock.

Miriam Noel Wright said, "Here I am at my own home, locked out so I must stand in the road!" Then she rounded on Weston and cried, "You always did Wright's dirty work! When I take over Taliesin, the first thing I'll do is fire you."

"Madame Noel, I think you had better go," said Mrs. Cupply.

"And I think *you* had better leave," replied Miriam. Turning to the reporters, she asked, "Did you hear her? 'I think you had better leave!' And this is my own home." In the silence that followed, Miriam walked close to Mrs. Cupply, who drew back a step on her side of the gate. Then, with staring eyes and lips drawn thin, Miriam said to the young woman, "You are ugly—uglier than you used to be, and you were always very ugly. You are even uglier than Mr. Wright."

The animosity expressed by such a scene had the penetrating quality of a natural force; and it gave Miriam Noel a fund of energy like that of a person inspired to complete some great and universal work of art. As if to make certain that Wright would be unable to pay any settlement at all, Miriam wrote to prospective clients denouncing him; she also went to Washington and appealed to Senator George William Norris of Nebraska, the Fighting Liberal, from whose office a sympathetic but cautious harrumphing was heard. Then, after overtures to accept a settlement and go through with a divorce, Miriam gave a ghastly echo of Mrs. Micawber by suddenly stating, "I will never leave Mr. Wright."

Under this kind of pressure, it is not surprising that

Wright would make sweeping statements to the newspapers. Miriam had not yet goaded him into mentioning her directly, but one can feel the generalized anger in Wright's remarks to reporters when he was asked, one morning on arrival in Chicago, what he thought of the city as a whole. First, Wright said, he was choked by the smoke, which fortunately kept him from seeing the dreadful town. But surely Michigan Avenue was handsome? "That isn't a boulevard, it's a racetrack!" cried Wright, showing that automobiles were considered to be a danger as early as the 1920's. "This is a horrible way to live," Wright went on. "You are being strangled by traffic." He was then asked for a solution of the difficulty, and began to talk trenchant sense, though private anguish showed through in the vehemence of his manner. "Take a gigantic knife and sweep it over the Loop," Wright said. "Cut off every building at the seventh floor. Spread everything out. You don't need concentration. If you cut down these horrible buildings you'll have no more traffic jams. You'll have trees again. You'll have some joy in the life of this city. After all, that's the job of the architect—to give the world a little joy."

Little enough joy was afforded Wright in the spring of 1925, when another destructive fire broke out at Taliesin. The first news stories had it that this blaze was started by a bolt of lightning, as though Miriam could call down fire from heaven like a prophet of the Old Testament. A storm did take place that night, and fortunately enough, it included a cloudburst that helped put out the flames. Later accounts blamed defective wiring for starting the fire; at any rate, heat grew so intense in the main part of the house that it melted the window panes, and fused the K'ang-si pottery to cinders. Wright set his loss at $200,000, a figure perhaps justified by the unique character of the house that had been ruined, and the faultless taste that had gone into the selection of the prints and other things that were destroyed. In spite of the disaster, Wright completed during this period plans for the Lake Tahoe resort, in which he suggested the shapes of American Indian tepees—a project of great and appropriate charm, that came to nothing. Amid a shortage of profitable work, the memory of Albert Johnson's $20,000 stood out in lonely grandeur—the money had quickly melted away. A series of conferences with friends and bankers began about this time; and the question before these meetings was, here is a man of international reputation and proved earning power; how can he be financed so that he can find the work he ought to do? While this was under consideration, dauntless as ever Wright set about the building of Taliesin III.

As he made plans for the new Taliesin, Wright also got on paper his conception of a cathedral of steel and glass to house a congregation of all faiths, and the idea for a plane-tarium with a sloping ramp. Years were to pass before these plans came off the paper, and Wright was justified in think-ing, as the projects failed, that much of what he had to show his country and the world would never be seen except by visitors to Taliesin. And now there was some question as to his continued residence there. Billy Koch, who had once worked for Wright as a chauffeur, gave a deposition for Miriam's use that he had seen Olgivanna living at Taliesin. This might put Wright in such a bad light before a court that Miriam would be awarded Taliesin; nor was she moved by a letter from Wright pointing out that if he was not "compelled to spend money on useless lawyer's bills, useless hotel bills, and useless doctor's bills," he could more quickly provide Miriam with a suitable home either in Los Angeles or Paris, as she preferred. Miriam sniffed at this, and

complained that Wright had said unkind things about her
to reporters. His reply was, "Everything that has been
printed derogatory to you, purporting to have come from
me, was a betrayal, and nothing yet has been printed which
I have sanctioned." What irritated Miriam was that Wright
had told the papers about a reasonable offer he had made,
which he considered she would accept "when she tires of
publicity." From her California headquarters, Miriam fired
back, "I shall never divorce Mr. Wright, to permit him to
marry Olga Milanoff."

Then Miriam varied the senseless psychological warfare
by suddenly withdrawing a suit for separate maintenance
that had been pending, and asking for divorce on the
grounds of cruelty, with the understanding that Wright
would not contest it. The Bank of Wisconsin sent a representative to the judge's chambers in Madison to give information on Wright's ability to meet the terms. He said
that the architect might reasonably be expected to carry his
financial burdens if all harrassment could be brought to an
end, and that the bank would accept a mortgage on Taliesin
to help bring this about. Miriam said that she must be assured
that "that other woman, Olga, will not be in luxury while I
am scraping along." This exhausted Wright's patience, and
in consequence he talked freely to reporters in a Madison
hotel suite. "Volstead laws, speed laws, divorce laws," he
said, "as they now stand, demoralize the individual, make
liars and law breakers of us in one way or another, and tend
to make our experiment in democracy absurd. If Mrs.
Wright doesn't accept the terms in the morning, I'll go
either to Tokyo or to Holland, to do what I can. I realize,
in taking this stand, just what it means to me and mine."
Here Wright gave a slight sigh of weariness, and continued,
"It means more long years lived across the social grain of the

life of our people, making shift to live in the face of popular disrespect and misunderstanding as I best can for myself and those dependent upon me." Next day, word came that Miriam was not going through with the divorce; but Wright stayed in the United States. His mentioning of Japan and Holland had been merely the expression of wishful thinking. No matter what troubles might betide him, this most American of artists knew in his heart he could not function properly outside his native land.

In a few weeks Miriam made another sortie at Taliesin, but was repulsed at the locked and guarded gates. By this time, Wright was frankly arguing his case in the newspapers, and he said of Miriam to reporters, "I have deposited money for her needs with the District Attorney. I stand ready to support her if she will give me the opportunity, but there is no place for her at Taliesin, where her real contribution has been only sabotage for ten years. This is not her home and never will be." The nightmare continued: Miriam set up a stronghold in a Madison hotel, where it was reported she was suffering from hysteria, while Wright made a public offer to meet her expenses at a sanitarium if she would enter voluntarily. Then Miriam swore out a warrant for Olgivanna's arrest; the sheriff found himself unable to serve it, though he searched high and low.

One of Wright's lawyers, Levi H. Bancroft, now issued a statement that "Mr. Wright is not attempting to shirk the money obligation. He is willing to support Miriam Noel Wright in luxury to which she was unused before she met him. He is willing that a judgment be entered in this case and the property settlement be made on the same basis as though he had been guilty of the misconduct charged. He is willing to mortgage his immortal soul, as far as life on this earth is concerned at least, to appease her, but she must cease her attack upon him, and let him get back to work as an architect to rehabilitate his home and earn money to support her. Through her letter writing to business associates, bankers, and creditors, she has been successful in destroying his business. She has boasted and threatened his absolute ruin and he is virtually without means at the present time, and he is faced with suits for her bills that would force him into involuntary bankruptcy." The lawyer went on to say that the last settlement offered and refused was for $20,000 in cash and an allowance of $250 a month.

In the dollars of 1926, that was not at all a mean offer, though conservative enough in view of Wright's potential earning capacity. But the phrase "luxury to which she was unused" in his lawyer's mouth showed how Wright's understandable bitterness had grown. It was quite true that he felt willing to mortgage his immortal soul to get this matter settled. Even so, he sometimes showed friends his remarkable self-discipline and will power in his ability to relax the nervous strain inflicted by Miriam and pass an hour or two cataloguing Japanese prints, or improvising at the keyboard of one of his pianos. Then he would assure his friends, and Olgivanna, that things would turn out all right in the end, somehow. And some people thought that even if they did not, there would still be an unconquerable place in the heart of Frank Lloyd Wright.

"There's one good thing about this whole mess," he would say, "and that is, that things can't possibly get any worse."

But in this, for once, Wright was mistaken. To begin the final sequence of trouble, Attorney Jackson made alliance with Mr. Hinzenberg, Olgivanna's former husband. Although there was no ground for it whatsoever, he represented Hinzenberg in suing Wright for an enormous sum, charging alienation of affections, and in seeking court orders

to take ten-year-old Svetlana from her mother. While the
much-enduring Olgivanna took the girl to the home of
relatives of Wright in Pennsylvania, Miriam and Jackson
whipped up the press to lurid articles about a nationwide
hunt for the child and mother.

An interview with Miriam at this period gives an idea of
the typical newspaper drivel of the day, and makes it
possible to theorize that a few metropolitan journals have
improved since that time. The piece began, " 'I made a mistake,' Miriam Noel sobbed, 'but I have paid for it—how I
have paid for it! Yet I would do it all over again!' Now for
a moment she was again that lovely young girl, fresh from
Parisian studios, who went to Taliesin, that house of tragedy,
to take the place of Mamah Borthwick Cheney. 'Mine was
a greater tragedy than Mamah Borthwick's,' she went on.
'She is dead—and I live on. Oh, how I loved him!' " Shortly
after this material appeared, Miriam Noel said that her
lawyer was working to get deportation proceedings started
against Olgivanna. Wright might have taken this as a
symptom of a turn for the worse, but his optimism was
such that he could not believe any action of this sort
would be taken.

Meanwhile, a great event took place in the lives of Wright
and Olgivanna when a baby girl was born, who was given
the name of Iovanna. Though this child was lucky in her
parentage, her arrival in the world caused such a sensation
that Wright's friends advised him to take Olgivanna and the
two children, and make a serious effort to drop out of sight
for a while. The Pennsylvania refuge had been discovered
by Attorney Jackson, and Wright decided to take a cottage
on the shores of Lake Minnetonka outside Minneapolis. His
retreat was covered by Bancroft, who did not deny rumors
that Wright had finally left the country for Mexico. Sum-

moning reporters, Bancroft spoke as follows: "The Wright
case is closed so far as my client is concerned. Mr. Wright
is out of the country, forced out by Mrs. Wright. His
earning power has been cut off by the very woman who
wants to get as much money as she can from him. But
he cannot return to this country and take up work at
Taliesin, not knowing at what moment he will be aroused
by sheriffs, lawyers, and photographers led by Mrs.
Wright." Bancroft might have added here that for the time
being, both Wright and Miriam were barred from Taliesin
by a court order obtained by the bank holding the mortgage;
but this was, perhaps, a minor detail in the general pattern
of frustration and mutual reproach. He went on, "The case
has come to the apex so many times, and each time Mrs.
Wright has thrown all reasonable legal suggestions to the
floor. She'd better make up her mind at once, and stick to it.
In a few weeks Mr. Wright will get to work in the country
where he now is. He will go back to his profession and he
will never return to this country. Mrs. Wright can then
have all the rhetorical vengeance she wants, but the dollars
she could now have simply won't be available. It's all wrong,
this idea that Mrs. Wright has been persecuted and neglected. From the moment I entered this case, months ago,
I insisted upon giving her every legal right, just as if she
had always been Mr. Wright's wife. She spit in our faces,
she turned down proposition after proposition. The climax
came when she turned down as big a monetary offer as Mr.
Wright could then give her, in spite of the fact that it was
guaranteed by the bank and asked, instead, for vengeance.
Even after this, Mr. Wright insisted on sending her money,
$125 a month, until she rushes up to Taliesin with Valdimar
Hinzenberg, armed with warrants which would land
Olgivanna and Wright in jail. Naturally they chose the

other alternative, flight. Olgivanna, Svetlana, and the new baby are back in Europe. Mr. Wright is probably in Mexico." Reporters then asked about the status of Hinzenberg's efforts to obtain custody of Svetlana. "Hinzenberg visited Taliesin last Christmas," the lawyer said, "and again later in the winter. He saw his daughter with her mother, who had been awarded the child by court order at the time of their divorce. He was pleased with what he saw. It was only when Miriam Noel Wright got control of him that he objected to leaving his daughter with Olgivanna. The inconsistent thing is that the little girl was all ready to go back to school this fall when her father, claiming he cares for her, charges her mother with adultery, sets upon her with a sheriff, and compels her to flee the country with Svetlana. And so, with Olgivanna in Europe, and Wright getting ready to take up his pen and blue prints down in Mexico, and Taliesin in the hands of a bank, the case is closed, unless Mrs. Wright decides to accept freedom and money in place of vengeance."

Although it came from counsel for one side in the matter, and was deliberately inaccurate as to Wright's whereabouts, this was rather a fair statement of the entire affair as it stood in the fall of 1926. In October, Jackson again sued Wright in Hinzenberg's name for alienation of affections. This time it was Svetlana whom Wright was alleged to have lured away. Jackson's temper was not improved when a Madison court slapped him with a bill for $50 in court costs when he failed to appear at a hearing he had requested for arguments that Miriam should be appointed receiver of Taliesin. Instead, the court granted the Bank of Wisconsin permission to sell Wright's art collection, chiefly Japanese prints at the time. The bank did not immediately go through with this sale, although the prints were later sold by Wright himself through a New York gallery. But now he had little room for objects of art in the small Lake Minnetonka cottage where he was established with Olgivanna, Svetlana, the baby, and a nursemaid.

On a chilly night toward the end of October, Wright heard a knock at the door, and when he opened it, found himself facing a party of law officers led by Harold Jackson. It has never been explained how the lawyer found Wright's whereabouts, and he volunteered no explanation as he walked into the living room, drawing legal papers from his pocket. Ten-year-old Svetlana was terrified when the marshals restrained Wright, who started for Jackson while the attorney was peering into the children's room.

"You have frightened her, and her heart will break!" said Olgivanna, and the marshals were decent enough to withdraw from the cottage, taking Jackson along for his own safety. Wright was a strong and wiry man, and capable of doing the attorney serious damage. But the officers were not going away; they had ordered Wright, Olgivanna and the children to prepare for the trip to the county jail. The two adults were arrested as fugitives from justice, and the children had to go along, since this masterpiece of legal effrontery had provided no other place for them. As the Wrights and the children left the cottage, newspaper cameras clicked and flashlights flickered like summer lightning.

Aside from hanging a man, the social community can make no greater gesture against him than by locking him in a cell. For this reason, the English Common Law and American Bill of Rights provide safeguards against indiscriminate confinement, which one would suppose to have operated in the case of Frank Lloyd Wright. That he was actually confined in prison seems as unlikely and unreal as the account of some fear or fantasy related to a psychiatrist, and retold in a clinical case history. But there was no questioning the reality of the experience: later that night Wright found himself walking down a long corridor in the Hennepin County Jail, his architect's eye noting the cells built tier on tier in a great empty space arched over by a high trussed roof. A warder opened a cell door—Wright stepped in. The door was closed and locked. Under the polished steel ceiling Wright observed that the principal furnishings were a dingy mattress and a filthy water closet. He thought it might clear his mind to grasp the bars, and as he did so, Wright said to himself, "Hold on to your sense of humor." But he passed several hours in black despair before that sense of humor began returning to him with the dawn. He found a clean corner of the mattress where he could sit between periods of pacing the floor, in stocking feet so as not to wake his neighbors.

After a breakfast of bread and chickory, the newspapers were brought in. The pictures were on the front page; and Wright realized his predicament had been brought about by arrangement between what was called the press and what was called the law. One immediate effect of the photographic display was to give Wright high status among the other prisoners. In that section of the jail, reserved for felons of the better sort, they were mostly bootleggers. They gave Wright the name of an able lawyer, W. M. Nash, who was used to clients in prison, and specialized in seeing that they spent the shortest possible period there. This attorney came at once when Wright sent for him, and reported that Wright and Olgivanna had been taken on the strength of a telegram stating that a warrant for their arrest had been issued in Wisconsin. Acting merely on the strength of this telegram, the press and sheriff's men had descended

on Wright at night, so as to make sure that he would
have to be held in jail on suspicion until the matter could
be brought before a magistrate. In other words, Wright was
held without charge. This part of the shabby affair was
concluded that morning when, after being interviewed in an
uproar of reporters admitted to the prison's anterooms by a
headline-loving sheriff, Wright and his counselor got their
hearing in court. The judge immediately threw out the case,
such as it was, against Wright and Olgivanna, who had
been cared for with the children in a women's ward. But
Harold Jackson was still at work, and Wright and Olgivanna
were called on to face the additional charge, especially
odious in this instance, of violating the Mann Act. A certain
LaFayette French, United States Attorney in those parts,
assured himself of a small place in history by proceeding
against Wright in this matter, so that the victims were held
in captivity a second night before being hauled before a
Federal Commissioner, who released them in bail of $15,000.
Harold Jackson stood by, asking for custody of both the
children, but this was denied, and Svetlana and her half-
sister were handed over to the Child Welfare Bureau pending their disposition. In Chicago, Miriam Noel waited at the
Southmoor Hotel for instructions from her lawyer. She said
to the swarming reporters, "I will never divorce Frank
Wright as long as I live, but if my attorney wants me to help
press these Mann Act and adultery charges against him, I
certainly will."

   In Minneapolis, Jackson gloried in the attention of the
press, finding that reporters would listen even to his statement that he was going to demand a grand jury investigation
of the seven deaths that occurred at Taliesin twelve years
before. When he saw the journalists actually writing this
down, Jackson continued, "I haven't scratched the surface

yet. There will be plenty more excitement. I am going to make sure that Wright is brought to justice. Up to this time Frank Lloyd Wright has considered himself above the law. He has flaunted [*sic*] and laughed at everything that resembled a legal process, or law and order. He has made his own morals. He has done that for seventeen years. I bear no animosity against him. It is just a question of a showdown with two figures—Frank Lloyd Wright or the law."

Jackson talked like a man with a handful of aces, but the dismissal of his application for custody of the children, and the admission of Wright and Olgivanna to bail, put them beyond his immediate reach. Attorney Nash crisply dismissed his Chicago colleague as one who was representing a wife who had abandoned her husband long ago, and was now persecuting him by threats and quasi-legal harassment. This was what a good many people were beginning to think. Wright's friends in Chicago and throughout the country, recovering from the shock of his imprisonment, began to rally to his defense, as did his two sisters and his son John Lloyd, who sent District Attorney French a copy of the letter Wright had written him shortly after meeting Miriam Noel, expressing fear that the relationship was not a sound one.

On his own account, John told the official, "You are not called upon to condone my father's past misguided mistakes in life, but it is your duty to condemn the mercenary, tricky, and vicious conspiracy that has dragged him before you at this time for prosecution. I have faith in his character and purposes and know he will justify that faith. My hope and trust is that you will sense the truth of his present situation and free him at once of the unjust charges against him under your jurisdiction."

Paying no attention to this letter, or to the other respectable and eminent voices raised on his victim's behalf, the bureaucrat continued preparations to have Wright committed for trial. Olgivanna also stood under the Federal threat, and was further embarrassed by at last being subjected to a newspaper interview, in spite of all Wright's efforts to spare her this questionable benefit. The result was a piece of fourth-class fiction.

But next day, one member of the press made an effort to undo some of the journalistic harm by arranging a meeting with Olgivanna, becoming aware of her quality, and paying close attention to what she said. This conscientious writer was Kathleen M'Laughlin, a star reporter of the Chicago *Tribune*. She saw a woman who had obviously lost weight that she could not afford to part with, looking dangerously thin in a gown of royal blue velvet which was set off by a string of jet beads, though "not of the latest mode." Olgivanna had many things on her mind, but started the conversation by saying, "Please, will you write that I am not a dancer? I have been called that to make a questionable atmosphere. I belonged to no cult, but was an instructor in rhythm, and taught exercises to build up the body." It was true that the papers had been calling her "the Montenegrin dancer," since presumably there was something outlandish about Montenegro, and the term "dancer" at that time had the pejorative value of "chorus girl"—if not immoral, distinctly flighty. Nothing could be less like the serious-minded Olgivanna, who now went on to identify her grandfather, General Milanoff, at the mention of whose name every Montenegrin patriot would remove his hat.

Olgivanna then described her education in Russia, and her early marriage, and told how they separated, with Hinzenberg coming to America. Olgivanna followed, and made a final effort at reconciliation, which failed. "I went ahead with my work and studies," Olgivanna said, "groping after those things I had begun to see I wanted. Philosophy fascinated me—I wanted to study. In Chicago I met Mr. Wright, and we had much in common. He told me many things, answered many questions that had been troubling me."

Olgivanna then spoke of the regard that quickly grew between them, and how they faced the fact that they were grown people in love. Mrs. Wright was in California, where she had gone after telling Wright she would never return to him—indeed, that she hated him. All this Miriam Wright reiterated in letters that Olgivanna had seen. Utterly confident that Wright would soon be free, they had gone ahead with their lives. Then came the crushing blow, when Miriam Wright sent a telegram, saying she had heard about Olgivanna and would never consent to a divorce. Olgivanna told the reporter it was not true that she had been living in luxury at Taliesin. "On the contrary," she said, "I was working, slaving about the house and grounds, doing both a man's and a woman's work, because I had made a bargain with Frank, that if he would dismiss his old housekeeper and let me take her place, I would ease my conscience by earning the $125 a month he paid her, and would support Svetlana and myself. I didn't want her to become a burden on him. I cooked and scrubbed, gardened, even painted and put in the screens in the windows. And I was glad to do it."

Olgivanna mentioned Iovanna's birth in a Chicago hospital on the second of December, 1925. Three days later, Miriam Wright made such a disturbance that Olgivanna and the baby were carried on a stretcher to an ambulance, and thus to a train that was to take the mother and her two daughters to New York and the first of a series of hiding places. In a narrow, dark room in a small New York hotel, Olgivanna read a newspaper statement by Miriam, charging that she was being maintained in opulence. "She should have seen me then," said Olgivanna. "There I stood in that damp, dark little room, my sleeves rolled up, my dress soaked clear down the front from the washing I was doing, and my tiny Iovanna asleep in one of the drawers of the bureau, which I pulled out to make a bed for her. Opulence indeed." The transcontinental hunt for Olgivanna and her older daughter followed; in her account of it, Olgivanna revealed that during her flight, she had stayed two months in Puerto Rico. And now, it seemed, this chapter of the story was over.

The sympathetic interview presaged a change in the way newspapers would handle Wright and his doings; eventually, he was to become a reporters' hero. And as he read the good account that Olgivanna had given of herself, Wright felt that the Minneapolis imprisonment was the lowest point to which his fortunes could possibly descend—after this, anything must be an improvement. But even Wright's courageous spirit quailed when it became evident that sanity had not yet returned to Minneapolis officialdom. They were forbidden to leave Hennepin County; and French, the Federal Attorney, continued his campaign to have prison sentences inflicted on Wright and Olgivanna.

It developed that the charges of being fugitives, on which they had been arrested, were based on a warrant sworn out the previous June in Iowa County, Wisconsin, by Miriam Wright for the purpose of instigating deportation proceedings against Olgivanna. Wright had thought there were no grounds for such action, and had continued to hope that the Mann Act charges would be set aside. It was therefore highly alarming to Wright and Nash when a second hearing was set for later in the week; the lawyer warned his client that it might be more than a mere formality. At this, Olgivanna suffered a collapse. Nothing was wrong with her courage, but her doctor said a month's rest was required to prevent serious injury to her nervous system. There can be no doubt that Olgivanna was near the end of her endurance, for the feeling that the entire might of the Federal Government was arrayed against her was a nightmare in reality. That this did not turn Olgivanna permanently against the United States is more credit to her than it is to certain officials of this country; with much grace, she later became an American citizen. Tired and distraught, Wright said, "God knows I would have saved her all this if I could. I never meant to drag her into such a mess."

The day of the second hearing before U. S. Commissioner Howard S. Abbott came swiftly. It seemed that this officeholder was something of a moralist. He allowed Olgivanna one week in which to recover her health, and refused to entertain Nash's plea that there was insufficient evidence to show that Wright had violated the Mann Act. Of course everyone in the country who took any interest in the case knew that the Mann Act could not be decently or logically applied to reputable private persons. Nevertheless, Abbott said to Wright, "I am binding you over to the April grand jury." After the hearing, Wright said, "This is just as I feared. It means that I can do no work until next spring— that my usefulness is curtailed until then, while my career waits on those of other men." It also meant that while waiting, he could consider the possibility of being sentenced to a Federal penitentiary. Next day, Olgivanna also was bound over to the grand jury, the dispenser of justice

deciding not to wait until she was able to appear before
him. Wright said that if his troubles could ever be com-
pounded, he would go to a foreign country and never
return. One can believe that he meant it, at the time.

The processes of the law now ground to a temporary halt.
Well pleased with himself, French allowed Wright and
Olgivanna to leave Minnesota under bond. They went first
to New York and stayed with Wright's sister Maginol. In
New York, more shapes from the nightmare loomed before
Olgivanna when officials of the Immigration Service appeared with a warrant arresting her for leaving the country
to go to Puerto Rico. Like most people, Wright had always
assumed that this island was part of the United States. So
far as Olgivanna was concerned it appeared that this was
not so, and he gave up the last of his Liberty bonds to be
posted for bail.

Everything Wright had was now in the hands of the
Bank of Wisconsin, which was in possession of Taliesin.
Utter confusion of financial affairs—one possible Federal
indictment looming over Wright, two over Olgivanna—in-
ability to attend properly to such work as might appear
through all the disturbance—this was the situation now
confronting a man who had, it should be noted, the orderly
mind of an architect. The untidy quality of all the circumstances surrounding him must therefore have been especially
painful; and the unshaken belief that he had great work to
do must have made the constant frustration of his efforts
to settle down to it doubly hard to bear. That Wright held
on to his sanity through this period, and actually got architectural plans on paper, is proof for all time that he was
made of indestructible stuff, as was his loyal Olgivanna.
With the bank's permission, they now went home to
Taliesin for a brief period; Wright wanted to put before

his counselors a scheme that he believed might bring order out of chaos.

This was simply that he should be incorporated, with shares sold to his friends and clients as though he were a stock company. The money thus raised would be used to satisfy all creditors and clear Wright's title to Taliesin, where he would settle down to repay the investors out of his future earnings. The recent troubles had shown that Wright had good friends; now they could show their faith in him by coming together to relieve an intolerable situation. Favorably impressed, the bank officials told Wright to proceed with his plan, reminding him that he was subject to eviction from Taliesin at their pleasure. Some of the directors were worried about Olgivanna's presence there, and all of them were uneasily aware of Miriam's continued campaigns of harassment; if she succeeded in bringing about Wright's complete ruin, the bank would be loser by the substantial amount already advanced. The bankers therefore instructed Wright to sell a block of his Japanese prints, and the sale was held at the Kennerly galleries in New York in January, 1927. A lawyer representing Miriam Wright appeared with a warrant of attachment to halt the sale, but allowed it to continue on condition that the courts would settle disposition of the proceeds; these amounted to some $37,000, less a commission in the neighborhood of 35 per cent. The money eventually found its way to the bank, along with Mitchell Kennerly's comment that the sale had brought in considerably less than the real value of the prints, because of unpleasant notoriety given the owner. This added to the feeling at the bank that sooner or later, Taliesin would have to be confiscated. In this crisis, the good friends Darwin Martin, Mrs. Coonley, and Professor Ferdinand Schevill of the University of Chicago

showed their quality by giving leadership to a group of
investors who subscribed $75,000 as proof of their faith that
Frank Lloyd Wright would live and function usefully in
spite of his trials and misfortunes. Their example was responsible for a slight but perceptible change in the climate
of public opinion—from that moment on, Wright began
to be respectable again, as his old enemy the man in the
street would see it, though dreadful embarrassments were
still to be faced and overcome.

One sign of better times, for example, came when Wright
made an anxious trip to Washington in hopes of tempering
the action of the Department of Immigration against
Olgivanna. Surprisingly enough, he found a high official
who had both sympathy and common sense. He was told
not to worry about the matter—it had been the result of
excessive zeal on the part of underlings, and would not be
pressed. With this load off his mind, Wright returned to
Taliesin, where he got word that Miriam had taken up a
position in Los Angeles, from which she was firing her
customary volleys of accusation and abuse. Another proffered settlement had been turned down, and Harold Jackson
had entered a claim against the proceeds of the print sale
for a $5000 fee, plus $1200 he had lent his client; also, the
Southmoor Hotel had made a claim for the $1500 owed by
Miriam when she left for California. All this was as if to
say, there has been no change; it might have reminded
Wright, who in happier days delighted in vaudeville humor,
of the celebrated comedy routine, "No News, or What
Killed the Dog." In this sketch, the owner of an estate returns to be told that there is nothing to report, except that
the dog died, and when he inquires how this came about,
is informed of one linked catastrophe after another until it
becomes evident that the entire place has been burned to

the ground. Indeed, this almost happened, when another serious fire tore at Taliesin's vitals on a cold night in February. The alarm went out in time for neighbors to rally, and most of the furnishings were carried out intact, so that the total damage was held to about $6000.

Meanwhile, in Minneapolis, LaFayette French was feeling a change in the atmosphere. A certain sanity of approach was beginning to make itself felt in the matter of Frank Lloyd Wright and Olgivanna, and it was now evident that these were no friendless derelicts, but persons for whom men of good repute had spoken up in voices loud and clear. The day before the grand jury convened, French announced that the Federal government would drop the Mann Act charges. After all, he explained, they were based only on a technicality; moreover, the State of Wisconsin had failed to prosecute Wright as a fugitive—therefore the whole affair, so far as he was concerned, might be forgotten. But no one ever apologized to Olgivanna or to Wright.

Thus another weight was lifted from Wright's mind as the possibility of long imprisonment receded into the region of the impossible; now he could almost forget the brief Minneapolis jailing. But when one mental burden was lifted, another seemed nearly always ready to take its place: this time it was an overdue note for $18,360 at the bank. And the latest shot from Miriam was in her usual tone, as she refused another settlement offer with a telegram from San Francisco that concluded, "MY HEART IS DEEPER THAN POVERTY OR STARVATION AND NO MONEY CAN HEAL IT WHEN YOUR HIRED RUFFIANS KEPT ME OUT OF MY HOME WHEN I WAS PENNILESS AND HEARTBROKEN YOU SHUT THE DOOR FOREVER ON A DIVORCE FROM ME."

Though this had the familiar sound, Miriam was beginning to turn in the direction of settlement; she had parted

with Harold Jackson, and retained a woman attorney, Miss
Tillie Levin, who brought matters almost to agreement by
the third of July. Only one piece of paper needed to be
signed—but Miriam insisted that it include a stipulation
that Wright should not marry Olgivanna until at least five
years after the divorce was granted. After a fortnight of
argument, Miriam suddenly withdrew this demand. The
newspapers said the architect and his wife had almost come
to terms—and late in August, the divorce that Miriam had
sworn she would never agree to was granted to her in Superior Court, on the ground—a legal fiction—that she had
been deserted. According to Wisconsin law, Wright and
Olgivanna would be free to marry in one year's time.
Miriam was to receive $30,000, of which the first installment
of $6000 would be paid within a week, and a trust fund
would be established for her benefit. Miriam's lawyer announced that she was going to adopt a baby boy, and return
to Paris, where she would resume her career as a sculptress.

Somehow when this news came out there was felt in the
surrounding air a perceptible breath of good will for Frank
Lloyd Wright. He took advantage of this by showing his
first glimmering of aptitude for what would later become
known as the art of public relations, in making announcement of the formation of Frank Lloyd Wright, Incorporated, under the laws of the State of Wisconsin. The
impact of the story was that Wright would be put back
to work by his friends; and the inescapable conclusion was
that he must be a good man to inspire such loyalty. Actually
the bank was in possession at Taliesin, but Wright was
living there, the story explained, while arrangements were
being made to return the estate to his complete ownership
and control. It was hard to see how anything could go

wrong now, but all concerned had reckoned without Miriam Noel Wright.

That they were dealing with an unbalanced person had long been clear—sympathy for Miriam's unhappiness could not deny this fact. But even the staunchest of Wright's supporters was aghast when, instead of going to Paris, Miriam turned up in Madison, and sent Wright a letter of such an extraordinary tone that he felt bound to turn it over to the authorities. Miriam was then arrested in the dining room of Madison's Lorain Hotel on the charge of mailing an obscene letter. She was placed in her room under guard of a woman deputy to await further action in the morning. Meanwhile, it was reported that before mailing the letter, Mrs. Wright had caused a scene in the office of the district attorney at Dodgeville, when he refused to send deputies to arrest Wright and Olgivanna at Taliesin. Next day, Wright asked to be excused from pressing the charges in connection with the letter, and Miriam immediately went to the State capitol and obtained a hearing from Governor Fred R. Zimmerman. Acting in Miriam's behalf, Lawyer Levin presented a demand that the Dodgeville district attorney be compelled to issue a warrant charging Frank Lloyd Wright with adultery. The governor stalled by saying he would order an investigation if Mrs. Wright would post $500 to guarantee the state against useless expense. The obsessed woman now hurried away to Chicago, and was not heard from for two months. Then, Miriam wrote to every member of the United States Senate, demanding an investigation by the Department of Justice of the circumstances surrounding the dismissal of the Mann Act charges against Wright in Minneapolis. Though nothing came of this, it showed that Miriam's malice was still unappeased.

Now it seemed that the bad dream would never end;

though friends had subscribed for shares in future earnings, and Darwin Martin and Professor Schevill had taken care of certain obligations not covered in the arrangement with the bank, the necessary peace of mind for consecutive work was still denied to Frank Lloyd Wright. This was made shockingly evident, one afternoon, when a man appeared at Taliesin and told the people there that they were now in the bank's employ. Next day came a long legal notice that carried in its coiling sentences a most odious conclusion: Taliesin was being used for purposes that outraged the mortgage. Would Wright and Olgivanna, therefore, kindly remove themselves from the premises?

"Do I have to take this lying down?" Wright asked his lawyers. They answered that it looked very much as though he did; and then, as always with the indomitable Wright, a way was opened for him—it seemed that his courage attracted answers in the nick of time. This reply to his need came from Albert Chase McArthur, a Chicago architect who had once been an assistant at the Oak Park studio, and was the son of an early client.

Four years before, McArthur's two brothers Charles and Warren had gone to Phoenix, Arizona, where they correctly saw many possibilities for development on various lines. Among their plans was one for a splendid resort hotel, for which they bought a tract of land at the foot of Camelback Mountain early in 1927. They employed their brother Albert to design the hotel, which was to be called the Arizona Biltmore. While working on the plans, McArthur thought of the concrete textile-block construction that had been used in La Miniatura and other California houses, a method he considered to be Wright's property. Accordingly he wrote to Taliesin, asking for permission to use the block technique. His letter arrived just as the bank trouble came to a head, in January of 1928, and Wright at once telegraphed the answer. "DEAR ALBERT CONGRATULATIONS TEXTILE BLOCK IDEAL FOR YOUR PURPOSE MAKE PLANS AND ELEVATIONS SIXTEEN INCH UNIT IN ALL DIRECTIONS TYPICAL MOLDS AVAILABLE IN LOS ANGELES PATTERN IDEAL FOR SYSTEM IF ACCURATE SIZE IN BLOCK UNIT CAN BE HAD ACCURATE SIZE NECESSARY TO COMPLETE SUCCESS SHOULD COME OUT TO HELP YOU START PERHAPS FRANK LLOYD WRIGHT."

Albert McArthur was glad to have his teacher and old friend come to Phoenix, and Wright and Olgivanna shortly arrived under the benign sky of an Arizona winter. The coldness, the disappointment, the weary struggle that centered at Taliesin lay behind them, and Wright's enthusiasm was unbounded as he looked over the work McArthur had done. Olgivanna and Mrs. McArthur became good friends. And best of all was the substantial fee that McArthur paid to Wright for the use of his block construction method. For six or seven weeks Wright came to the office, but Charles McArthur, head of the enterprise, felt that he disturbed the routine, and tactfully suggested that he suspend his visits. Soon afterward, Wright and Olgivanna found a pleasant cottage at La Jolla, California, and retired there so that Wright could at last enjoy a period of rest and meditation. What makes his connection with McArthur especially interesting is the fact that it led to widespread reports that he had designed the Arizona Biltmore—reports that persist to this day, when visitors who come to the Phoenix area to see the work Wright did at a later period of his career are advised, "And don't miss the hotel that Mr. Wright designed—the Arizona Biltmore." Not only guides and citizens are under this misapprehension —published lists of Wright's work have included the hotel, and it has been credited to him in at least two books.

Wright did design an Arizona hotel—but it was not the Biltmore, and it was never built. This glittering project was called San Marcos in the Desert, and Wright put it on paper for a promoter who planned to make a resort center in the small town of Chandler, about twenty miles outside Phoenix. The general pulling back of speculative funds that accompanied the depression of 1929 put the Chandler plans on the shelf, apparently forever. It also brought ruin to the McArthurs, for the Eastern millionaires who were expected to fill the luxurious Biltmore after its completion in February 1929 stayed at home that year—or at least did not come to Phoenix—and the promoters started their second season only on the strength of a loan from P. K. Wrigley, the chewing gum magnate, who later took over the property. The gentle Albert McArthur left Phoenix for California, where he was distressed to find the word passed from time to time along channels of architectural gossip that the Arizona Biltmore was really the design of Frank Lloyd Wright. Just why Wright would plan a major piece of work and sign it Albert McArthur was never explained; but in this field the matter of professional credit is sometimes delicate, and many people found it possible to believe that for some indefinable reason, McArthur might have acted as a front for the older architect. It is the kind of thing that people like to repeat, for it gives an air of being in the know.

At last, after the appearance of the two books that flatly assigned the Arizona Biltmore to Wright, McArthur wrote to the *Architectural Record* in an effort to establish the truth. His letter said, "Now that these false statements have found their way into the public record, I am placed in an equivocal position . . . I have in my possession, besides all the originals of the plans, specifications, contracts and correspondence incident to the project, sufficient other documents to prove that I was the architect of these buildings,[1] and that Mr. Wright's relation to the project was no more than that of a private consultant to me, and to me only, for the specific purpose of the technical application of his invention, the 'Textile-Block-Slab Construction.' " McArthur went on to state that he became aware in 1930 that his authorship of the Arizona Biltmore was questioned, and asked Wright at that time for a letter about his part in it. Because of its sense of fair play the *Record* also published Wright's note:

> "All I have done in connection with the building of the Arizona Biltmore, near Phoenix, I have done for Albert McArthur himself at his sole request, and for none other.
>
> "Albert McArthur is the architect of the building—all attempts to take the credit for that performance from him are gratuitous and beside the mark.
>
> "But for him, Phoenix would have had nothing like the Biltmore, and it is my hope that he may be enabled to give Phoenix many more beautiful buildings as I believe him entirely capable of doing so.
>
> "Frank Lloyd Wright"

This letter should have set the record straight so far as the architectural profession was concerned; but McArthur had reason to feel that the public misconception would never be entirely corrected. A few months after the letters were printed, he suffered a heart attack, and lived the remaining ten years of his life as an invalid. During this time,

---

[1] The hotel included cottages.

he devoted himself to metaphysical studies, mathematics, and the partial working out of a theory of color.

After leaving Phoenix, Wright recruited his spiritual forces as he studied the varying shades of tan in the California foothills. He had first felt the impact of the Great American Desert on the trip with Albert Johnson to visit Death Valley Scotty—now, with Arizona and California before him, he began to think of an architecture of the wasteland, something that would blend the dehydrated colors into the brilliance of the sun and sky, that would take its sense of shape from the towering mesas that he saw on his way between Phoenix and the coast. Wright meditated on this in the quiet cottage at La Jolla. Nature was the prime creator, Wright told himself, and in his mind's eye he saw, beyond the prairies and the badlands, against a blue sky with high floating clouds "a distant architecture, ethereal, touched, only touched with a sense of Egyptian, Mayan drift and silhouette." The blaze of sunshine was an asset, as Wright saw it; in these regions, sun acceptance rather than sun defiance was the condition of survival. This meant that "wall surfaces must eagerly take the light and play with it, break it up, or drink it in until the sunlight blends the building into place with the creation around it." Trees and vines, carefully watered, should cover these sun-drinking walls, and as for ornament, that would be integral— an organic pattern learned from nature itself through the example of the rattlesnake, the Gila monster, and the cactus.

All of this was to be demonstrated in the fulness of time; and as he sat in his wicker armchair at La Jolla, with an Indian pottery jar of colored pencils near at hand, Wright had only one nagging worry to impede the progress of creative thought: Miriam Noel Wright was still in the United States. She had not gone to Paris and the baby boy she had proposed to adopt and bring up in the artistic atmosphere of her studio remained in the realm of fantasy. In fact, Miriam seemed not to have made the slightest alteration in her behavior after the divorce and settlement, and still gained newspaper space in various unpleasant connections. A private detective, for example, sued for the fees he had earned in shadowing Wright and Olgivanna; and Harold Jackson, the displaced attorney, also presented an unpaid bill. News came from Chicago that this was satisfied by the sale, in the bailiff's rooms at the Municipal Court, of a collection of Japanese prints that Wright had given to Miriam as a property reserve. These prints, indeed, seemed like the scriptural widow's cruse of oil that yielded unending sustenance; and their value on the American market is unshakable testimony to Wright's taste, and to his skill as a buyer.

At this point, Miriam was in Washington, hoping to stir up governmental action against Wright; she then started west, and although Wright and Olgivanna did not know it, arrived at La Jolla the second week in July. Here she decided to find Olgivanna and recite her grievances face to face; she went to the cottage, but providentially both Wright and Olgivanna were away. Miriam entered and raged through the rooms, pulling pictures from the walls, upsetting and breaking furniture, tearing up letters, and hurling Olgivanna's clothes and personal possessions to the floor. A frightened housemaid called police, who put Miriam under arrest, then released her on a $250 bond. Next day the police judge gave her the choice of thirty days in jail, or putting up $3000 to pay for the damage, allowing a period of ten days during which Miriam could decide which penalty she preferred. As usual, she swore a warrant for Wright's arrest, charging him with being a lewd and dissolute person. The endless nightmare went on; friends hid Wright and Olgivanna in a vacant house, and brought them food, so that the police were unable to serve the warrant. In a few days, Miriam left town and went to Hollywood, where she boasted that she had settled the entire affair by paying $69 in court costs.

Terrifying as this latest assault had been, Wright and Olgivanna took comfort in one thought that may have saved their sanity, which was that the time during which they could be harrassed for their quiet domestic existence was drawing to a close. The statutory year following the Wisconsin divorce would be up on the twenty-fifth of August. When the day of deliverance at last arrived, a Congregational minister made Wright and Olgivanna man and wife. The service was performed at midnight, in the patio of a hotel at Rancho Santa Fe, a small place near La Jolla. Present were the minister's wife, Mr. and Mrs. Charles McArthur, and Olgivanna's two daughters. Wright sent Chicago friends a telegram of announcement that ended on a buoyant note: "WE ARE ALTOGETHER WELL AND HAPPY GOING TO PUT NEW LIFE INTO NEW BUILDINGS IN THE GREAT ARIZONA DESERT SPACES DURING THE NEXT YEAR OR TWO." Evidently he saw no evil auspices in another midnight wedding ceremony; and he was perfectly correct, for no man ever married a better helpmate than Olgivanna Lloyd Wright.

After this marriage, it could be said that one of the few men in the United States to whom the depression of 1929 made no difference was Frank Lloyd Wright. He was already broke, deep in debt, out of work, and in danger of seeing the bank take over his home and studio. Against this he had a considerable number of assets, though they were not the sort that could be listed on a balance sheet. They included first of all his genius, indestructible courage, and energy; this was supported at all points by the loyalty and understanding of his gifted and competent Olgivanna; and there was the good will of friends, such as Darwin Martin in Buffalo and Professor Schevill in Chicago. No man should be called poor who counted such items in his favor; but he certainly could be out of funds. In the month of May preceding Wright's marriage to Olgivanna, the announcement was made that Taliesin and its contents would go up for public sale. All that came of this was that a number of curious persons wandered through the house and grounds; the few bids submitted were too low to be considered. When word came that Wright was married, the bank vacated the premises, and the directors ruled that he might live there while he made the effort to begin earning a steady return on the practice of his profession. Though on financial probation, and under the eyes of bankers no farther away than Madison, it now could be said that Frank Lloyd Wright was once again making his headquarters at Taliesin.

"There is no substitute for Frank Lloyd Wright," said Darwin Martin, as staunch as he had been that day in Chicago years before when he decided that this man was his architect and friend. Martin was pleased with the house, Graycliff, on Lake Erie, that Wright had designed (though he had not supervised the construction) in the time of troubles. Another who showed confidence was Richard Lloyd-Jones, a cousin who was a newspaper publisher in Tulsa. He commissioned a house, which was completed in 1929, and turned out to be one of Wright's most effective pieces of work. Made of concrete, the Lloyd-Jones mansion was designed by Wright in a mood to avoid anything remotely resembling artifice, with results that can only be described as uncompromising; and yet, the more one studies this house, the more one likes it. It pleases by not seeking to ingratiate itself, and seems to be refreshed by the passage of time, while progressive designs of less integrity have dated year by year. Another interesting point about the Lloyd-Jones house is that it is the only considerable commission, from which Wright may be assumed to have made a comfortable fee, of which there seems to be record from the year 1924 until 1936.

The lean years interpreted from the dream by Joseph before Pharaoh could not have been more severe. Taliesin was unkempt and in need of repair; weeds choked its fields, and the buildings of the Hillside School were vacant and neglected. All in all, Wright's race with actual want was to become, as the Duke of Wellington reported of Waterloo, "A damned close-run thing." Estimates of historians and architects have been made from the time of the Barnsdall commission to 1936, and they present a very discouraging picture for any young person planning to go into the business of being a great and inventive genius. Wright had said that he charged as high as 15 per cent of the total construction cost. Assuming that he always received this, the historians calculate that he earned about $18,000 on the Barnsdall job, and something in the neighborhood of $4000 each for the Ennis and Freeman houses, the major works aside from La Miniatura and the Barnsdall mansion in his early California practice. No further work of this size, except for the house in Tulsa, was to come his way during the period under examination, and it averages out at about $2000 a year, small money indeed for a man of his quality. All this was borne with dignity, for Wright never abated a manner that indicated he considered himself a person of worth and consequence, and also never pretended to have money when he did not. During the period immediately after his return with his wife to Taliesin, he wrote that "The next move, even the next meal, is becoming a problem to be solved without money. There is less than none." He was happy to receive the modest checks that his writing brought in, and delivered lectures for startlingly small fees. In Wright's later years the distinguished architect Harwell Hamilton Harris remarked to him how much he had profited from a lecture Wright delivered in Philadelphia in 1929. "I'm glad to hear that," said Wright. "I remember that lecture well. I needed the money. They paid me thirty-five dollars."

As always with Wright, there was no lack of optimism; and hopes rose high when he went to work for a stimulating client, the Rev. Dr. William Norman Guthrie, rector of St. Mark's-in-the-Bouwerie, New York City. This clergyman had earned Wright's respect by his broad vision of pastoral responsibilities. Holding that all religions are essentially one, Dr. Guthrie enlivened the services with Greek folk dancing, American Indian chants, and other ceremonials not usually encountered in the Episcopal order of worship. He also established a "Body and Soul Clinic," planning to minister simultaneously to physical and spiritual ills. For some reason, Dr. Guthrie lost the unanimous support of his vestry; and with the depression, the drawings for St. Mark's apartment tower were added to Taliesin's pile of uncompleted plans.

To broaden the financial base, Wright's friends extended the stock company to Illinois, where papers of incorporation were taken out with the help of Harold McCormick and others. The newspapers, in the benevolent tone that they would use in referring to Wright from now on, reported that he was happily established at Taliesin and quietly at work on many projects. Wright, however, soon learned that though malign publicity had failed to break him, the friendly articles certainly did not make him; the greatest gain from the altered attitude of the press was that Wright was no longer emotionally torn by sensational sharpshooting in print. The corporations now held all his assets, including Taliesin—including his brain, if one read beyond the legal language. And the bank stood near at hand, watching with what Wright felt was a singularly cold and expectant eye. All that was early-American in Wright was gathering to meet this challenge, and in the back of his mind echoed the folk sayings, "The Lord helps those who help themselves"—"Plough deep while sluggards sleep"—"Root, hog, or die." The indomitable man promised himself nothing less than to bring back the days of lavish spending, and many houses and buildings rising under the sun, with himself striding through the work, altering here, rebuilding there, flourishing his cane as though it were a pencil that could trace against the sky.

As he gradually got the hang of using the press in his own behalf, even though the results might not be readily apparent, Wright floated from time to time what might be called a trial balloon of publicity. One such was an announcement by Charles L. Morgan, a faithful Chicago associate, that Wright had worked out a plan for cantilever construction of tall buildings that would permit the use of glass as an outer cover, and eliminate the need for heavy masonry walls. Indeed, Wright had conceived this some years before, for Johnson's unbuilt insurance headquarters. Morgan said that the recommended method would place the stress on masonry removed to the interior of the building, thus leaving the outer surface to opalescent glass that allowed maximum light while cutting down the glare. The story went on to tell how the Imperial Hotel had survived the earthquake, giving the impression that it had been alone in doing so, and concluded by promising an early announcement as to the location of Mr. Wright's new Chicago skyscraper. But this structure was not heard from again; as in the theater, the projects of the building industry sometimes get no farther than the printed page. At any rate, Wright stated soon after that his hours were filled with important work, making it necessary for him to divide his time between Taliesin and New York. He had a "concrete slab skyscraper process in mind that he believed would greatly change architectural methods." Also, he was thinking of re-establishing the school for architects he conducted from 1919 to 1925. This was the first hint of an important development in Wright's later career. But Wright as the head of a school of architecture was a startling thought to many; some of the ablest of the architects who had been associated with him agreed with the eminent Barry Byrne that the greatest benefit one got from association with Frank Lloyd Wright was that of seeing a tremendously capable professional at work—and drawing one's own conclusions, a privilege that Wright liked to extend freely to those about him.

The Illinois incorporation was accompanied by other news, that struck a deep pang of mixed emotion into Wright's heart: Miriam Noel, it turned out, would never get to Paris. She had come to Milwaukee, for the purpose of entering a suit against Wright in connection with the trust fund that had been established for her out of the proceeds of the first stock issue. While in Milwaukee, Miriam was taken to the hospital, where the doctors found her suffering from a grave abdominal complaint. They operated; the patient rallied, then got rapidly worse, and early in January 1930, death came as a friend to the incurably unhappy Miriam Noel Wright. That she had followed Wright like a fury in the last years of her life did not take away the fact that she had once been a person of beauty, talent, and sensibility. During the time she was associated with Wright she was, in a way, the personification of his own folly; and all of it that did real harm perhaps was buried with her.

Released in this melancholy way from the constant threat that Miriam represented, Wright began to prepare for the delivery of the Kahn lectures at Princeton, one of the most important speaking assignments he had ever received. To the surprise of some, Wright did not denounce the architectural medley that spread before his eyes in the town and university. This was at the height of the Collegiate Gothic boom in American institutions of higher learning, and at Princeton he saw Colonial and Victorian structures side by side with the Holder Hall and Tower, designed by Day and Klauder, that crowned the new western development of the campus. This frankly derived and historical building was perhaps too assured and successful to be directly attacked—handsomely supported as it was by the Campbell Hall of Cram, Goodhue, and Ferguson, and the connected system of Blair and Stafford Little leading down to the mass of the Gymnasium, the last three buildings being the work of Walter Cope and John Stewardson. A mile away stood the high point of an architecture that was academic both in purpose and inspiration—the Graduate College, by Ralph Adams Cram. Lying at the crest of a low hill and surveying the Springdale golf course, these towered courtyards were supremely accomplished work by a man who disregarded the element of time: a local wit said that the great hall of the college was five hundred years old the day the doors were opened.

As he was taken to see the sights of Princeton, Wright may have privately observed that this graduate college, as opposed to Taliesin, was most decidedly on the hill rather than of it. But he made no public comment; and the six lectures, setting forth his philosophy of design, the use of materials, and planning in general, were later published by the university press. In the lectures, he stated the inner meaning of his attitude on design when he said, "Repose is the reward of true simplicity, and organic simplicity is sure of repose. Repose is the highest quality in the art of architecture, next to integrity, and a reward for integrity." Thirty years now in the past—a past that flowed on inexorably into the future—the Oak Park houses stood to bear him out.

It should be noted that what he saw at Princeton did nothing to convert Wright to the Collegiate Gothic revival. Some years later, he excoriated similar buildings at Yale and the University of Chicago; it was true that these had not come off with the aesthetic success achieved at Princeton, but in Wright's mind the whole movement was a mistake. Amazing results were to come when Wright himself was commissioned to design an entire college plant in Florida; and it is entertaining to imagine what he might have done, had the opportunity come his way, on the hillside above the Springdale golf course.

At this time Wright made a penetrating remark: "Keep your eye on the little gas station. This is the advance agent of decentralization; a new integration made by the advent of the automobile." Wright had his own ideas for a gas station, and it, too, was planted like a seed to appear as a full growth some years later. But more important was the trend of Wright's thinking; his agrarian cast of thought now hardened to a distrust of metropolitan concentration that led him to theorize that cities as they now exist could be altogether dispensed with.

"Broadacre City"—that was the conception that Wright built up in his mind, so titled as to indicate that what he had conceived was a city spread and flattened out so that each householder had the impression he was living in broad lands. Indeed, each man would have an acre on which he would raise most of his family's food. Here and there would be shopping centers, and for those who preferred them, tall apartment buildings. He finally was able to rationalize his feeling about tall buildings by saying, "The skyscraper is no longer sane unless it is in free green space. In the country it may stand beautiful for its own sake." The Swiss painter and architect Charles-Édouard Jeanneret, better known by his pseudonym Le Corbusier, was not ahead of Wright in this idea. Le Corbusier's Unité d'Habitation de Grandeur Conforme on the Boulevard Michelet in Marseilles was not opened until 1953, at which time Le Corbusier argued that similar tall concrete apartment houses should be built in open country, dominating the neighboring villages, and allowing as many as 2000 inmates to look out over green fields. For some reason, Le Corbusier attaches great importance to the fact that all users of his Unité d'Habitation come and go through a single entrance. Twelve years younger than Wright, Le Corbusier worked on theories of housing for many years. At the time he was conceiving the Broadacre City thesis, Wright thought of Le Corbusier and the men around him as useful and valuable in at least one way—they were enemies of ornament. But a slavish worship of straight line and flat plane, Wright warned, might lead to mechanism, a result as much to be feared and shunned as that of the old dishonest ornamented buildings.

The lean year of 1930 saw Wright scoring a number of successes in ways that emphasized his stature and importance while putting little or nothing in his pocket. Having lectured with great success side by side with Barry Byrne before the Chicago chapter of the American Institute of Architects, he was invited to exhibit his work at the Chicago Art Institute, and showed among other things the models of the Richard Lloyd-Jones house, the ill-fated St. Mark's tower, and a little contilevered filling station. At the conclusion of the show, people overflowed the Institute's Fullerton Hall to hear Wright talk. He had by now perfected his platform style—it was easy and informal, and his voice had its accustomed Welsh music; when he rose to heights, he could sound like a fine, old-fashioned preacher, and in the conversational passages, he gave the impression of being a kindly uncle, an experienced man quite willing to give advice from a store of worldly wisdom. There were many practicing architects in the tightly-packed audience; observers were also interested to see that the crowd included a large number of young people. This was significant—with his energy, his indestructible optimism, and his belief that the future might hold more of value than the past, Wright himself was young, and would always be so. "There must be no conflict between architecture and nature," he said to his young hearers. "A building should conform to the contour of its surroundings."

The lofty halls of the Art Institute were appropriate surroundings for Wright, as he walked about with his straight back and commanding air. It was in one of these halls, while he was inspecting a model, that he heard a woman's voice say, "Why, Frank—how are you?" He

turned and saw a tall, slender and handsome lady coming
toward him with outstretched hand. For a moment he did
not place her, and then he knew it was Catherine. Wright
was aware that Catherine had married a man named Ben
E. Page, for it happened that Page was one of his admirers,
and the secretary of the Illinois Taliesin corporation; but
he had not seen Catherine for fifteen years. Now she
showed a streak of gray in her hair, and was poised and
self-possessed in stopping for a brief and friendly chat.
Catherine had been reading good things about Wright
in the papers, and she hoped that all was well with him; he
expressed similar sentiments, and they parted. Wright
would never see her again; nor could he ever fully realize
what Catherine had gone through in a former time so that
she was able to dismiss him so lightly with a moment of im-
personal social talk. Her friends knew that in the years
immediately following Wright's departure from Oak Park,
Catherine would sometimes see Wright walking down the
aisle at Orchestra Hall concerts, and tremble like a girl.

As though a ghost had been disturbed by this chance
meeting, one final evidence of Miriam Noel Wright's emotional tragedy arose to menace the security of Taliesin. In
that same year Morris Fromkin of Milwaukee came forward
—from the woodwork, some of Wright's friends thought—
with an old claim to press. Fromkin alleged that he had
represented Miriam in her last legal action against Wright.
On his testimony, a Milwaukee court awarded a judgment of $7,018.70 and summoned Wright to appear and
pay up in thirty days. This appearance coincided with
a lecture date, which was also notable in furnishing an example of how Wright provided entertainment by expressing
disrespect for things that were taken for granted by ordinary people—in this case, a new Milwaukee courthouse in

the official, pillared style. When a reporter asked for his opinion of it, Wright replied, "I think this building is neither a gentleman nor a scholar. These millions of tons of stone will set back the cause of architecture in Milwaukee from fifty to a hundred years." This set off a considerable uproar, for the average Milwaukeean liked the new courthouse very well, and thought it grand and impressive, as a seat of justice should be. A less palatable example of the workings of justice now came when a Federal catchpoll sprang from behind a pillar at Wright's hotel and placed him under arrest. The warrant had been sworn out by Fromkin, who said he was afraid Wright would not appear at the appointed time. The officer took Wright before a United States Commissioner, who was moved to release him on his pledge that he would be present at nine o'clock the following morning. Wright seemed hardened to this sort of thing, remarking to Fromkin, "Let's cut out this nonsense about my running away, and let me get about my business."

Next day, Fromkin took the role of investigating prosecutor, asking Wright how it was that he looked so prosperous.

"I've been wearing this suit for the last four years," Wright replied, "It looks pretty good, eh?" But Fromkin insisted on being told how Wright lived. Wright answered that he gave his services for nothing to the corporation, which kept him going. He explained that the corporation had earned nothing during the past year, though a number of important projects had been started. "Until I have paid off the preferred stock I own nothing," Wright said. "Whenever I need money for food, clothing, or shelter, the corporation pays it."

"You own Taliesin, don't you?" Fromkin asked.

"No, I don't. Taliesin is owned by Ben E. Page, who is secretary of the corporation, and by a man in Buffalo."

"But you have your genius, Mr. Wright," said Fromkin, with a smirk.

"Well, they call it that."

"And those talents are bartered away to this corporation for fifteen years!" cried Fromkin.

"I am to donate all my talents to the corporation," Wright said patiently. "It is to the stockholders' interests to keep me working, to keep my shop open."

"Will you be paid for your lecture here in Milwaukee, at the Layton Art Gallery?"

"I don't know. I hope so."

Thus it went until the Commissioner stirred himself into ascertaining a few facts. It turned out that Wright had deposited $15,000 in a Madison bank to meet the payment that Fromkin claimed. In view of this, it could not be determined why the money in question had not been paid. Twitching on the official woolsack, the Commissioner grew tired of the proceedings, and ruled that Wright obviously could not meet this demand; he therefore threw the case, and Fromkin, out of his court. One wonders what it all amounted to, and can only conclude that it served as another demonstration of how a distinguished and gifted man, in certain circumstances, could be humiliated and annoyed.

After undergoing such an experience, Wright might well have taken stock of the projects he had mentioned before the Commissioner; one of them had seemed especially promising. It was for a newspaper plant in Madison, and featured an interesting treatment of the concrete columns that supported the ceilings of the big pressroom. Those were to be cast with a hollow core, and to spread out at the ceiling like giant water lily pads. The plant was not built and again a valuable idea went into the capacious file that was Wright's architectural mind. Like a long-lived composer, he was never to waste a theme. But the crowds of young and progressive people who came to hear Wright speak were there because of his past performance rather than for the schemes that thronged in his head. The auditors turned out in such numbers now that his daughter Catherine, whose family nickname was Taffy, tried in vain to get through a crowd of admirers to speak to her father after a lecture he delivered at the New School of Social Research in New York City. "Time's up now, I really must go to catch my train," said Wright, and he left without noticing Taffy in the back row. There was talk, too, of a gleaming tower of glass for the Chicago Century of Progress Exposition; again Wright was associated with Charles Morgan in the announcement. And that was as far as the project went, for Wright was not asked to join the Exposition's committee on design. He showed what he might have had to offer in a brief talk at a meeting that was called at Town Hall in New York to protest against his exclusion from the Chicago Fair. Alexander Woollcott presided, and Lewis Mumford, who had succeeded Montgomery Schuyler as America's most penetrating critic of architecture, made the principal speech, in which he stated the case in his usual well-informed and understanding way. Then Wright found himself on his feet, and he decided, as a form of constructive criticism, to sketch spontaneously three schemes for the fair's design—to work them up, so to speak, in the presence of the audience, as a composer might improvise variations at the piano.

First, Wright suggested, since this was the age of the skyscraper, why not have a tall building utterly beyond anything yet conceived, so vast that the Empire State Building might stand free as an incidental structure in its interior court space.[2] Have mechanized parking space in great tiers from which the central tower would rise. Put an enormous auditorium at the base, and in the rising stories have garden restaurants behind walls of translucent plastic from which the view across the prairies and the lake might extend in clear weather for hundreds of miles. At night, shoot light against this tower, and surround it by great fountains, pumped from the lake to prodigious heights, and irradiated with light. By day, when the clouds themselves did not gather around the summit of the tower, have colored ribbons of smoke laid across it by aeroplanes.

"This, my friends, would be a permanent landmark on the Chicago lake front," said Wright, "and beautiful as the Eiffel Tower never was." He added that the Eiffel Tower would reach only well below the middle of the structure he had in mind; and as a final thought, that after the fair was over, the city government might move into the building and use it as permanent headquarters. But perhaps a tower wasn't wanted; and so Wright went on to another possibility.

This was the age of steel in tension, after all, and one of its marvels was the Roeblings' Brooklyn Bridge. So why not make the fair in the form of an immensely long bridge? Build huge pylons 500 feet apart on the lake front, and link them with canopies anchored in steel cables—"an architectural canopy more beautiful and more vast than any ever seen." Underneath, moving walkways would carry the spectators through the various shows; overhead, the restaurants, bandstands, and pleasure domes would rise between

---

[2] James Bogardus, an American pioneer in iron-framed buildings, predicted in the 1840's that they might attain a height of ten miles.

the pylons. And the pylons might remain as lighting features of the lake front parks.

The third scheme that Wright sketched out suggested the use of a piece of engineering already in existence, the part of the Chicago harbor that was enclosed against the turbulence of the lake. This version of the fair was to be floated on pontoons that would be connected by steel chains so that all would be joined, and yet might rise and fall in gentle undulation as the water moved beneath. All this was to be lit by translucent colored glass that would make the night magical with dreamlike moving patterns, while banners would float over the festive scene by day. As with the tower suggestion, Wright saw fountains projected to great heights and in enormous quantity, as a becoming salute by the lakeside city to its inland sea.

At the close of the fair, Wright proposed, certain units of this project might be detached from the general mass and towed to the various park lagoons, there to be used as restaurants or places of recreation. Of course, Wright said, he could hear designers of the fair saying that they had thought of these ideas, and they were impractical. Nevertheless, these were the things that had come to his mind. Actually the only question to be answered if Wright had been empowered to put one of these ideas in practice would have been that of cost. But Wright was not to be troubled by any practical problems of the fair. The organizers said "he had never been much of a team man." And had not Walter Gropius, the eminent German designer of the Fagus shoe-last works, and founder of the Staatliches Bauhaus (State School of Architecture) announced that architecture is a collective art? He had indeed, and the rise in the profession of the umbrella practice—one firm including engineers, landscapists, and other specialists as well as architects—underlined the point. The discouragements began to alter Wright's appearance—Richard Neutra had the opinion that "Wright appeared older and more worn in his late fifties than in his late eighties."

In considering men's lives, the Spanish philosopher Ortega y Gasset wrote: "Every life is, more or less, a ruin among whose debris we have to discover what the person ought to have been. The matter of the greatest interest is not the man's struggle with the world, but his struggle with his vocation. How does he behave when faced with his inexorable vocation? Does he subscribe to it basically; or, on the contrary, is he a deserter from it, does he fill his existence with substitutes for what would have been his authentic life? Perhaps the most tragic thing about the human situation is that a man may try to supplant himself, that is, to falsify his life."

Turning from his vital vocation was the one tragedy that would never overtake Frank Lloyd Wright. And in 1932, he decided that if he was no longer to advance his calling by serving clients, he would do it by training students. He had always had young associates around him; why not set up as educator on a systematic plan? Accordingly, in August 1932, Wright announced the Taliesin Fellowship, in which acceptable trainees would work as apprentices in learning *"essential architecture"* against a background of "Philosophy, Sculpture, Painting, Music and the Industrial Crafts." Wright's prospectus was headed:

AN EXTENSION OF THE WORK IN
ARCHITECTURE AT TALIESIN TO INCLUDE
APPRENTICES IN RESIDENCE

The announcement went on to say that more than one hundred young workers in architecture had already come to Taliesin at various times from all parts of the world. Now the reception and employment of such persons would be systematized; they would be accepted as trainees, each of whom would undergo "a direct work-experience." To make sure that prospective applicants understood what would be required of them, Wright emphasized that "*Apprenticeship* not *Scholarship* is to be the actual condition and should be the attitude of mind of the Fellowship." A simple home life would underlie the daily round of work and study, and the beautiful region itself would be a "never-failing source of inspiration and recreation for all concerned." Studios and galleries for the collateral work in philosophy, painting, drama and rhythm were already built or under construction; shops were planned for practical use in molding or casting, woodworking, and typography—what Wright described was to be a synthesis of life, philosophy, art, and craftsmanship. The connection with nature would be direct, for the farm and garden were to be "so managed to employ the help of the apprenticeship that a substantial portion of the living of members may come from their own labor on the ground, thus enabling apprentice fees to remain as low as possible."

At first glance this might look as though Wright were offering nothing more than a chance to pay for the privilege of being put to hard labor; but neither he nor the many persons who came to him under these conditions saw it that way. What he was offering was a chance to be associated with Frank Lloyd Wright; and with superb assurance, he made it plain that he and not the apprentice must be satisfied: "The right to reject any applicant at any time is reserved—either before or after being formally received into the Fellowship. The Fellowship, however, is not on trial. The Apprentice is. A personal testimonial, only, will

be given to each worker at the end of his or her apprenticeship."

When he first thought of the organized Fellowship,
Wright reckoned on a force of seventy student apprentices
at Taliesin. But when he took a realistic view of the housing
on the estate, he reduced the number of available appointments to twenty-three. Every place was filled when the
Taliesin Fellowship started its first year on October 1, 1932.
Wright had been recognized as a great architect and a remarkable man for more years than most of these young
people had lived; and that, of course, was why they were
there.

A powerful influence on Wright was the fact that the
Taliesin farm and grounds had been used for educational
purposes before. The Hillside School, conducted by his
aunts, had been a remarkably fine place; and Wright never
forgot how the aunts often would suspend classes and lead
the pupils out to see some unusual bird of passage, or the
blooming of a tree or flower, or a newly dropped calf or
foal. He also knew that one reason for their eventual bankruptcy was their leniency in the matter of fees; they were
especially likely to keep orphans or children from broken
homes, even when payments became irregular or stopped
altogether. Now the sisters had died, but Wright remembered their generosity. He set the annual fee expected from
an apprentice at $650, and next year raised it to $1100; but
he reduced this, or remitted it altogether, when he saw
indigence handicapping talent. Young people from all
over the world immediately began to apply for permission to come and live at Taliesin, and some 1500 of them
have entered the Fellowship since its founding. They stayed
for periods varying from two hours to twenty years. In
a typical year Taliesin had residents from Hawaii, China,

Canada, Egypt, Greece, India, Italy, Holland, Japan, Mexico, and Venezuela, as well as from the United States.

The buildings of Hillside School were another heritage from the aunts, and a most welcome one, as they would serve Wright's purpose admirably. However, they were in ruinous condition at the time Wright launched the Fellowship. First comers to his academy, therefore, would start their courses of instruction by helping in the repair of these houses; it was obvious that a man's knowledge of building would be deepened by the practical work of sawing timber and laying stone. So far as the farm chores were concerned, there was precedent reaching back to the Transcendentalist communities of the early nineteenth century; a hundred years before, for example, the Oneida Community had ruled that "each student pay part of his expenses by working on the school farm." It was pointed out that this not only reduced financial burdens, but protected the health of the student, which might be endangered by long hours at his books without wholesome exercise in the open air.

Wholesome exercise in plenty awaited the Taliesin apprentices, and left them so tired they did not mind the fading of the electric lights at half-past eight each evening. Wright not only rebuilt the Hillside School, but was continually altering and adding to the main house. The sound of builders at work was soothing to his ears, and apprentices noticed that he could take his afternoon nap in perfect composure with saws and hammers going all around him, but any cessation of the noise would wake him like an alarm clock.

The share-the-work feature of Fellowship life was soon extended to include all domestic services for Mr. and Mrs. Wright. This followed a suggestion by Olgivanna, who pointed out that "servants were vulgar, and had no place at

Taliesin." As a result, the apprentices learned to set tables, serve dinners, and get up at 2 A.M. to start fires in the kitchen. They were encouraged to compete in pleasing the master with flower arrangements for their lunch table, which stood on a balcony overlooking the general mess hall at Hillside. Mr. and Mrs. Wright dined up the hill at Taliesin, usually with several apprentices as guests, for the domestic tasks rotated. It was thus possible for Fellowship members to meet Wright's visitors from the outside world, as well as wait on them, the work schedule determining which role the apprentice would play. In this connection a difficulty arose when a young Italian prince was serving a turn as butler, and one of his countrymen came to dine. The apprentice peered out at the caller and refused to go on. He explained, "It wouldn't be right for me to wait on that fellow—he's only a marquis."

The nobleman was not so disgruntled as a student who had come from Thailand, and was known as the old school Thai. After six weeks of chopping trees and sawing green timber, he inquired, "When do we start on organic architecture?" He was told, "You've been absorbing it ever since you got here." The Thai immediately went to his room, packed his bag, and left Taliesin. This was one case of a student's rejecting the basic Taliesin idea. But in general Wright sold his doctrine of adding tired to tired not only to the apprentices, but to the wives of those who were married. He said to a young woman who arrived with her Paris-trained husband during the first hard winter of the Fellowship, "My dear, I'll make an architect's wife of you —but it won't be easy, you'll have to work as you've never worked before."

"But Mr. Wright, I have a little baby," said the girl.

"Get someone to take care of the baby," said Wright.

Whether or not he meant the suggestion seriously, the young mother hired a village woman to look after the child, and devoted her own time to working for Frank Lloyd Wright.

Apprentices who lived in the Fellowship through the winters of its early life speak of the period as Revolutionary War veterans might recall Valley Forge, or marines a boot camp. Some remember eating an unusual number of boiled turnips, while others can only recollect how the generator would freeze, and fail to function even through the short period before the lights officially went out. During one such emergency an apprentice said he had read somewhere that heat was stored in compost heaps, haystacks and dunghills, and he suggested insulating the generator with manure. The book proved to be correct, and this measure prevented freezing through an especially trying cold spell.

"Don't tell Mr. Wright how it was done," said the resourceful apprentice. "He'll claim he invented it."

But whatever claims Wright might have made about the generator, every apprentice understood how strongly the master was rooted into the house and land. When Taliesin stopped growing, Wright said, "The pencil will fall from these fingers, and I'll be ready for the box." He had always hated boxes, and now he identified them with death. What Wright was getting at and hoping to bring alive in the minds of the apprentices was a dedication to unity in life and work. He would expound this philosophy at any odd moment, as well as in the discussions that traditionally followed Sunday morning breakfast. His message was that an architect must be equally strong in body and character, and that he had to know life by both studying and living it. Wright said it took a long time to develop his kind of architect. On one occasion he remarked that it might take as long as ten years for a young man to grow in this sort of rigorous training until he stood above the average in the profession. At other times, when apprentices asked if they were making progress, he would answer, "If you weren't making progress, you wouldn't be here. You can't pull yourself up by the roots to see if you're growing."

Nature was the thing; and Wright seized every opportunity to make this ethical and esthetic point. An example of how he went about this was given when Wright delivered an extemporaneous talk with a tray of sea shells as illustration. "Speaking of human housing," he said, "here is a good lesson you young architects may now get." He exhibited the shells as the housing of a lower order of life, but "a housing with exactly what we lack: inspired form." Each shell was different, and this "multitudinous expression indicates what design can mean." The declared enemy of sterile uniformity, Wright said with emphasis, "There is no reason why our buildings and the housing of human beings, which we so stupidly perpetrate all alike as two peas in a pod, shouldn't be quite as fertile in imaginative resource as these little sea shells. Why do we ever take any one formula, carry it out to a dead end, and execute it as though that were all? Here in this collection of little houses is one of the best lessons you could possibly find. Study them." After commenting on the variations appearing in the shells, Wright went on that here was humble innate evidence of the genius of nature in low forms of life. It followed that if "we go into the human phases of what we call our divinity and consider the inherent element at work in us, as in all of life, you may find the same idea. Therein lies the value of these little things to us, if we study them as artists should. Here, in nature, is an architect's 'school.' "

As the apprentices intently followed Wright's voice, and watched his strong fingers moving over the smooth helical

forms, he drove home his conclusion: "Once you understand the principle upon which this differentiation depends,
you will astonish your kind by your own prolific capacity.
To always turn out a different design from the one you did
before will become inevitable. The secret of that variety is
inherent in nature. She is jealous of it! If an architect does
not have that secret, he will not be a great artist. He is miss-
ing essential quality. The key to creation is not in him."

It would be hard to improve on this as an inspirational talk
for young artists in any medium. But whether that prolific
capacity that Wright possessed could be taught was a question that Wright did not attempt to answer. The paradox
of the Taliesin Fellowship was never resolved; on the whole
the apprentices felt that they were being educated; and
without doubt they *were* being educated, by listening to
Wright, by hearing music, by working on projects, and
by doing the farm chores. They also learned, on occasion,
from Olgivanna, who perhaps represented Philosophy in
the Fellowship curriculum as it was first planned. Olgivanna
wrote a highly commendable book on achieving mental and
spiritual balance called *The Struggle Within*, and could
lead discussions on related subjects when the occasion
seemed to warrant it. But like her husband's, Olgivanna's
greatest contribution to the apprentices may have been as
an example of high human competence; this lady worked
early and late as house-mother, dean of women, catering
manager, and hostess to a stream of visitors both humble
and great. And it may be that Wright was never quite comfortable in the role of instructor. In later years, he stated
it flatly: "I'm no teacher. Never wanted to teach, and don't
believe in teaching an art. A science, yes; business, of
course; but an art cannot be taught. You can only inculcate
it. You can be an exemplar. You may be able to create an

atmosphere in which it can grow. But I suppose I being an exemplar would be called a teacher in spite of myself. So go ahead, call me a teacher."

Since the head of the Fellowship was a teacher in spite of himself, an exact definition of the Taliesin learning process is probably forever out of reach. But Wright had a definite idea of the daily routine, and in the later 1930's, after the Fellowship had survived its hard early years, he told an audience in England that "a boy may be in the kitchen one day, and the next day driving a tractor, and the next day laying stone, but nearly every day he spends some time in the drafting room making plans. Leadership rotates from fortnight to fortnight so all have a turn at leading others. We have as little organization as possible—too little, I suppose. We are trying to develop initiative in these young people—that special interest in his work—getting a feeling of the stone and wood, into his hands on his way to his mind." Then Wright made a statement that was to be of considerable interest when the question of making a legal definition of the Fellowship arose. "Don't get the idea that Taliesin is a school, or a community," he said. "It happens to be our home, and where we work, and these young people are my comrade apprentices—no scholars. They come to help, and if they can learn—well, we are very happy."

In the early days of the Fellowship, Wright needed local and transient labor, as well as that of the apprentices, to keep Taliesin growing. The financial Indian clubs were still flying into the air, and now and then Wright missed one as it descended. He was able for a time to hire men for board and lodging, plus $35 a month in cash, and Taliesin scrip for the balance at $4 a day. This scheme served well enough until the appearance of the Works Progress Administration, when the labor force understandably went to Uncle Sam, not nearly so exacting a boss as Frank Lloyd Wright. The question lingers as to whether Wright settled accounts to the satisfaction of everyone around Spring Green. Weighing his eccentricities against natural human malice, and considering the conflicts of interest that are the inevitable accompaniment of all relations between employees and employers, one must withhold judgment.

As late as 1951, the Dodgeville *Chronicle* prefaced a long article about Taliesin and Wright's career with a rather tart remark. "Some citizens prefer to ignore Mr. Wright," the paper said, "because of his disregard of the usual codes governing financial obligations and marriage." However, the article itself was highly favorable, and the same issue of the paper carried an advertisement by a farm machinery dealer stating that it was a pleasure to do business with the people at Taliesin. Long after the days when money was short, some of the senior drinkers in Spring Green's six barrooms limit themselves to saying, "Old Frank—he *finally* paid everybody off." Others avoid the subject; and there are admirers of Wright, among the Taliesin alumni, who merely remark that new money always carried an immediate suggestion of new possibilities to him, so that he found it hard to apply funds to matters past and gone. "Sometimes new income was just too fascinatingly available to Mr. Wright," is the way one of these people put it.

The well-known rapidity with which Wright could spend money when he had it caused his wife to make a heartfelt remark on one occasion, when he was talking with a group of apprentices about some great plan for the future. One million dollars, Wright estimated, would be his fee. "Oh, Frank!" cried Olgivanna. "I couldn't *bear* to be in debt for a million dollars!"

Wright's most regrettable dispute over money occurred

in early Fellowship days when a man named C. R. Sechrest
said that Wright owed him $282 and refused to pay. Coming
up behind Wright on a Madison street, he knocked the
architect down and kicked him in the face, breaking his
nose. Wiry and game at sixty-three, Wright got up and
wrestled his man into the gutter, covered him with blood
from the broken nose, and seemed to have the upper hand
when bystanders stopped the fight. That night several apprentices went to Sechrest's house and struck him with a
whip, or so he complained next day in swearing warrants
against them. Sechrest said he escaped injury only by standing off the Taliesin party with a butcher knife. The judge
fined the apprentices from $50 to $100, and postponed hearing on Wright's countercharges of assault with intent to
maim.

Next week, a letter came to Taliesin, signed by "The
Vigilantes" and demanding a payment of $5282 on the threat
of cutting Wright's fingers off. The source of this letter, and
the reason for the precise amount demanded, were impene-
trable mysteries. Next month, the charges against Sechrest
were dismissed.

This was the most violent attack made on Wright by a
representative of the community in general; but even his
Lloyd-Jones kinsmen could turn raised eyebrows in his
direction when they saw cause. Family disapproval was
shown, for example, on the day a boy and girl of the Fellowship were married in the Lloyd-Jones chapel. The charming little shingle structure, designed by Lyman Silsbee,
with the ceiling by Wright himself, was filled with fresh
flowers and green boughs. All went well until the apprentices carried the organ into the churchyard and started a
square dance. Hands were clapping and bright skirts flying,
when a delegation of Lloyd-Joneses rushed up and dispersed

the dancers. Wright was sorry the pleasant day ended in anger, but not in the least surprised; though public opinion in the country at large was slowly swinging his way, he knew but too well that there are some prejudices never to be overcome by a hero in his own home town. It was part of the price he paid to settle down as a celebrity amid the fields and villages that had known him as a boy.

Though he felt currents of sympathy stirring, Wright had misunderstandings to contend with beyond the boundaries of Spring Green. A most distressing controversy, for example, arose in 1931 when a California exhibition of work by Wright, Neutra, Schindler, and others was arranged. The matter progressed smoothly until Wright saw the catalogue, and was displeased at its statement that Schindler had been in charge of his Los Angeles office while Wright was in Japan. Wright felt that this gave Schindler undeserved prominence and credit, and became so incensed that he demanded his work be taken out of the exhibition. He also wrote Schindler a letter in which he allowed himself to say that the Austrian architect had been a nonentity whom Wright had befriended, and to cast aspersions on his conduct in regard to the military draft. Schindler's reply showed how keenly he was hurt. He wrote, "The structural features which hold the Imperial Hotel together were incorporated only after overcoming your strenuous resistance." He said that after Wright went to Tokyo, he drew up seven jobs without Wright's help. "You were informed of all this work by letters and blueprints I sent to Japan," the outraged Schindler continued. "You accepted it and paid for it (as little as you could). You officially identified yourself with it by including my scheme and drawing of Mr. Hardy's workingman's colony unretouched in your personal exhibit as your own." Wright never saw Schindler again.

Another thing that displeased Wright during these years was the manner of his inclusion in a general exhibition of American design, art, and architecture by the Museum of Modern Art. It was all very well to be represented here, but what distressed Wright was the way that he felt the Museum was presenting him as an influence from the past. Wright liked to think that big achievements still lay ahead of him, and in this, as it turned out, he was entirely correct. Being bracketed with Richardson and Sullivan was flattering, to be sure; but being buried beside them was entirely unwelcome. Wright was somewhat soothed when he found that he could raise the money from patrons to finance the building of a large model of Broadacre City. This landscape of houses, shops, and apartment buildings was destined to visit many American cities, and at last, turned on edge, to become a strikingly effective wall decoration in a room at Taliesin.

What did the Taliesin Fellowship really do for its members? One can hardly escape the conclusion that its influence has been one of great good in many lives and careers; and yet one is hard put to it for an answer to those who say it was an essentially unreal atmosphere. Still, the atmosphere of any retired institution might be called unreal, if reality is to be the irritating turmoil of ordinary life. The question has been raised, too, if the Fellowship was the sort of thing that Wright himself would have been attracted to, had such an opportunity been suggested when he was a young man. Probably the youth who gloried in being Chicago's highest-paid draftsman would have hooted at the suggestion that he himself should put down money to be a member of a working group. Wright's tuition charge was certainly a reasonable one, even adding in the value of the unskilled labor furnished by the apprentices, when one reflects that it included food and lodging for a year; that he grew rich from the fees of students, who also largely contributed to work that he sold for his own profit, is simply not true. The fact is that Wright kept up a professional architectural organization at all times, paying salaries— though in the lean years they were meagre—to the associates who rose from the ranks of the senior apprentices, or came to him with professional credentials from outside.

It seems clear that to those who found the Fellowship worth while, there was a highly satisfactory emotional content in the life of Taliesin, and the heart of it was love and respect for Frank Lloyd Wright. The moral and physical benefits of hard work, and sharing the chores of the establishment, cannot be questioned. Again, it has been pointed out that this enabled Wright to live like a potentate with a staff of attendants, when he was actually quite a poor man and perhaps technically bankrupt. This too is beside the mark. Though the members of the Fellowship saw a movie on Saturday night, sitting in a jewel-like little theater after it was built in the middle thirties, they provided the rest of their entertainment by producing their own music, or composing, rehearsing, and presenting their own dance recitals. And they might arrange the tables with flowers and brightly colored cloths, but the food for both master and apprentices was farm fare, and they were more likely to drink homemade wine than cocktails or expensive liquors. (A known teetotaller was appointed keeper of the wine cellar.)

Some notion of the soundness of Wright's essential Taliesin idea is indicated by the cry that goes up continually from pulpits and in the press for home-centered amusements other than television, and for some substitute in the lives of modern young people for the household responsibilities and chores of former days. One cannot fault Wright for his

conception of Fellowship life as that of an old-fashioned
American family. He had something there, with or without
the teaching of architecture and the building arts. The question was, how long should adults stay in such an atmosphere? We have seen that Wright mentioned ten years as
none too long a time to season a man who wanted to take
a serious place in the profession. This matter of when to
leave was delicate; it was known that Wright especially re-
gretted the departure of a good musician or a good carpenter. It was also known that Wright talked such things
over with Mrs. Wright; this would sometimes be reported
by those who waited on the family dinner table, which
seems to give a slightly below-stairs flavor to the household
arrangements that is unfair both to the Wrights and the
members of the Fellowship. But it is true that when an
apprentice left Taliesin and went out into the world, an
emotional tie was severed, sometimes not without pain.
Were those who came to Wright a little more serious-
minded, a little more intense in their reactions than the
average run of young people at work or in college? Probably so; they were looked on as a breed apart by the native
populations in southern Wisconsin and later in Arizona, at
the winter Taliesin, which we shall describe in its place.
Consider the case of a young man at a western university
who finds something amiss with the architecture the professors are trying to teach. He cannot define his objections,
and can only say, this isn't it. Then, in the library, he comes
upon books and pamphlets by Frank Lloyd Wright. This
is it—and so completely, that within a few days he leaves
for Taliesin, though he is almost penniless, and half the
width of the continent lies between him and Spring Green.
He arrives broke and hungry on Wright's birthday: "Mr.
Wright, you've got to take me!" After a conversation,

Wright admits the penniless young man; he stays for seven years, then goes out to a useful career; and there is about him something of a man who has been a Templar, or a Knight of the Hospital of St. John.

When such a member of the Fellowship left Taliesin, he must have left something of himself behind. What he took with him, as we have seen, defies analysis. On the question of planting talent and taste, Wright was in the position of Mr. Valiant-for-truth, who remarked before passing through the river that he left his courage and skill "to him that can get it." One way of arranging a departure from Taliesin that also carried an accolade was to send out a seasoned apprentice as the overseer of a large building commission; but this method of launching a young man's independent career had to wait until the time came when there were commissions to be looked after. In the first years, those who left Taliesin went out on their own.

Sometimes those who had worked at Taliesin as members of the Fellowship tried to put their experiences into words. A girl who found the life to her liking said that it had been like living with wealthy parents who provided the finer things of life, including philosophy, interior decoration, literature, and travel. All this was available, plus practical work in masonry, drafting, wiring, and plumbing—a solid background indeed, whether for an architect or housewife. A successful Chicago architect looked back on Taliesin during its rough years as a better professional education than what he had been exposed to at Princeton and the Beaux Arts in Paris. He also said that Taliesin Fellowship men were better hiring prospects for his office than others: "they understood building, and have a faith in the creation of a sound indigenous architecture for the United States." Another practicing architect maintained he had sorted out his ideas while pitching hay, pulling weeds, or laying up stone —such activities were of equal value with his work under Wright's eye in the drafting room. "Architecture was a lost art in the nineteenth century until Mr. Wright came along," said another. This man added that Taliesin had developed beyond a mere studio into a laboratory where new materials were tested and new methods worked out; not only the apprentices and associates, but the visitors to Taliesin had a part to play, as this man saw it: important people from all over the world came there and saw what was going on, then returned to their own communities where they influenced the awarding of large architectural contracts. Looking forward to his own practice, this apprentice decided that the great developments in architecture would come from the jobs handed out by big business and the government. Whether he debated this point with Frank Lloyd Wright, he did not say; for Wright always seemed much happier when working for a single client rather than a committee, and his detestation of bureaucrats was instinctive and intense.

A western architect who was trained at Taliesin said that he had never seen anything to equal the way Wright could take the spiritual and philosophical implications of an abstract discussion and translate them into reality through the medium of the hammer and saw. "Mr. Wright never thought of architecture as a profit-making business," said this former apprentice, and added that no profit ever accrued from the Fellowship, as the entire amount collected from apprentices went out again for food and shelter. Summing up what most of those in the Fellowship felt, a student who came from Switzerland stated that he had studied with eminent architects in Europe, but that none of them furnished the inspiration that came from Frank Lloyd Wright. He added, "This great master is the best known ambassador of American thought in the whole world." The sentiments were heartily endorsed by a Hindoo, who saw Wright as a prophet who had much in common with Buddha, Lao Tse, Tagore, and Ghandi, as well as Lincoln, Whitman, Emerson, and Thoreau.

What was Wright's deepest feeling about Taliesin and the Fellowship? Undoubtedly the receiving of apprentices kept him going and in the position of a laird, like Scott at Abbotsford, during the period when work was scarce and money almost impossible to come by. It is true that few architects prospered in the two or three years following the panic of 1929, and many who came from the schools to enter the profession had to find other work. But it is also true that few architects, or Americans in any line of business, were able to enlarge their houses and land estates through the bad years, as Wright was able to, and this was due to the presence of the Taliesin Fellows.

Continually he astonished the more perceptive among the disciples by the way he could detach his mind from ordinary troubles, freeing it to explain his large basic ideas of art and life—ideas that were grand for all that they lacked crisp or precise definition—his version of truth, against the world. These young people saw something indestructible in the master, as though he were a rock that would remain after the tide ran out; and their faith was justified when at long last, the tide began to turn. Gradually at first, but perceptibly, Wright's practice began to revive, and there slowly came in sight a final period of numerous clients, large commissions, countless official honors, and a general renown that was unprecedented even for Frank Lloyd Wright.

31. Residence of Lowell Walter, Quasqueton, Iowa, 1949

32. Boat House for Lowell Walter, Quasqueton, Iowa, 1949

33. First Unitarian Meeting House, Madison, Wisconsin, 1951

34. Interior, First Unitarian Meeting House, Madison, Wisconsin, 1951

35. Residence of Mrs. Clinton Walker, Carmel, California, 1952

36. Dining Alcove, Residence of Mrs. Clinton Walker,
Carmel, California, 1952

37. H. C. Price Tower, Bartlesville, Oklahoma, 1953-56

38. Administration Building, Florida Southern College,
Lakeland, Florida, 1948

39. Pfeiffer Chapel, Florida Southern College, Lakeland, Florida, 1940

40. Roux Library, Florida Southern College, Lakeland, Florida, 1942

41. Interior, Administration Building, S. C. Johnson & Son, Racine, Wisconsin, 1936-39

42. Research Tower, S. C. Johnson & Son, Racine, Wisconsin, 1951

43. Congregation Beth Sholom, Elkins Park, Pennsylvania, 1959

44. Interior, Congregation Beth Sholom, Elkins Park, Pennsylvania, 1959

Chapter Seven

THE OLD GREAT MAN

THE EXACT POINT at which Wright's luck began to turn cannot be pinned down, but it may well have been when a young man named Edgar Kaufmann, Jr., walked down the hill from Taliesin to the Hillside buildings as a newly accepted member of the Fellowship. This young man was later to become an authority on art and architecture and would edit books on Wright's work. But when he entered the Fellowship, Edgar Kaufmann knew that its director's career was practically halted, so far as serving clients was concerned. The force that Kaufmann brought to bear on this inertia was the suggestion to his father, a Pittsburgh department store owner, that Wright should design his weekend retreat at Bear Run, Pennsylvania.

The result was Falling Water, one of the most famous modern houses in the world. Completed in 1936, the house was a natural continuation of the site, with concrete porches cantilevered over the mountain stream from which the estate takes its name. The Kaufmann house was frankly a luxury item, as might be expected when the given problem was to design a country lodge for a wealthy merchant. With its dramatic handling of site and materials, it also gave a direct demonstration of how a fine architect benefits from a client of taste and imagination; houses like Falling Water are seldom built for committees or institutions. At about the time that Falling Water was finished, Alexander Woollcott wrote that if he were so rationed in the use of the word "genius" that he might apply it to only one man, he would be compelled to reserve it for Frank Lloyd Wright. The same remark would have fitted the Kaufmann house and the word "masterpiece."

Then came one of the most important commissions of Wright's career, the administration building for S. C. Johnson and Son, makers of wax products in Racine, Wisconsin. Herbert F. Johnson, head of the company founded by his grandfather, put aside plans by another architect after talking to Wright. When Johnson's letter of commission arrived at Taliesin, along with a $1000 advance to bind the bargain, the apprentices working in the fields were startled to see the master lean out of his study window, flourishing a check.

"It's all right, boys," cried Wright, "we got the job!"

The Johnson Adminstration Building, one of the nation's notable sights, was completed by 1939. Along the way, the Johnson people and the citizens of Racine found Wright a vigorous, salty, and often entertaining man who was obviously giving them his best. The look of unbreakable endurance—which he had worn so long—was altered now to an air of optimism and authority. Old friends thought he actually looked taller, climbing around the scaffolds on the Johnson job as nimbly as any young workman.

Wright's finest day on this project came as climax to a dispute with the building license authorities. He planned to support the roof of the main workroom on twenty-four-foot concrete columns that looked like giant water-lily pads with slender stems. The officials feared these were too thin to hold up their calculated loads of six tons each, and it was announced that Wright would publicly test a sample column. The general interest Wright had roused was shown at this demonstration by the gathering of so many spectators that the police had to put up barricades.

Wright gave a tremendous show, directing a crane as it dropped ton after ton of scrap metal on the wide top of the slender shaft. Sixty tons were piled on before the column crumpled, establishing the factor of safety at almost ten to one. Since four to one is generally accepted in static construction, everybody was happy—the officials for the exceeding of requirements, Wright for the confounding of those who had doubted him, and his clients for the good publicity.

When the building was opened, 30,000 people went through in the first two days, and since then many thousands more have experienced the strange but stimulating feelings that come from walking through this great sealed structure. To some people, the oddly exhilarating interior spaces and forms are the visual equivalent of two or three dry Martinis; and all are struck by such unforgettable Wrightian oddities as the chairs that gently urge the sitter out of the seat with their inwardly leaning hinged backs, or shoot from under him on wheels; the round bird-cage elevator from which passengers may survey the main floor as they rise; and the huge *"Santa Maria"* desk in the advertising department, so called because of pooplike structures at each end. Engineers have an idea that the bands of Pyrex tubing that admit exterior light to this building, in place of windows, have a different rate of contraction from the surrounding brick, which raises problems in the Wisconsin winters. At any rate, it is interesting to note that the company manual for tourist guides tell them to answer the question "What construction faults, if any, have been found?" by replying, "High maintenance costs."

Following the administration structure, Wright was commissioned to do the Johnson Research Tower, a design by which he set great store because its floors were cantilevered from a central steel mast, as he had planned for the St. Mark's apartment house. The windowless tower was built in this form after Wright accepted Johnson's suggestion that he build the research area tall and narrow, instead of long and flat. Just why the cantilevered floors as he used them here (and later in the Price Tower in Oklahoma) are better than ordinary floors, is a question to which only Wright may have had the definitive answer. At any rate, they were very dear to Wright, and the wax company's tower forms an interesting abstract shape in contrast to the lower and heavier mass of the Administration Building.

Another good contract resulting in a remarkable structure was the great house Wingspread, built for Herbert Johnson and his bride in a fold of land at Wind Point, a few miles north of Racine. Wright designed Wingspread with long horizontal lines and a massive brick chimney-stack, opening into four fireplaces at the heart of the house, all in the best manner of his prairie period. Until the work was three quarters finished a white dove frequented the site, then flew away and did not return. An old stonemason said this meant, "The young lady will never live in this house." The prediction came true; Mrs. Johnson died before Wingspread was completed. Today the mansion is maintained by the Johnson Foundation as a meeting place for boards, committees, and discussion groups.

Soon after the Johnson Administration Building was finished, a college president came to Wright's door. Dr. Ludd M. Spivey, of obscure Florida Southern College, introduced himself by saying, "Mr. Wright, I have no money —but if you'll do me some plans, I'll give you money when I get some." Perhaps Dr. Spivey did not know that Wright had once said, "If I had unlimited wealth, I would use it in buying up and closing universities." But there was something about Dr. Spivey that Wright liked, and he decided to design an entirely new center of learning for him. And the educator raised money in satisfactory amounts—Wright's fee in the end was more than $100,000. Needless to say, Florida Southern is no longer obscure.

During this period, Wright showed what he could do in the way of designing houses that could be built for a moderate price. One of the best was the Jacobs house in Madison, as good an example of Wright's taste and touch, on its scale, as the largest mansion in Oak Park or California. Characteristically, Wright preached lengthy sermons on these smaller houses, and called them "Usonian," from the coined word meaning the United States of North America. A curious aspect of the Usonian houses was that banks and building loan institutions at first made trouble about financing them. Since then they have increased 100 per cent and more in market value, like the architectural blue chips they are.

What might be called the public rediscovery of Frank Lloyd Wright now took on the aspect of a bandwagon, with eager passengers clambering aboard at every street corner. Some of this was due to the late Howard Myers, publisher of *Architectural Forum*, who had respected Wright for years and decided, in 1938, that the time had come to devote an issue of the magazine to his work. Next came the news weeklies, passing the word throughout the land to the nonprofessional public. The daily papers, no longer featuring accounts of sensational troubles, were now more than ever recognizing Wright as a maker of copy, eagerly interviewing him wherever he went and filling many columns with his opinions and ideas. In 1939, the Royal Institute of British Architects gave Wright their medal, which he called "the best I ever got—real guinea gold," as though he could still find his way to the pawnshop if it became necessary.

There was a lengthening procession of honors—degrees from such institutions as Yale, Princeton, and Wisconsin, and a place in the Masters of Four Arts Exhibition at Harvard's Fogg Museum that presented Wright along with Maillol, Picasso, and Stravinsky; and in 1948, another entire issue of *Architectural Forum.*

But Wright was understandably displeased to reflect that many people thought he had *now* arrived—he whose work was first published in 1900, and recognized abroad by 1909. This matter of foreign recognition was very odd: Wright had been a strong influence in Europe, as a look at the factory building designed by Gropius for the Cologne Exhibition in 1914 would show; and presumably Wright's work was one of the roots of what was now called the international style. Assuming this, Wright was not happy about it. To say the least, Wright and the newer moderns looked at life in different ways; in general, he saw their product as inhuman, bureaucratic, and boxy. He hated the box. And when his own pronouncements about art and the machine were quoted in support of modern doctrines, Wright replied, "Why should architecture or objects of art in the machine age, just because they are made by machines, look like machinery? Because they were so made might be the best of reasons why they should not. Nor is there good reason why forms stripped clean of all considerations but function and utility should be admirable beyond that standpoint. They may be abominable from the human standpoint. Let us have no fear, therefore, of liberalism in our art of architecture nor in our industries. Dogma is still, as always, deadly."

What Wright decried in much of the modern European work was a sense of emptiness. Paul Klee himself, the remarkable artist who was also a teacher at the Bauhaus, seemed to have satirized this in the Kafkaesque canvas called "Hall C. Entrance R2," that he painted in 1920. This haunting scene is nothing but a system of architectural perspectives—an elaborate entrance to a habitation without life. Much as this aspect of the Bauhaus repelled him, Wright expressed personal respect for Miës van der Rohe, the German architect and teacher who had told Bauhaus men they should cut down to essentials, according to his famous maxim, "Less is more." As economical with words as with materials, Miës acknowledged Wright's European influence by remarking of the Robie house, "It saved us twenty years." On his first visit to Taliesin, in the late 1930's, Miës was walking through the place with his friend Bertrand Goldberg, a young architect who was later to add two sixty-story skyscrapers to the Chicago skyline. Goldberg was not a member of the Fellowship but a visitor, like Miës, and he expressed surprise when they noticed some defect of construction due to the informal manner in which Taliesin had been built. "Goldberg, just thank God it exists," said Miës van der Rohe.

In addition to being sometimes called the father of an architecture of which he disapproved, Wright received another distinction that he was willing to do without when he was identified by many as the hero of a work of fiction. Whether or not Miss Ayn Rand, author of the best-selling novel *The Fountainhead*, had noted the facts of Wright's career, readers saw a resemblance between certain of his tribulations and some of those endured by Miss Rand's gloriously independent architect hero. Published in 1943, the story soon reached the screen, with Gary Cooper in the leading role. Though Wright was fond of moving pictures, his comment on this one was scarcely a rave notice, since he called it "a grossly abusive caricature of my work."

A more acceptable recognition came when the American Institute of Architects, over internal opposition, conferred its highest award on Wright at the 1949 convention in Houston. This award, like its British counterpart, was a gold medal; Wright eventually had enough of them to make the surface for a tray. But there was significance in organized American architecture giving the prize to Wright, who had said that many of the most eminent A.I.A. members were "old men afraid to go out without their rubbers," and had refused to give any opinion at all of another Institute leader —on the grounds that he did not wish to use profanity over the telephone. It was obvious enough that his professional brethren were honoring Wright's works rather than his words, and Wright would have been the first to acknowledge this. In accepting the medal, he followed such men as McKim, Bertram Goodhue, Sullivan, George B. Post—of the Wisconsin State Capitol—and Sir Edwin Landseer Lutyens, who not only designed the city of New Delhi but added a phrase to the language by saying that certain houses in London had "Queen Anne fronts and Mary Ann backs." Wright never equalled this, the most durable humorous remark yet made by an architect, but he had a try at it when friends were driving him around Houston and the towering Shamrock Hotel came in sight. Wright said, "I can see the sham, but where's the rock?"

The A.I.A. award marked a truce rather than a permanent cessation of hostilities in Wright's long verbal war against the organization. On their part, many of those who honored him at Houston believed that Wright was his own best client. In support of this they pointed not only to Taliesin in southern Wisconsin but to Wright's winter residence and workplace near Scottsdale, Arizona. As we have seen, the architect became conscious of the American desert in the 1920's, and was disappointed in the construction of a resort hotel especially designed for this terrain, in the town of Chandler, Arizona. As his practice began to come back in the 1930's, Wright returned and bought land not far from Chandler on Maricopa Mesa under McDowell Peak. Here he raised the astounding walls of Taliesin West. The world offers no visual experience comparable to coming on this camp, rising from the desert in the diamond-clear Arizona evening. Wright said these buildings in stone and canvas were "pole-and-boulder Gothic," but he was proud of them, as he revealed in a remark he made to his friend, Charles Laughton, after showing him the wonders of the place. The actor said, "It's magnificent, Frank."

"Yes," said Wright. "I have given Arizona a voice."

Every man and woman in the Taliesin Fellowship went from Spring Green to Scottsdale in the fall, and stayed till the following spring. Wright became a well-known figure around Phoenix, and watched with pleasure as the region grew in population, and in stature as a resort area. The region also watched Wright with fascinated attention. He once astounded a dinner-jacketed guest at the Camelback Inn, an exclusive and conservative resort, by taking him (or feigning to take him) for a waiter, and tossing him his cloak. He fought a battle with Federal bureaucracy, this time without success, over a power line that was run across the desert so that his eyes fell on it from Taliesin West. Its towers were not unlike the totem-like structure that Wright himself had erected at the gates of Taliesin, but he was not quite enough of a constructivist to take any comfort from this. It was during the days of this controversy that Wright's Phoenix lawyer began to be aware of his regal habit of disregarding receptionists, and directly entering the private office of anyone he wished to see. Wright now was able to travel between the two Taliesins like a ruling monarch, selecting one from a stable of cars to be driven by shifts of apprentices—perhaps "the prideful Cord," the specially built Cadillac, the Jaguar, or the Mercedes. In later years a Diesel-powered freighter was added to the caravan. But by this time, the age of air travel had arrived, much to Wright's satisfaction. He liked to fly from Wisconsin to Arizona, and it was observed that he always looked a little reproachful on reaching the desert to find that those who were coming by road had not already arrived.

But whether in the desert or at Spring Green, Wright was a noble figure in his closing years, busy at the work he was born to do, and surrounded by freely expressed affection and respect. The three great events on the Taliesin calendars were Christmas, Easter, and Wright's birthday. The latter was celebrated by carefully rehearsed entertainments, with music and dancing; on one occasion there was a great garden party at Taliesin, with guests from all over the world, outdoor music, a pageant, fireworks, and illuminated barges on the pond. A permanent feature was the laying before the master of the "birthday boxes" containing projects prepared by apprentices in honor of the day. The boxes themselves were works of art, designed and built for this single purpose.

Wright returned all this good will in good measure; he "made people be at their best," as his friend Mrs. Lloyd Lewis saw it. But his unfailing appeal was to the young, even when he did not know them, as could be noticed when troops of adolescents followed him through the streets of Florence and Rome, begging for his autograph. These young people sensed, as did their counterparts in America, that here was one unalterably on their side against the authorities. Wright's youthfulness of spirit may explain why he suggested that the high school students of America should be appointed to select the nation's public buildings, deciding on the plans by vote. He brought this idea out as part of his blast against the Air Force Academy, which struck him as a collection of factories that had mistakenly wandered into Colorado.

This downright manner of condemnation, always a part of Wright's approach to his profession and art, had grown with the years. Sometimes one got the impression that Wright felt he was the sole proprietor of the truth about architecture, graven on the tablets and brought down from the summit of Taliesin. His writing has flashes of insight and vivid pages, notably in the account of boyhood days in his *Autobiography*, but when taken in large amounts has a suffocating quality. As we have seen, his philosophy of design and materials was to a considerable extent *ex post facto* —an explanation of the reason why, after he had done the thing. In the Prairie houses and his other best works, it was, after all, the incomparable thing itself that counted. But Wright, like other architects, loved to discuss his work, and to point out why it had to be what it was rather than what it was not. In this he was following a mighty army of critics, scholars, and historians. Sir Henry Wotton, the first English writer on architecture, had begged the builders of his day to provide structures of "commoditie, firmness, and delight," and Sir Thomas More reported that the inhabitants of Utopia lived in houses that featured flat roofs, plaster fronts, and "great quantities of glass." This material was widely used from the time of its invention, and windows taking up most of the wall space were familiar by the end of the sixteenth century, as a glance at Hardwick Hall in Derbyshire will demonstrate. Concrete had been used by the Romans, by medieval builders, and by the Spaniards in the New World. As for iron, the forerunner of steel, the American Victorians had worked freely with this material; in the 1850's, James Bogardus used it to make a basic functional pattern of columns, spandrels and windows, remarking that "the plan of construction has been to bring out the beautiful construction of the building—to decorate construction rather than to construct decoration." At this time Professor Joseph Henry was bearing him out: "Our houses are for *use*, and architecture is substantially one of the useful arts. In building, we should plan the inside first, and then plan the outside to cover it." Abroad, Karl Friedrich Schinkel of the Old Museum in Berlin had summed it up nearly thirty years before: "Emphasize construction by its articulation; use materials frankly; no useless parts; all clear and natural."

Philosophers were constantly weighing the subject of architecture and coming to conclusions similar to those that Wright worked out in practice as well as in prose. The English writer Edward Carpenter sounded like Wright addressing the Taliesin Fellowship when he said, in 1889, that "Men often ask about the new architecture, what and of what sort it is going to be. But to such a question there can be no answer till a new understanding of life has entered into people's minds, and then the answer will be clear enough. For as the Greek temples and the Gothic cathedrals were built by people who themselves lived but frugally as we should think, and were ready to dedicate their best work and chief treasure to the gods and common life; and as today when we must needs have for ourselves spacious and luxurious villas, we seem unable to design a decent church or public building; so it will not be until we once more find our main interest in the life of the community and the gods that a new spirit will inspire our architecture." When that time comes, houses will spring up "for the use of free men and women . . . companionable with the trees and the rocks." As to style, "their form and structure will quickly determine themselves, and man will have no difficulty in making them beautiful . . . and giving them form by a law unfolding from within."

Henry David Thoreau had come to a similar conclusion in 1854, in the pages of *Walden*: "Before we can adorn our houses with beautiful objects the walls must be stripped, and beautiful housekeeping and beautiful living be laid for a foundation: now, a taste for the beautiful is most cultivated out of doors, where there is no house and no housekeeping. "What of architectural beauty I now see, I know has gradually grown from within outward, out of the necessities and character of the indweller, who is the only builder,—out of some unconscious truthfulness, and nobleness, without ever a thought for the appearance; and whatever additional beauty of this kind is destined to be produced will be preceded by a like unconscious beauty of life."

All this was a small part of the heritage of thought and writing on architecture that supported Wright as he laid down his theories and made his exhortations. But where he stood far ahead of all mere theorists and, indeed, needed to make no explanations whatsoever, was in his completed work; no architect had equalled it for copious variety; and Wright was not afraid of being mentioned in the same breath with Michelangelo, a man he considered to have offended structural purity by anchoring the dome of St. Peter's with a chain.

Indeed, Wright's confidence in his own achievement has been equalled by no other artist, Benvenuto Cellini excepted.

This was illustrated one evening during the great final period at Taliesin, when Wright entertained a client at dinner, and a number of the young apprentices were present. Respectfully silent during the early courses, these young people came to conversational life when the visitor remarked that he had read a book in which a historian identified Wright as the greatest architect since the Renaissance.

The apprentices promptly began to analyze this statement like literary critics puzzling over a passage of James Joyce. They asked each other, "Who of the Renaissance could the historian have had in mind as greater than Mr. Wright? Was it Michelangelo? Bramante? Raphael? Brunelleschi of the Chapter House at Florence?" In the end their only agreement was that the writer must have been singularly ignorant not to know that the entire Renaissance had failed to produce anyone who could surpass the master of Taliesin. In the midst of this sat Frank Lloyd Wright, flashing his penetrating glance from face to face, and holding his white head high. While the discussion continued, it was observed that Wright, who had never been known to keep silence in the presence of anything with which he disagreed, did not interrupt the apprentices with so much as a murmur of deprecation. His attitude was not complacent, but merely convinced; it had long been known that where the great men of the Renaissance were concerned, Wright's policy was that of Huckleberry Finn, who took no stock in dead people.

As the Michelangelo of the present, Wright would have been willing to undertake any government project, such as the Air Academy, but his experience in federal housing during the war was not happy; cities and counties were the largest governmental units with which he was able to work successfully, and the largest public project that he planned

45. Residence of David Wright, Phoenix, Arizona, 1952

46. Kalita Humphreys Theater, Dallas, Texas, 1960

47. Entrance, Guggenheim Museum, New York City, 1959

48. Interior, Guggenheim Museum, New York City, 1959

49. Guggenheim Museum, New York City, 1959

was the civic center for Marin County, California, at which ground was broken after his death. His usual experience with bureaucracy may be illustrated by the letter he received from an official who was interested in having Wright take on a federal assignment. "Tell us about some of your work," said the letter, in a kindly tone. "We'd like to know what sort of person you are. Tell us something about yourself." Wright wrote back, "Try the nearest library."

Such obtuseness was understandably trying to Wright's temper, nor was there any obligation to suffer fools gladly attached to his position as creative artist. But as his national renown rose to the point at which he turned into a public oracle, he also turned into a public scold, on the lines of George Bernard Shaw. He made it plain that he seldom saw a building he wished to look at twice—the Metropolitan Museum was "a Protestant barn," the Radio City complex "the crime of crimes against humanity," the Seagram Building on Park Avenue "a whiskey bottle on a card table," the University of Mexico "a good place for a trainload of dynamite," and the United Nations Secretariat "a gravestone." A grand municipal structure "had a great deal of taste—and all of it bad." An office building in California struck him as "a dish of tripe." The skyline of Dallas in the 1930's, spectacular then as later, appeared to Wright to be "composed of rubbed bath-mats." The collegiate designs of Cobb and Goodhue were so much "cast-iron Gothic." In Chicago he said that the respectable Michigan Avenue building of the University Club was "an effete gray ghost with less vitality than a smokestack." Chicago was hopeless, to be sure, but the plague spot of American architecture was the lower Broadway and Wall Street area in New York. Though this obliterated the Woolworth

Building, the Singer Tower, and the beautifully proportioned New York City Hall, Wright seemed to be quite
serious in what he said.

He would occasionally admit, however, that some of his
verbal mortar shells were merely the advertising needed in
competitive trade. It could be pointed out that Richardson
himself had said the first principle of architecture was
"Get the job." For this there was a tradition almost as
old as the profession: the Macedonian architect Dinocrates
presented himself before Alexander the Great wearing a
lion's skin, carrying a club, and followed by a crowd of
curious onlookers. He told Alexander that he proposed
to carve Mount Athos into a colossal statue of a man,
and while the potentate did not have the project carried out,
he was so impressed with the grandeur of the idea that he
made Dinocrates his town planner and consulting architect.
That Dioncrates lead his honorable descendants Wright
would have been the last to deny. Nevertheless, he once
charged a publicity man of his acquaintance with dealing
in charlatanry. The publicity man replied, "I have heard
that a genius and a charlatan can be combined in one
person."

"I wouldn't fight you on that," said Wright.

He was equally candid with a client, the writer Arch
Oboler, to whom he said, "All you need do to become a
grand old man is live long enough." He paused and then
continued, "I am a grand old man."

And after a television appearance with Carl Sandburg,
Wright remarked, "We'd better get out of here, Carl—
before somebody starts telling the truth."

Wright thought he was telling the truth, to be sure, on the
occasions when he ventured on large generalities, though
he was sometimes grossly in error. This would come about

because he had not made the mistake of burdening his mind with too much factual information in any field other than his own. So he was able to say, on his return from a visit to the Soviet Union in 1937, just after the appalling purge trials and executions, "If Comrade Stalin, as disconcerted outsiders are saying, is betraying the Revolution, then in the light of what I have seen in Moscow, I say he is betraying it into the hands of the Russian people." This might rank with Wright's dictum on the purposes of the Japanese, delivered after he returned from building the Imperial Hotel; in justice to him, however, it should be noted that he was following a well-worn intellectual path. Generally speaking, his common sense and instinct for spotting personal frauds kept him out of the clutches of professional leftists. It is true that he was duped into allowing himself to be listed as a sponsor of the "Science and Culture Conference for World Peace," generally known as the Waldorf Conference, that was held in March 1949, amid the familiar chorus of vilification of the United States and applause for the foreign policy of the USSR. Wright fell into this trap because he regarded himself as a liberal and progressive man; his political ignorance was almost a perfect thing. Yet it should be recorded, too, that after the Russian trip he refused to allow the Communists on the faculty of the University of Wisconsin to use the history of his financial troubles at Taliesin as an indictment against the United States. "I am inclined to see any 'ism' as alien," said Wright.

But Wright did not invariably claim infallibility in his great closing years. A case in point arose at Taliesin when he pointed to a handsome fir tree growing outside his bedroom window and said, "It doesn't look right. Cut it down." The apprentices asked, "Are you sure?" Yes, Wright was positive, and the tree was levelled. Then he came back and had a look. "My God," he said, "did I do that? What a boner!" The apprentices thereupon searched the woods for an exactly similar tree, which they transplanted into the place where the other one had been. Readiness to own up to such occasional visual errors, which he called "dropped stitches," was characteristic of Wright, but it was best that he himself should be the one who first pointed out the mistake. A man approaching and entering his ninth decade might be allowed small errors when his work in general was taking on the dazzling quality of a fireworks display. He would tap his forehead, with a twinkling look in his eye, and say, "Plenty more up in the attic—plenty more."

Among the startling luminosities of the final period was the meeting house for the Unitarians of Madison, with a tall folded roof, to represent hands folded in prayer, and a prow of stone and glass, aimed out over the lake. Like all Wright's major buildings, it is signed with a small red square carrying his initials. It is also signed, to the discerning eye, in every edge and surface, as well as in the roof overhang, characteristically so low that if the members of the University of Wisconsin crew were to attend service, only the coxswain could walk under without bumping his forehead.

Then there is the Price Tower in Bartlesville, Oklahoma, a descendant of the aborted tower for St. Mark's-in-the-Bouwerie, and one of the most romantic structures in the country. This tower changes color under varying light like a northern lake; its horizontal elements give it certain aspects of a pagoda, and when the apartments that share its floors with offices are lit up at night, they seem to be a cluster of Chinese lanterns in the sky. Its outer decoration is interesting, as it shows that Wright's "T-square" ornamentation, though highly refined in the Coonley and Dana houses, is essentially akin to folk art. Students of American needlework could testify to this, by comparing the incised motifs on the exterior elements of the Price Tower balconies with the traditional patterns known as Dolly Madison's Star, California Star, Missouri Puzzle, and Kansas Trouble, among others. The patchwork patterns and Wright's T-squared angles result in a similar effect.

A notable domestic composition of the final years was the Sol Friedman house at Pleasantville, New York, in round rough stone like a Welsh castle; another circular house for David Wright, the architect's son in Phoenix, Arizona; the Lowell Walter house along the river at Quasqueton, Iowa; Mrs. Clinton Walker's house by the sea at Carmel, California; and many others, each one eloquently telling who its author was.

Of large structures, there was the massive concrete Kalita Humphreys Memorial Theater in Dallas, which may perhaps be the theater that Norman Geddes hoped to have, for it is an unqualified success. Its gifted director, Paul Baker, was consulted on the plans, and its wiring and lighting, by theater technicians, contribute to the total impact of what well may be, aside from Professor Baker's workshop at nearby Baylor University, the living center of present-day drama in the United States. Another large commission was the Wrightian-Byzantine Greek Church in Milwaukee, left unfinished at his death. There is also a Synagogue Beth Shalom in suburban Philadelphia that owes something to Wright's steel and glass cathedral of all faiths conceived a third of a century before, and something to the train sheds in the great railroad stations of youthful Chicago. As a non-Jew designing a synagogue, Wright could not claim to be learned in the Torah, but he applied himself so diligently to the client's problems that the correspondence, over several years, filled many folders. Wright's interest, in fact, was so great that the rabbi has been compelled to deny the persistent story that he got approval of the plans from his trustees by insisting, "We pray the way Mr. Wright *says* we pray."

The fabulous center of culture for King Faisal of Iraq, a $10,000,000 project, had to be abandoned when the client was murdered by a revolutionary mob. Here there was lost a grand and strange conception—Wright's fantastic drawings put one in mind of the idea of Jerusalem recorded by Hieronymus Bosch in his altarpiece of the Adoration of the Magi in the Prado at Madrid. Another large project, the Monona Terrace, a system of gardens, towers and driveways for the Madison lake front, had a curious history. The proposal was first postponed while the voters considered in a public referendum whether Wright should be retained. They agreed to that by a good majority, but before work could start, the state legislature passed a law limiting the dimensions of such structures in a manner that was obviously designed to prevent the building of Wright's terrace. After much controversy, the Wright faction again prevailed, the law was rescinded, and Madison now may be destined to have a unique though expensive stretch of shore front with terraces, pavilions, and hanging gardens.

The controversy over Lake Monona Terrace suggested that while Wright might be deferred to throughout the country and the world, he was still on probation around the old home town. At any rate, that was the way he felt when the Supreme Court of Wisconsin ruled that local tax collectors were correct in saying, "The Taliesin Fellowship is not an educational institution within the meaning of the law." The troubled traced back to the formation, in 1940, of a Frank Lloyd Wright Foundation, which was something on the order of a successor to the incorporations of previous years. This Foundation included the Fellowship, and the main points in the decision were that the Fellowship had no entrance examinations, no set course of study, no credits recognized elsewhere, and no diplomas or degrees. Perhaps forgetting that he himself had said Taliesin was his home and no school, Wright was outraged at Iowa County's bill for $18,000 in back taxes. "Very well," he said, "I'll tear the whole place down and leave the land idle. Let them tax that."

Among those who rallied to Wright's side at this time was Cary Caraway, a Chicago architect who had been in the Taliesin Fellowship. Knowing Wright well, Caraway could see that he was serious about destroying Taliesin and leaving Wisconsin. Thinking it over, Caraway waked at three o'clock one morning with an idea—why not hold a banquet, where people could gather to reassure Frank Lloyd Wright of his place in Wisconsin, and raise all or part of the tax money for him as a solid token of regard? Helped by many volunteers, Caraway went to work, and the dinner was held in Madison on the bitter cold night of February 10, 1955. Wright got a standing ovation and a check for $10,000. He said he was overwhelmed, and added, "I never would have known how high I stand in the esteem of my friends and neighbors in Wisconsin but for the adverse decision of the Supreme Court."

He stayed on in Spring Green, and experienced further gratification the following year, in his other home town of Chicago, when friends, architects and leading citizens turned out to celebrate Frank Lloyd Wright Day. At this time Wright unveiled the plans for Mile High Illinois, a building to point into the sky like a sword, 528 stories high. Working sideways on a table twenty-six feet long, he prepared the largest of his drawings for this project. It is the only plan by Wright that has something frightening in it. The promoter withdrew when he saw how far Wright had carried his original suggestion, which was merely for a television tower some 1200 feet tall. But Mile High Illinois is possible from an engineering point of view. All it needs is a builder with $30,000,000 to invest.

A welcome commission was the V. C. Morris china and glassware store in San Francisco. This city, though noted for enthusiasm, outdid itself in paying attention to the store. When the elegantly simple brick façade was completed on the shopping thoroughfare called Maiden Lane, people turned out in such great numbers for the opening that the police had to rope off the block to prevent dangerous congestion in the narrow street. Inside the store the surging crowds saw a helical ramp along whose walls the rare and costly merchandise was displayed under a central skylight. This was highly effective, but in time the owners began to ponder the economics of it, for as the years went on, it became evident that more visitors came in to see than to buy.

The most widely discussed of all Wright's later buildings, of course, is the Solomon R. Guggenheim museum on Fifth Avenue, New York. Wright got this remarkable building largely finished, though not ready for public use, before his death. Though Wright may or may not have been aware of it, the outward shape of the Guggenheim was similar to that of the main body, minus the spire, of the Great White Dagoba that had stood for 300 years in Peking. As the museum took form, the American public was keenly aware that a highly unusual building was going up in the country's largest city, and began to take full stock of its designer, who by his own count had completed more than 700 structures, and who was credited with having somehow led the nation out of architectural bondage. One thing was clear: Frank Lloyd Wright had achieved personal fame beyond that of any other American artist.

In fact, Wright was one of the most renowned Americans in any line of work, as would be impressed on those who came to hear him speak and expected to be seated without turning up three-quarters of an hour early. And even those who had no desire to hear him lecture recognized Wright in the street as readily as if he had been a champion athlete or a television star. It might even be maintained that he *was* a television star, for he entered that medium with easy mastery, presenting to camera and microphone a pleasing voice, a graceful presence, and a handsome face topped by a head of snowy white hair. Curiously enough, he had a close resemblance to Sir Christopher Wren, as those who knew Wright and had also seen Godfrey Kneller's portrait of the English architect could testify.

The personality wrapped in this aristocratic exterior grew so impressive that Wright was said to fill any space he occupied, and during his later years people got to their feet when he entered a room, as though before royalty or a prince of the church. Such a commanding personality gave myth-makers plenty to work with, and the absurd legends that came to surround Wright might almost make one forget that the facts were even more extraordinary. Some of the myths had to do with the boundless authority Wright was supposed to have claimed over his clients, even to the extent of ordering one patron to buy ten more acres so as to give his house a better setting, or instructing a woman in what kind of clothes to wear so as not to clash with his decoration. People have actually dined out on such preposterous tales as the one which had Wright sleeping all night on the ground under a tree, to get the feel of a client's property, or the story that he invited friends to lunch and refused to let them have knives, forks, or spoons, insisting that they use a combination eating tool of his own invention. This suggestion of the White Knight was engaging, but far from Wright's real personality. Guests at his winter home or at his Wisconsin estate were received with great consideration and not only given the customary number of knives and forks, but were waited on by Taliesin apprentices, as we have seen. These apprentices could deny another story about the master, to the effect that an Oriental ruler sent him a harem as a token of regard. The tale sprang from the Imperial Hotel; another legend, of course, was the one that made the Imperial the sole survivor of the 1923 earthquake. More homely than the tale of destruction with the hotel as sole survivor were the hundreds of spurious Wright anecdotes involving leaky roofs.

Some among the many such coverings built from Wright's plans must have sprung leaks from time to time, but putting the blame on the architect seems rather like reproaching Sibelius if someone should blow an E with too much F in it during a performance of *Finlandia*. However, the most widely believed of all the spurious Wright anecdotes had it that a leak occurred during a dinner party at Wingspread, and the owner rushed to the telephone and called Wright, who said, "Think nothing of it—rise above it." According to the tale, Herbert F. Johnson then said, "But the rain is falling into the lady guest of honor's soup plate!" To this plea Wright was supposed to have replied, "Tell her to move her chair."

This yarn had such wide circulation that Wright despaired of catching up with it, remarking that "Hib Johnson

has told that story so often he's beginning to believe it."
However, it was known that Wright was quite capable of
treating clients in an offhand way. A typical experience was
that of Harold C. Price, the pipe line engineer who commissioned the Bartlesville tower, and sometimes found it hard to
make contact with the architect at his Arizona lair. At last
Wright agreed to install a radio telephone hookup, and Price
was pleased, when he put in his call, to hear the voice of a
secretary in the desert, and then the measured tones of
Wright himself.

"Hello, there, Hal," said Wright. "Isn't this wonderful?
Over."

"Yes, it certainly is wonderful, Frank. I'd like to talk
about the plans. Over."

"I can hear you perfectly, Hal. Don't you think this is a
remarkable thing? Over to you."

"Highly remarkable," Price answered. "Now about those
plans. Have you made any decision in the matter I wrote
about? Over."

There was a pause, and Price repeated, "Did you get my
letter? What do you think? Over." Another long pause
ensued, and then the client heard the secretary say: "I'm
sorry, Mr. Price, but Mr. Wright has gone." All this left
Price reflecting that, to say the least, Wright had his own
way of doing things. But Wright's clients usually let the
world know they liked him as much as they respected him,
reacting almost without reservation to the architect's competence and charm. And the respect amounting almost to
adulation that was accorded Wright by his associates
was well known. However, the people who dealt with
Wright every day could also have their own ways of doing
things. One of these, a veteran draftsman, saw a visiting

architect shudder when Wright slashed a soft pencil over part of a perfectly finished drawing that was ready to go out of the shop. As Wright walked away, the draftsman said to the visitor, "He always does that. But I always have three coats of lacquer on a finished drawing, so it wipes right off."

On the whole, though, even Wright's careless slashings were sacred at Taliesin. Visitors reported how the members of his claque applauded everything he said and did, praising him for the arrangement of knickknacks on his desk, or for the artistic effect that resulted when he tossed his overcoat on a chair, forgetting that any window dresser on Michigan Avenue or Wilshire Boulevard could do the same. For such loyal support, Wright rewarded his disciples and friends with warm appreciation and vivid humor, turning on a current of excitement that could be felt like an electric charge. Wright could convince his younger followers that he had a personal interest in each one of them, and they were not mistaken in his sympathy, for all his life he remained young in heart.

Wright's ever-youthful sense of fun could be seen when he turned his talents to designing a chickenhouse for a friend, or a doghouse for a child who wrote to request it. Related to this sense of humor was an irreverance for the pretentious that caused him to walk out in the middle of a solemn avant-garde movie with the remark, "We've had about enough of that." Wright applied the same devastating disrespect to a portenous art expert who made the mistake of patronizing him during a visit to Taliesin. In return, Wright summoned his students and organized the Great Picasso Contest, selecting the most convincing sketch by an apprentice in one of the Spanish painter's styles. On his next visit to Taliesin the critic found this drawing in the midst of a pile of prints and cried, "But this is wonderful! Wright, you don't realize what you have here!"

"Oh, yes I do," said Wright. "Come into the drafting room and meet the artist."

Such drastic treatment might be given those he considered to be in need of it, but Wright could be graciously tactful in quieting the fears of persons who were overpowered by his presence. At the height of his fame, he was taken to call on an elderly lady who jittered that she supposed he would condemn her Victorian house and furniture.

"I wouldn't change a thing," said Wright. "All this suits you perfectly. I couldn't do nearly so well."

This was Frank Lloyd Wright at his most attractive, in the mood which prompted him to crawl under the house to rescue a child's kitten, and permit a tame duck to waddle in and out of his study at Taliesin. In the same engaging vein was his stock answer to the question, "Mr. Wright, which do you consider the greatest of your buildings?"

"The next one," Wright would reply with a twinkle. "Always the next one."

For all the geniality and charm that was a natural aspect of his personality, Wright still intimidated many of his fellow citizens, in his last golden age, by the acidulous manner in which he commented on any person or event that failed to please him. Growing as he aged, this habit of objurgation at last reminded some Americans of Rip Van Winkle's rueful conclusion that a sharp tongue is the only edged tool that grows keener with constant use. Before an audience of advertising men, for example, he remarked, "There's not enough integrity in the whole bunch of you to make one decent man." To a group of clubwomen he said, "Those hats you are wearing are monstrosities. I can't understand why you don't throw them away."

Wright's comment on an address by no less a personage

than the dean of the Massachusetts Institute of Technology was that it had been "an unctuous falsification of modern architecture." He dismissed Ernest Hemingway, who had questioned a Wrightian conception for the Grand Canal in Venice, as nothing more than "a voice from the jungle." And he said that Le Corbusier was "only a painter—and not a very good one."

It is true that the cutting remarks were usually accompanied by a twinkle in Wright' eye; but his ameliorating expression could not be reproduced in newsprint. Therefore it was assumed that Wright was serious when he informed the citizens of Los Angeles that their town was "much worse than the average American city because there is so much more of it to be ugly." To make sure no crumb of comfort was extracted from the remark, he added that in general "Los Angeles looked as though you had tipped up the United States so that all the commonplace people in the country slid down into Southern California." But perhaps Wright's greatest piece of civic condemnation was his reply to the interviewer who asked what might be done to improve Pittsburgh. Wright snapped, "Destroy it and start over."

It is not surprising that one who could make such stinging remarks about cities was capable of rebuking the entire country when he felt like it. Wright deployed on America by first assailing "Mrs. Alderman Schmutzkopf," "Mrs. Gablemore," and "Mrs. Reggie Plasterbilt," who had committed the offense of preferring American Queen Anne and neo-classic styles to Wright's domestic architecture. A nation that harbored such beings, Wright maintained, must be "the ugliest civilization in the history of the world."

But perhaps it was not even civilized. After all, the capital itself "did not contain a single example of democratic architecture." The more Wright thought of it, the fonder he became of quoting "a certain witty Frenchman" who had said that "America was the only great nation that went from barbarism to degeneracy with no culture in between." Wright's friends hoped he would forget this witty Frenchman, but he liked the statement so much that he clung to it all his life, relying on the twinkle to lessen the shock. And Wright undoubtedly felt that he made amends for all the sarcasms when he began to remark, from time to time in later life, in what sounds like the echo of a lyric by Oscar Hammerstein, "I find it still good to have been born and lived as American as corn on the cob."

American he was to the bone, and this was what his countrymen instinctively recognized. Where Henry James had written of the struggle of the artist against society, this man from Wisconsin had lived it; and where James speculated on the impact of European culture on Americans, Frank Lloyd Wright made his own resounding and undeniable impact, as an American, on Europe. Thus Frank Lloyd Wright had scored a monumental victory for his native land.

In New York City, early in 1959, Frank Lloyd Wright spent an exhilarating day, that showed how he stood with the public, at the nearly completed Guggenheim Museum. Its 7000 tons of concrete had been poured, and the gently rising ramp inside was finished. The newspaper account of his activities said that workmen and foremen showed high respect for Wright—also a sort of amused affection, smiling at his cane, and at the flattened, wide-brimmed object he called a "cantilevered hat." Walking down Fifth Avenue later, Wright came upon a group of college girls who asked for his autograph. A man stepped up and asked the privilege of shaking his hand. An architectural student begged

Wright to pose for a photograph, a request that was granted with evident enjoyment. "Nature is the thing, young man," said Wright. "I spell that with a capital 'N.' I pay reverence to it." Then Wright stepped into a taxi for the ride to his New York home of many years, Suite 223 at the Plaza Hotel. "Wait till I tell the wife Frank Lloyd Wright was in my cab!" cried the driver. "She thinks you can do no wrong."

Wright smiled benignly and said, "That's notoriety. But it isn't fame. Do I have fame, I wonder?"

Three months later a lady came with some hesitancy to Taliesin West. She was Louise Elliott Rago, a teacher of art in the Wheatley School at East Williston, Long Island. Escorted by Dr. Harry Wood, head of the art department at Arizona State University, who was painting a portrait of Wright, Mrs. Rago hoped to get material for an article in an art teachers' magazine. Wright bowed courteously, but said, "Oh, no! Not another interview!" Then it was mentioned that the lady was a teacher. Wright smiled and said, "You know, my mother was a teacher too. Come into my study."

Here, on a thronelike chair of his own design, Wright gave his last interview. As Wright talked, small birds flew in and out; his blue eyes brightened, and the interviewer felt a "warm, generous rapport."

"A creative teacher," said Wright, "is one of the finest examples of humanity." Then he said a child should begin to learn what is called art at the earliest possible age. "Put blocks in the child's hands," he said. "Let the child hold a sphere, a ball—and get a sense of the universe, a sense of God." He was thinking of the Froebel kindergarten blocks that had stayed in his own fingers all his life. He impressed Mrs. Rago as "gentle and generous, spiritual, willing to share"—and frail. But his grey suit and tie were perfect, his starched collar just right, his voice level, his hands steady. He seemed permanent.

The sun was going down behind the McDowell Range when the callers left. Taliesin West had given them the impression of being out at sea. But it seemed firmly enough anchored to the members of the Fellowship when they rose next morning and went to their tasks. Wright sat at his drawing table, took up his colored pencils, turned them in his hands, and scattered them before him; then he went to work on the Donahoe project—three connected circular houses for a desert moraine. In a little while, he was stricken with pain; it became so severe that his doctor took him in to St. Joseph's Hospital in Phoenix.

That was Saturday, April fourth. On Monday the surgeons operated to correct an intestinal stoppage. The old great man made a good recovery, but on Thursday, at a quarter of five in the morning, his nurse heard Wright give a sigh—and he was gone. The doctors said it must have been something like a heart attack that caused his death, but many people thought his case was like that of Edgar Lee Masters' Lucinda Matlock, who at a great age "had lived enough, that is all." Wright was in the last months of his ninth decade when he died. But, in a sense, much of him continued to live: Mrs. Wright and her daughter Iovanna, with some of Wright's colleagues, announced that they would complete his contracts and carry on the educational and architectural work of the two Taliesins.

Frank Lloyd Wright was buried in the Lloyd-Jones family churchyard at Spring Green on April 12, 1959, a bright and chilly Sunday afternoon. The minister of the Madison Unitarian Church spoke a few words and read portions of the Bible that mention truth and genius. Six apprentices lowered the box into the grave beneath the pine trees. Later the place was marked with a rough-cut slab of native stone, like that which built the walls of Taliesin. And the *Journal* of Wright's old admirers and adversaries in the American Institute of Architects had this to say: "His place in history is secure. His continuing influence is assured. This century's architectural achievements would be unthinkable without him. He has been a teacher to us all."

BIBLIOGRAPHY

BIBLIOGRAPHY

WORKING his way through the published and unpublished material on Frank Lloyd Wright, the author mined extensively at the Newberry Library in Chicago, and owes a debt of gratitude to the director, Dr. Stanley Pargellis, and his staff. There is also much Wright material in the Burnham Library at the Art Institute of Chicago, the Fine Arts Room at the New York Public Library, and the Avery Library at Columbia University. The list of books which were illuminating to one or many aspects of this subject must be headed by Wayne Andrews' *Architecture, Ambition and Americans*, and the same author's *Architecture in America*. Grant Carpenter Manson's *Frank Lloyd Wright to 1910*, the first volume of a projected trilogy, is a necessity for the serious student, as is Henry-Russell Hitchcock's *In the Nature of Materials; the Buildings of Frank Lloyd Wright, 1887-1941*. Other works of general or particular value included the indispensable *History of Architecture on the Comparative Method*, by Sir Banister Fletcher; *Architecture: an Introduction to the History and Theory of the Art of Building*, by W. R. Lethaby; *Guide to Western Architecture*, by John Gloag; *European Architecture*, by Nikolaus Pevsner; *Early Victorian Architecture in Britain*, by Henry-Russell Hitchcock; *Roots of Contemporary American Architecture*, edited by Lewis Mumford; *The Shingle Style*, by Vincent J. Scully; *The Railroad Station*, by Carroll L. V. Meeks; *The Golden City*, by Henry Hope Reed, Jr.; *My Work*, by Le Corbusier; *Louis Sullivan As He Lived*, by Willard Connolly; and *Prairie Avenue*, by Arthur Meeker.

Two anthologies of Wright's literary output, gathered from his lectures, magazine articles and books, are *Frank Lloyd Wright on Architecture: Selected Writings* (1941), edited by Frederick Gutheim, and *Writings and Buildings* (1960), selected by Edgar Kaufmann and Ben Raeburn. Wright's major books are *Modern Architecture* (1931); *An Autobiography* (1932, revised and expanded in 1943); *The Disappearing City* (1932); *Architecture and Modern Life* (with Baker Brownell, 1937); *An Organic Architecture: the Architecture of Democracy* (1939); *When Democracy Builds* (1945); *Genius and the Mobocracy* (1949); *The Future of Architecture* (1953); *The Natural House* (1954); *The Story of the Tower: the Tree That Escaped the Crowded Forest* (1956); *A Testament* (1957); and *Drawings For A Living Architecture* (1959).

INDEX

INDEX

Adler, Dankmar, 20, 41 ff., 148
Adler & Sullivan, 42 ff., 64, 145, 172
American Institute of Architects, 222, 256
Annunciation Greek Orthodox Church, Milwaukee, Wisconsin, 267
Architectural Record, 72, 101, 127-130, 159, 109-10
"Architecture, In the Cause of," 127-30
Arizona Biltmore (Project), Phoenix, Arizona, 207-10
"Art and Craft of the Machine, The," 74-76
Auditorium (Sullivan), Chicago, Illinois, 43-45

Bancroft, Levi H., 188-91
Bank of Wisconsin, 187, 191-92, 201 ff.
Barnsdall, Aline, 162-65, 172
  house, Hollywood, California, 162-66
  theater (Project), Hollywood, California, 163-64
Bartlesville, Oklahoma
  H. C. Price Tower, 252, 266-67, 273
Barton, George
  house, Buffalo, New York, 87
Bear Run, Pennsylvania
  "Falling Water," Edgar J. Kaufmann house, 249
Beman, Solon Spencer, 37, 50, 106, 148
Blossom, George
  house, Chicago, Illinois, 63
Bok, Edward, 68, 82

Borthwick, Mamah (*See* Cheney, Mamah Borthwick)
Bradley, B. Harley, 73, 99, 107
  house, Kankakee, Illinois, 73-74, 77-78
Broadacre City (Project), 221, 241
Brodelle, Emil, 136-37
Brunker, Thomas, 137-38
Buffalo, New York
  George Barton house, 87
  Larkin Building, 86
  Darwin D. Martin house, 86-87, 214
Burnham, Daniel A., 39-41, 50, 65
Byrne, Barry, 59, 93, 129, 218, 222

Caraway, Cary, 269
Carleton, Gertrude, 135 ff.
Carleton, Julian, 135 ff., 143, 145
Carmel, California
  Mrs. Clinton Walker house, 267
Cary, Alice, 4
Cary, Phoebe, 4
Charnley, James
  house, Chicago, Illinois, 49-50, 53, 65, 70
Cheney, Edwin H., 94, 119, 123-24, 134-35, 139
  house, Oak Park, Illinois, 94
Cheney, John, 135-37
Cheney, Mamah Borthwick, 94, 104, 108-09, 112 ff., 143-45, 147, 173, 190
Cheney, Martha, 135-37
Chicago, Illinois
  George Blossom house, 63
  James Charnley house, 49-50, 53, 65, 70

287

Chicago, Illinois (*Cont.*)
E-Z Polish Plant, 88
A. W. Harlan house, 63
Isidor Heller house, 69-71, 91
Warren McArthur house, 63-65
Midway Gardens, 132-35, 138,
145, 151-54
Frederick C. Robie house, 101-
104, 225
Chicago Architectural Club, 76,
82, 95, 170
Chicago, Art Institute of, 222-23
Chicago Century of Progress Ex-
position, 226-28
Chicago World's Columbian Ex-
position (World's Fair 1893),
40, 50-53
Congregation Beth Sholom, Elkins
Park, Pennsylvania, 186, 267-68
Conover, Allen D., 14
Coonley, Mr. & Mrs. Avery, 99-
100, 202-03
house, Riverside, Illinois, 99-101,
127, 267
Corwin, Cecil, 31-34
Cupply, Frances (Wright's daugh-
ter), 183-84

Dallas, Texas
Kalita Humphreys Theater, 164,
267
Dana, Susan Lawrence
house, Springfield, Illinois, 85,
267
Donahoe Project, 279

E-Z Polish Plant, Chicago, Illinois,
88
Elkins Park, Pennsylvania
Congregation Beth Sholom, 186,
267-68
Elmslie, George Grant, 41-43, 145
Emerson, Ralph Waldo, 15, 23-24,
79, 124, 246
Ennis, Charles
house, Los Angeles, California,
215

Faisal, Cultural Center for King
(Project), Iraq, 268
"Falling Water" (*See* Kaufmann,
Edgar J.)
First Unitarian Meeting House,
Madison, Wisconsin, 266
Florida Southern College, Lake-
land, Florida, 220, 252-53
Francke, Dr. Kuno, 104-05
Freeman, Samuel
house, Los Angeles, California,
215
French, La Fayette, 195, 201, 204
Friedman, Sol
house, Pleasantville, New York,
267
Fritz, Herbert, 137-38, 145
Froebel blocks, 9, 50, 60, 278
Fromkin, Morris, 223-25

Geddes, Norman Bel, 97, 163-65,
267
Golf Club, River Forest, Illinois,
70-71
"Graycliff" (*See* Martin, Darwin
D.)
Griffin, Walter Burley, 59, 117,
129
Guggenheim Museum, New York
City, New York, 270, 277

Hardy, W. P.
house, Racine, Wisconsin, 88-90,
107
"Harem House, The" (*See*
Thomas, Frank)
Harlan, Dr. A. W.
house, Chicago, Illinois, 63
Heller, Isidor
house, Chicago, Illinois, 69-71, 91
Hennepin County Jail, Wisconsin,
193-95, 204
Heurtley, Arthur
house, Oak Park, Illinois, 84

Hickox, Warren
house, Kankakee, Illinois, 73-74, 77
Highland Park, Illinois
Ward Willitts house, 76-78
Hillside Home School, Spring Green, Wisconsin, 80-82, 215, 231-32
Hillside Home School Tower, Spring Green, Wisconsin, 80-81
Hinzenberg, Svetlana, 190, 192-93, 195, 198-99, 213
Hinzenberg, Valdimar, 189, 191-92, 197
"Hollyhock House" (See Barnsdall, Aline)
Hollywood, California
Aline Barnsdall house, 162-66
Barnsdall theater (Project), 163-164
Holst, Hermann von, 116-117

Ianelli, Alfonso, 134, 151-57
Imperial Hotel, Tokyo, Japan, 157-162, 167-70, 172, 218, 240, 272

Jackson, Harold, 183, 189-90, 192-193, 195-96, 203-04, 212
Jacobs, Herbert
house, Madison, Wisconsin, 253
Japanese print collection, 91, 116, 202, 212
Johnson, Albert M., 177-80, 186
Johnson, Herbert F.
house, Wind Point, Wisconsin, 252, 272
Johnson, S. C. & Son
Administration Building, Racine, Wisconsin, 250-52
Research Tower, Racine, Wisconsin, 251-52
Johonnot, Dr. Arthur, 96, 98
Jones, Owen, 35-36, 47

Kahn Lectures, Princeton University, 219-20
Kahn, Otto, 164
Kalita Humphreys Theater, Dallas, Texas, 164, 267
Kankakee, Illinois
B. Harley Bradley house, 73-74, 77-78
Warren Hickox house, 73-74, 77
Kaufmann, Edgar J.
"Falling Water," house, Bear Run, Pennsylvania, 249

"La Miniatura" (See Millard, Mrs. G. M.)
Ladies Home Journal, 68, 82-83
Lake Tahoe Resort (Project), California, 186
Lakeland, Florida
Florida Southern College, 220, 252-53
Larkin Building, Buffalo, New York, 86
Levin, Tillie, 205-06
Lincoln Center (Project), Chicago, Illinois, 95-96
Lindbloom, David, 137
Lloyd-Jones, Anna (See Wright, Anna Lloyd-Jones)
Lloyd-Jones, Ellen (Wright's aunt), 7, 15, 80, 231-32
Lloyd-Jones, Jane (Wright's aunt), 7, 15, 80, 231-32
Lloyd-Jones, Jenkin (Wright's uncle), 7, 14, 31, 33-34, 48, 80, 94-96, 138
Lloyd-Jones, Richard (Wright's cousin), 214
house, Tulsa, Oklahoma, 214-15, 222
Lloyd-Jones, Richard (Wright's grandfather), 5-7
Los Angeles, California
Charles Ennis house, 215
Samuel Freeman house, 215
Lowell, James Russell, 4

Madison, Wisconsin
  First Unitarian Meeting House,
    266
  Herbert Jacobs house, 253
  Monona Terrace, 268
Mahoney, Marion, 59, 116
Mann Act, 149, 195, 199-200, 204,
  206
Marin County Civic Center (Project), California, 263
Martin, Darwin D., 86-87, 202-03,
  207, 214
  house, Buffalo, New York, 86-87,
    214
  Larkin Building, 86
Martin, W. E.
  E-Z Polish Plant, Chicago, Illinois, 88
  house, Oak Park, Illinois, 86
McArthur, Albert Chase, 207-11
McArthur, Warren
  house, Chicago, Illinois, 63-65
McCormick, Harold and Edith
  Rockefeller, 105-07
  house (Project), Lake Forest,
    Illinois, 106-07
McKim, Mead & White, 19, 51, 63,
  70, 157
Midway Gardens, Chicago, Illinois, 132-35, 138, 145, 151-
  154
Mile High Illinois (Project), Chicago, Illinois, 269-70.
Millard, Mrs. George Madison,
  166-167, 172
  house, Pasadena, California, 166-
  167, 207, 215
Milwaukee, Wisconsin
  Annunciation Greek Orthodox
    Church, 267
Monona Terrace, Madison, Wisconsin, 268
Moore, Nathan G., 69
  house, Oak Park, Illinois, 69, 172-
  173
Morgan, Charles L., 217, 226

Morris, V. C., Store, San Francisco, California, 270
Morris, William, 64, 66, 68, 75

Nash, W. M., 194-96, 200
National Insurance Skyscraper
  (Project), Chicago, Illinois,
  177-80, 217
Neutra, Richard, 180, 229, 240
New York City, New York
  Guggenheim Museum, 270, 277
Noel, Miriam (See Wright, Miriam Noel)

Oak Park, Illinois
  E. H. Cheney house, 94
  Arthur Heurtley house, 84
  W. E. Martin house, 86
  Nathan G. Moore house, 69, 172-
  173
  The Studio, 57-59 (See also
    Studio, The)
  Frank Thomas house, 83
  Unity Temple, 73, 96-99
Okura, Baron, 161-62, 167, 169
Orchestra Hall (Office), Chicago,
  Illinois, 130, 132, 146

Page, Ben E., 223, 225
Pasadena, California
  Mrs. G. M. Millard house, 166-
  167, 207, 215
Phoenix, Arizona
  David Wright house, 267
Pleasantville, New York
  Sol Friedman house, 267
Porter, Andrew T.
  house, Spring Green, Wisconsin,
  139
Prairie Style, 78 ff., 167, 172, 259
Price, H. C., Tower, Bartlesville,
  Oklahoma, 252, 266-67, 273

Quasqueton, Iowa
  Lowell Walter house, 267

Racine, Wisconsin
W. P. Hardy house, 88-90, 107
S. C. Johnson & Son Administration Building, 250-52
S. C. Johnson & Son Research Tower, 251-52
"Red square," 88
Richardson, Henry Hobson, 19, 36-37, 39, 63, 241, 264
Richland Center, Wisconsin
A. D. German Warehouse, 162
River Forest, Illinois
Golf Club, 70-71
Tennis Club, 70
C. L. Williams house, 68, 84
William H. Winslow house, 64-65, 84
Riverside, Illinois
Avery Coonley house, 99-101, 127, 267
Roberts, Charles E., 96
Robie, Frederick C.
house, Chicago, Illinois, 100-04, 255
Robinson, David, 146
"Romeo and Juliet" tower (See Hillside Home School Tower)
Root, John Wellborn, 39, 41, 50, 148
Royal Institute of British Architects, 253
Ruskin, John, 15-16, 68, 75

St. Marks in the Bouwerie Tower (Project), New York City, N. Y., 216, 222, 251, 267
San Francisco, California
V. C. Morris Store, 270
San Marcos in the Desert (Project), Chandler, Arizona, 209, 257
Sandburg, Carl, 103, 180, 264
Schevill, Ferdinand, 202, 207, 214
Schindler, R. M., 172, 180, 240

Scottsdale, Arizona
Taliesin West, 257 (See also Taliesin West)
Silsbee, Joseph Lyman, 31-35, 41, 63, 239
Spivey, Dr. Ludd M., 252
Spring Green, Wisconsin
Hillside Home School, 80-82, 215, 231-32
Hillside Home School Tower, 80-81
Andrew T. Porter house, 139
Taliesin East, I, 122-24 (See also Taliesin East); II, 145 (See also Taliesin East); III, 186 (See also Taliesin East)
Taliesin theater, 242
Springfield, Illinois
Susan Lawrence Dana house, 85, 267
Studio, The, Oak Park, Illinois, 57-59; Life at, 62, 72, 88, 90, 92, 95, 122
Sullivan, Louis Henri, 20-21, 40 ff., 62-65, 70, 76, 89, 148, 170 ff., 241, 256

"T-Square and Triangle Verses," 92-93
Taliesin East, Spring Green, Wisconsin
I, 122-24; Life at, 130-31, 135; Massacre, 136 ff., 145-48
II, 145; Life at, 148, 179-80; Fire, 185-86
III, 186; Life at, 186 ff.; Taken over by Bank of Wisconsin, 191-214; As a school, 229 ff., 250 ff.
Taliesin Fellowship, 229 ff., 247 ff.
Taliesin theater, Spring Green, Wisconsin, 242
Taliesin West, Scottsdale, Arizona, 257; Life at, 258, 273, 278-79

Tennis Club, River Forest, Illinois, 70
Transportation Building (Sullivan), Chicago, Illinois, 51-53
Thomas, Frank
house, Oak Park, Illinois, 83
Tobin, Catherine (See Wright, Catherine)
Tokyo, Japan
Imperial Hotel, 157-62, 167-70, 172, 218, 240, 272
Tulsa, Oklahoma
Richard Lloyd-Jones house, 214-215, 222

Unity House, Oak Park, Illinois, 99
Unity Temple, Oak Park, Illinois, 73, 96-99
"Usonian" houses, 253

Voillet-le-Duc, Eugène-Emmanuel, 35, 46-47

Wainwright Building (Sullivan), St. Louis, Missouri, 48-49, 89, 95
Walker, Mrs. Clinton
house, Carmel, California, 267
Waller, Edward, 132-34
Waller, James B., 65
Walter, Lowell
house, Quasqueton, Iowa, 267
Warehouse, A. D. German, Richland Center, Wisconsin, 162
Wasmuth, Ernst, (Monograph of Wright), 104, 120, 130
Wasmuth Office, Berlin, Germany, 117, 119
Weston, Ernest, 136-37
Weston, William, 136-37, 183-84
Williams, C. L.
house, River Forest, Illinois, 68, 84

Willitts, Ward
house, Highland Park, Illinois, 76-78
Wind Point, Wisconsin
H. F. Johnson house, 252, 272
"Wingspread" (See Johnson, Herbert F.)
Winslow, William H.
house, River Forest, Illinois, 64-65, 84
Wright, Anna Lloyd-Jones (Wright's mother), 5-10, 13, 16, 24, 48, 122, 167
Wright, Catherine (Wright's daughter), 226
Wright, Catherine (Wright's first wife), 34-35, 48, 57 ff., 117-19, 122, 126, 157, 173, 222-23
Wright, David (Wright's son), 267
house, Phoenix, Arizona, 267
Wright, Frank Lloyd, Born, 3; Association with Sullivan, 40 ff.; Marriage to Catherine Tobin, 48; Elopement with Mamah Borthwick, 109, 116-117; Taliesin massacre, 137 ff.; Divorce from Catherine, 109, 122, 173; Marriage to Miriam Noel, 173 ff.; Divorce from Miriam, 177-205, 213; Marriage to Olgivanna, 213 ff.; Frank Lloyd Wright Incorporated, 202 ff.; Foundation of Taliesin Fellowship, 229 ff.; Death, 279-80
Wright, Frank Lloyd, Day, 269
Wright, Frank Lloyd, Foundation, 268-69
Wright, Frank Lloyd, Incorporated, 202 ff
Wright, Iovanna (Wright's daughter), 190, 192-93, 195, 198-99, 213, 279
Wright, Jane (Wright's sister), 10, 196

Wright, John Lloyd (Wright's son), 58, 88, 131 ff., 151-52, 155, 158, 196

Wright, Llewellyn (Wright's son), 60

Wright, Maginol (Wright's sister), 10, 196, 201

Wright, Miriam Noel (Wright's second wife), 146 ff., 177 ff.

Wright, Olgivanna (Wright's third wife), 181 ff., 279

Wright, William Russell Cary (Wright's father), 4-10, 12-13, 116

PHOTOGRAPH ACKNOWLEDGMENTS

The figures refer to the plate numbers.

WAYNE ANDREWS, 2, 3, 8, 10, 11, 13, 14, 18-36, 38-49

J. W. BAXTRESSER, 6

CHICAGO ARCHITECTURAL PHOTO. COMPANY, 4, 5, 9, 12, 15

P. E. GUERRERO, 1

JAPAN TOURIST ASSOCIATION, 16

MUSEUM OF MODERN ART, NEW YORK, 7

JOE D. PRICE, 37

SATO PHOTO., 17